T0327337

RESEARCH IN MARITIME HISTORY
NO. 29

THE BRITISH WHALING TRADE

Gordon Jackson

International Maritime Economic History Association

St. John's, Newfoundland
2005

ISSN 1188-3928
ISBN 0-9730073-9-7

Research in Maritime History is available free of charge to members of the International Maritime Economic History Association. The price to others is US$15 per copy, plus $3.50 postage and handling.

Back issues of *Research in Maritime History* are available:

No. 13 (1997)   Paul C. van Royen, Jaap R. Bruijn and Jan Lucassen, *"Those Emblems of Hell"? European Sailors and the Maritime Labour Market, 1570-1870*

No. 14 (1998)   David J. Starkey and Gelina Harlaftis (eds.), *Global Markets: The Internationalization of The Sea Transport Industries Since 1850*

No. 15 (1998)   Olaf Uwe Janzen (ed.), *Merchant Organization and Maritime Trade in the North Atlantic, 1660-1815*

No. 16 (1999)   Lewis R. Fischer and Adrian Jarvis (eds.), *Harbours and Havens: Essays in Port History in Honour of Gordon Jackson*

No. 17 (1999)   Dawn Littler, *Guide to the Records of Merseyside Maritime Museum, Volume 2*

No. 18 (2000)   Lars U. Scholl (comp.), *Merchants and Mariners: Selected Maritime Writings of David M. Williams*

No. 19 (2000)   Peter N. Davies, *The Trade Makers: Elder Dempster in West Africa, 1852-1972, 1973-1989*

No. 20 (2001)   Anthony B. Dickinson and Chesley W. Sanger, *Norwegian Whaling in Newfoundland: The Aquaforte Station and the Ellefsen Family, 1902-1908*

No. 21 (2001)   Poul Holm, Tim D. Smith and David J. Starkey (eds.), *The Exploited Seas: New Directions for Marine Environmental History*

No. 22 (2002)   Gordon Boyce and Richard Gorski (eds.), *Resources and Infrastructures in the Maritime Economy, 1500-2000*

No. 23 (2002)   Frank Broeze, *The Globalisation of the Oceans: Containerisation from the 1950s to the Present*

No. 24 (2003)   Robin Craig, *British Tramp Shipping, 1750-1914*

No. 25 (2003)   James Reveley, *Registering Interest: Waterfront Labour Relations in New Zealand, 1953 to 2000*

No. 26 (2003)   Adrian Jarvis, *In Troubled Times: The Port of Liverpool, 1905-1938*

No. 27 (2004)   Lars U. Scholl and Merja-Liisa Hinkkanen (comps.), *Sail and Steam: Selected Maritime Writings of Yrjö Kaukiainen*

No. 28 (2004)   Gelina Harlaftis and Carmel Vassallo (eds.), *New Directions in Mediterranean Maritime History*

Research in Maritime History would like to thank Memorial University of Newfoundland for its generous financial assistance in support of this volume.

For my mother
and in memory of
my father

Contents

PART ONE:

The Traditional Whaling Trades, 1604-1914

PART TWO:

The Modern Whaling Trade, 1904-1963

Tables in the Text

Appendices of Statistical Information

New Introduction

When, in the 1970s, Ralph Davis asked me to write this book for a series of British trade histories, we agreed that since whaling was more akin to fishing than, say, to the timber or wine trades, it should be more than a blow-by-blow account of mercantile entrepreneurial activity and competition between British companies and ports, or a repetition of the patriotic school-boy tales of "derring-do," exploration, sturdy ships and human suffering that passed for whaling history. Ralph had taught me that facts are only important in context and tell us little until analysed as part of a pattern. So I set out to find patterns, first in my study of Hull whaling and then for this book.[1] In fact, although the bibliography was huge, there were few publications that could inform my generalizations. Most interest was in seventeenth-century explorations or the 1750-1840 era, when Great Men performed Great Deeds and helped to found the British Empire.

One result of the paucity of economic information on the early rise and fall of British whaling was that I may have under-valued technical problems on the supply side, which have since been examined in great detail by Dutch scholars at the University of Groningen's Arctic Centre, and particularly in the impressive contributions of Louwrens Hacquebord.[2] Indeed, detailed archaeological work at Smeerenburg by Hacquebord, Fritz Steenhuisen and Henk Waterbolk recently produced a convincing case for adjusting my conclusion that British incompetence in early *catching* caused their failure.[3] Instead, their examination of British and Dutch processing plants shows that the Dutch were capable of producing a *better class of oil*, which was reflected in the tendency to import Dutch oil into Britain. Nonetheless, the argument that the British could not catch (or perhaps find) whales may still be justified for the dark period from 1670 to 1740. Elking was adamant that this was the case in the late seventeenth century, and the failure of the massive operation of the South Sea Company bears him out. Moreover, a Glasgow company, noting an earlier failure in 1673-1674, was convinced that

---

[1]G. Jackson, *Hull in the Eighteenth Century* (London, 1972), chapter vii.

[2]L. Hacquebord and R de Bok, *Spitsbergen 79° N.B.: Nederlandse Expeditie in het Spoor van Willem Barentz* (Elsevier, 1981); and Hacquebord and W. Vroom (eds.), *Walvisvaart in de Gouden Eeuw* (Amsterdam, 1988). The latter is the best book on Spitsbergen.

[3]L. Hacquebord, F. Steenhuisen and H. Waterbolk, "English and Dutch Whaling Trade and Whaling Stations in Spitsbergen before 1600," *International Journal of Maritime History*, XV, No. 2 (December 2003), 117-134.

there was "more probability of the company's succeeding...when they use the right means...in short the encouraging of foreigners to settle in Scotland, and to learn us many of the arts and mysteries we are still ignorant of would tend much to our temporal happiness." (infra, chapter 2, section IV). Once blubber rather than oil was brought home, it would presumably have been as easy for Glasgow to hire Dutchmen to run a cookery as it was for the Sugar House and other industrial ventures. Dutch whaling officers were indeed enticed (against Dutch law) for what at that time was essentially pelagic whaling, but with no success, and I suspect that this was because of excessive costs of British compared with Dutch whaling.[4] On the other hand it may be that the British went whaling only when imports of oil were threatened. It is significant that for most of Britain's whaling history imported oil augmented domestic supplies. What was lacking was an international whaling history which would allow comparisons, and this was provided in 1995 by Jurien Leinenga's wide-ranging comparative study of the chief European participants in Greenland and Davis Straits' whaling in the eighteenth century.[5] As well as useful details on whaling from Anstruther, Newcastle, Whitby and Exeter, his tables reveal Britain as a minor participant in whaling, not least because British owners, unable to employ foreigners, faced higher wage bills than Dutch owners who recruited half their men from the north European littoral. He also confirmed the rise of British activity towards the end of the eighteenth century when bounties could make a difference and British industrialization raised demand while American supplies were cut off by war. At the same time the Dutch, suffering from a shortage of labour (and international troubles), were unable to compete with cheaper British oil entering the Continent.

For the 1733-1824 bounty period there were, in the 1970s, antiquarian urban histories and government statistics of total activity at the national and local levels, but with notable exceptions little academic research was done on individual ports, and nothing on the relative Customs returns. Yet shortly after *British Whaling* was published two important articles appeared on Scottish east-coast whaling,[6] and work has since been undertaken on several ports (including my own

---

[4]Jackson, *Hull in the Eighteenth Century*, 112. For whaling as part of the early industrialization of a port, see G. Jackson, "Glasgow in Transition, c. 1660-c. 1740," in T.M. Devine and G. Jackson (eds.), *Glasgow, Volume I: Beginnings to 1830* (Manchester, 1995), 7-85.

[5]Jurjen R. Leinenga, *Arctische Walvisvangst in de Achttiende Eeuw* (Amsterdam, 1995). This book is in Dutch, with an English summary, but the tables and graphs should be understood easily. For a lengthy review, see *International Journal of Maritime History*, IX, No. 1 (June 1997), 274-277.

[6]W.H.R. Duncan, "Aberdeen and the Early Development of the Whaling Industry, 1750-1800," *Northern Scotland*, III, No. 1 (1977-1978), 47-59; and R.C. Michie, "North-east Scotland and the Northern Whale Fishing, 1752-1893," *ibid.*, 61-85.

on Montrose)[7], most notably that of Tony Barrow on the English whaling ports from Newcastle to Whitby.[8] The progress of whaling in individual ports can now be followed in Customs and shipping records in regional archives or the Public Record and Scottish Record offices. Whaling bounty certificates in the latter contain a wealth of detail about ships, owners, crews, voyages and produce. Barrow printed muster rolls and crew lists for his English ports, and the way now seems clear for an examination of the career structure and development of crucial whaling officers. But there is still a lack of private whaling company papers generated in the ports themselves, beyond collections of log books found in whaling museums. Where available these offer information about crews, whaling technology and climate.[9]

Insofar as it deals with the vibrant activity of the Scottish ports, Michie's Scottish article and other material accumulated since the late 1970s has led to a re-examination of my original argument that the British in the last phase of traditional whaling in the nineteenth century were as incompetent as in the first. At an international whaling conference in Sandefjord in 1992 I laid more emphasis on changing internal markets for oil and bone, and on competing demands for mercantile capital in an age of booming steamship companies.[10]

Moreover, Scotland's lead over England requires more emphasis on the "private markets" of Dundee and Peterhead and the increasing Scottish interest in sealing. Here as elsewhere it was the domestic market, expressing itself in rising and falling prices for whale oil, baleen and sealskins, as well as the recurring climatic changes in both Arctic and Antarctic, that influenced whaling, a point clearly made by Chesley Sanger in one of his recent important contributions to whaling history.[11] It is unbelievable that the booming industrial economy

---

[7]G. Jackson, "The Battle with the Arctic: 1785-1839," in G. Jackson, and S.G.E. Lythe (eds.), *The Port of Montrose: A History of its Harbour, Trade and Shipping.* (Tayport, 1993), 200-224.

[8]T. Barrow, *The Whaling Trade of North-East England, 1750-1850* (Sunderland, 2001). This book is based upon the author's PhD thesis.

[9]A multiple-indexed list of all 5018 logs known to exist is in J.M. Downie and V.M. Adams (eds.), *Whaling Logbooks and Journals, 1613-1927: An Inventory of Manuscript Records in Public Collections* (New York, 1986).

[10]G. Jackson, 'Why Did the British Not Catch Rorquals in the Nineteenth Century?" in B.L. Basberg, J.E. Ringstad and E. Wexelsen (eds.), *Whaling and History: Perspectives on the Evolution of the Industry* (Sandefjord, 1993), 111-119.

[11]C.W. Sanger, "'Oil is an Indispensable Necessity of Life:' The Impact of Oscillating Oil and Baleen Prices on Cyclical Variations in the Scale and Scope of Northern Commercial Whaling, 1600-1900," *International Journal of Maritime History*, XV, No.

of Scotland could not have adopted and perfected the dreams of Thomas Welcome Roys in the 1860s of rocket harpoons, floating factories with cookers and steam catchers with steam winches. Significantly, his vessels were built in Glasgow and Dundee and his rockets made in Dundee![12]

The fact that Roys was a failure does not affect the argument. Why were Roys' inventions perfected by Svend Foyn rather than by a combination of British shipbuilders and whaling owners in an economy awash with money and engineering skills? It is obvious that the declining market for whale oil and the availability of imports were important, and so was the easy availability of investment opportunities in developing temperate grasslands in the Empire and the Americas. Moreover, it seems increasingly clear that we should look at the nature of the transition from "old" to "new" whaling. I was mesmerized by pictures of capital-intensive floating factories. But that was not the start of modern whaling, which was not pelagic but rather a mechanized version of Spitsbergen – or Biscay – bay whaling. Improvement meant land-based catchers going further, faster and with an increased likelihood of killing and recovering a whale. This was possible because the coast of Finnmark was conveniently near migration routes, and oil and meat could be processed rapidly. No one in the northwest of Britain showed any interest in building shore stations, even when Norwegians built one at Bunaveneader and Salvesens of Leith (deeply involved with its Norwegian homeland) opened its facility at Olna. Not until 1922 did Lord Leverhulme think it worth buying Bunaveneader, and Britain's sudden interest in whaling sprang from the international fat crisis of 1904 and the huge potential of Antarctic whaling stations that would have to be in territory claimed by Britain. I may have thought more carefully about whaling stations had I known about the two in Ireland: the Norwegian/British Arranmore (1907) and Blacksod (1910) stations described in detail by James Fairley in 1981, a feat which added greatly to our knowledge of whaling in British home waters.[13]

In this, and other omissions and mistakes, it will be obvious to anyone who knows much about twentieth-century whaling that I did not benefit from J.N. Tønnessen and A.O. Johnsen's *Den Moderne Hvalfangsts Historie*, which was not translated until 1982.[14] *British Whaling Trade* would have benefited from access to its huge store of international detail, though some of its Norwegian-oriented

---

2 (December 2003), 147-157.

[12]See F.P. Schmitt, C. de Jong and F.H. Winter, *Thomas Welcome Roys: America's Pioneer of Modern Whaling* (Charlottesville, VA, 1980), especially chapter 10.

[13]J. Fairley, *Irish Whales and Whaling* (Belfast. 1981).

[14]J.N. Tønnessen and A.O. Johnsen, *Den Moderne Hvalfangsts Historie* (4 vols., Sandefjord, 1959-1970). This volume was ranslated in shortened form as *The History of Modern Whaling* (London, 1982).

assessments would have been questioned. It was certainly pleasing to see that I had unwittingly followed their approach to balancing the supply and demand sides of whaling and emphasising the importance of technological and chemical advances on sea and land. To some extent I accommodated their ideas in a lecture published in 1994.[15]

The success or failure of whaling was clearly interlocked with British industrial developments and social changes, not least in the fickleness of fashion, as appeared in the chapter on whaling in my thesis on Hull, which Ralph had supervised. Its advances were stimulated by other and various advances in economic and political life. Yet because its products were secured in the open sea or ocean, it followed the paths of explorers – or did its own exploring. It was facilitated by the "expansion of Europe," the invention of maps, compasses and, indeed, cannons. But because it was a ship-oriented trade, and those ships were good, bellicose governments periodically subsidized it as a "nursery of seamen" and a source of auxiliary armed transports, though the demands of the naval press gangs upset it gravely. While offering valuable new information which would fill-out this volume and make possible more on the social side, and on the structure of companies, there is no reason so far to adjust the basic generalisations which were made in this volume.

It was also clear that competition between companies and ports for the domestic market was not a crucial matter compared with two exogenous factors beyond the control of entrepreneurs. Fishing on the high seas was open to all comers, and from the start there was rivalry, sometimes violent, between British and Dutch whalers. More important, merchants involved in the whale oil trade had the option of employing their own expensive whalers or importing the oil and bone from Holland and, eventually, from British colonies in America and Australasia. In other words, the whaling "industry" was only one of the suppliers in the British whale oil "trade."

In the modern period the highly capitalized pelagic "expeditions" faced competition from foreign vessels and companies about which little was known in the 1970s. The publication *International Whaling Statistics* was available, as were Mr. Geddes' papers, but the structure of companies was vague; in particular, the interlocking financial affairs of many British and Norwegian companies were little understood. The work of Klaus Barthelmess has revealed not only the German whaling stations on the coast of German South West Africa but also the increasing German interest in factory whaling in the 1930s.[16] Jaap Bruijn has emphasised the

---

[15]G. Jackson, "The Rise and Fall of the Trade in Edible Whale Products," in K. Friedland (ed.), *Maritime Food Transport* (Köln, 1994), 434-448.

[16]K. Barthelmess, "A Century of German Interests in Modern Whaling, 1860s-1060s," in Basberg, Ringstad and Wexelsen (eds), *Whaling and History*, 121-138.

importance of state assistance for recreating Dutch whaling after WW II.[17] Ian Hart's huge book on Compañia Argentina de Pesca Sociedad Anónima tells us a great deal about the complexities of international whaling finance, company formation and the interplay of personalities from various nations.[18] Created with Argentinian funds by the pioneering Norwegian C.A. Larsen to exploit the whaling potential around Grytviken (British) to provide products chiefly for Britain, managed by Norwegians, and finally by an Irish Argentinian, it ran Grytviken with some success from 1904 to 1962 but ruined itself by dabbling in floating factories, supporting President Perón by building one of the largest, *Juan Perón* – which never caught a whale. It was not a happy history, but this is a valuable detailed analysis of a company doomed in the wind-down of whaling.

The purpose of this book was to write about *British* whaling, and the best approach seemed to be to set it a firmly within the context of the national economy on the one hand and international whaling on the other. Recent work has tended to support the generalizations contained in it, and I am happy that younger researchers have shown such interest in the subject. The main thing now, it seems to me from our ivory tower in Argyll, is for someone to link the increasing material on the whaling of all varieties, for all purposes, by all involved nations, from start to finish. It should link the economics and technologies, politics and personalities within a huge international industry that played an important part at various times in providing oil, foodstuffs and fashion. It might start with a list of all those (British – but not Dutch) economic history books in whose indices whaling does not appear.

Gordon Jackson
University of Strathclyde
January 2005

---

[17]J.R. Bruijn, "Dutch Whaling after the Second World War: Private Initiative and State Involvement," *Mariners' Mirror*, LXXXVIII (2002), 307-322.

[18]I.B. Hart, *Pesca: A History of the Pioneer Modern Whaling Company in the Antarctic* (Salcombe, 2001).

Preface

It is doubtful if any trade, save that in human beings, has attracted so much attention as whaling. There is a huge bibliography, which in 1948 filled ninety-five pages of the *Journal of the Society for the Bibliography of Natural History*. From its major advance in the 1780s, and especially during the last century, whaling – described by one of its earliest participants as "the greatest chase which nature yieldeth" – appealed to a readership searching for tales of exploration, adventure and hazard in romantic, far-off places. In the present century interest has to some extent shifted, and scientists working for or against the trade have produced a vast number of monographs on whales and various aspects of whaling. A number of books have combined a zoology of the whale with a brief outline of the trade, either to instruct a popular audience or to secure its condemnation of the ruthlessness of modern whaling. So far there has been no modern history of the whole of Britain's three hundred and fifty year involvement – sometimes extensive and sometimes slight – in whaling. In endeavouring to fill this gap, I have tried to steer a course between intricate science and exaggerated adventure. While recognising the appeal – and importance – of the human side of whaling, I have avoided lengthy accounts of the daring, bravery and suffering that appear in so many original and secondary sources. Nor have I dwelt on the bloody side of whaling. D'Arcy Thompson, the distinguished naturalist and member of the Scottish Fishery Board, once remarked that "the whale, for all its great size, has no voice with which to cry out when it is harpooned and lacerated by the whalermen, and no man can tell what suffering the poor creatures silently endure as they die of their wounds." There is no evidence that whalermen were ever impressed by the whale's silence, but they were commonly awestruck by the incongruity of their activities, and many men, to slave their conscience or enhance their prowess, told of the sufferings of the whale. That the Leviathan, with such bounding energy, could be overcome by puny men was more likely to be thought of as an Act of God rewarding sabbath observance than as capital in the pursuit of profit; and its heroic struggles have entered classical literature in Herman Melville's *Moby Dick*. Recent books have continued to describe every twitch of the stricken whale, with technicolor illustrations to bring home the enormity of what one recent observer – R.B. Robertson – called a "brobdingnagian Butcher's Shop." But that, after all, is what whaling was all about, and to introduce too much emotion is no more sensible than spending a chapter in a history of farming on the intricacies of slaughterhouse techniques. Although some account of catching methods – and of the hazards facing the crews – is essential to an understanding of the trade, I have written a relatively bloodless account from the point of view of an economic historian, using the normal sort of historical evidence which has, to some extent, been neglected. In particular, I have made use of official statistical material to show something of the size, and performance over time, of the whaling fleet. Such statistics must be approached with a degree of caution, for though they are supposedly accurate, based on certificates and the like, in practice there are a number of internal complications (for instance, some ships claimed their bounty late, and so are counted in the total for the following year). It would be unwise to assert the absolute accuracy of any particular figure without allowing some margin for error, but it remains true that the differences between various official tables are not statistically significant, and have no effect on the trend patterns deduced from them. Statistics after 1918 are assumed to be accurate.

The history of British whaling falls naturally into two parts. The first covers the original and traditional whaling trade which varied from time to time in region and in intensity, but which employed techniques that changed little in three centuries. Its purpose was to provide oil as a rudimentary material chiefly for illumination, lubrication and cloth-making, and whalebone for corsets. In the eighteenth century it was divided into two legally distinct trades – the old Northern Whale Fishery and the new Southern Whale Fishery – with different entrepreneurs, different systems of organisation and, by and large, different whales: the Right whales of the Arctic, and the sperm whales of the mid-Atlantic and the Pacific. For the sake of clarity these two divisions will be dealt with separately, though they co-existed and obviously affected each other to some extent. The second part covers the modern trade, with new sorts of whales, new techniques, new ships, and a totally different order of magnitude which justifies the relatively greater attention paid to it here. The purpose now was to provide oil for soap and margarine, and whaling therefore became involved with modern oil technology which played a vital role in the expansion of the trade.

For the early history, I have been forced to rely on the eye-witness accounts and the state papers which have formed the restricted basis for histories over the last two centuries. For the eighteenth and nineteenth centuries, however, it is possible to use the very extensive records kept by the Board of Customs and the Board of Trade, and these allow a more systematic study. It remains true, nevertheless, that any work on the traditional whaling trade must be deeply indebted to William Scoresby, whaling captain turned Divine, whose monumental work, describing every aspect of the Northern Whale Fishery, will never be surpassed. The most difficult period to write about is, in fact, that which follows Scoresby's terminal date around 1820. The state was already losing interest in the trade, and it more or less disappeared from Board of Trade notice, though indirect evidence occurs in several of the Parliamentary enquiries that became common after the Napoleonic war. Published accounts of whaling, though quite common, never rise above the anecdotal. The greatest drawback for that, as for the previous century, is the lack of adequate merchant papers to throw light on whaling from the point of view of the entrepreneurs, though I have been able to draw heavily on the collections of whaling log books in Hull for the descriptive material on conditions in the whaling grounds.

For the modern period there are fortunately papers surviving from the two major British firms set up early in the present century: Southern Whaling Company and Salvesen (the latter name will be used throughout, in preference to the variously named subsidiaries that were formed for each of Salvesen's operations). The historical papers of Lever Brothers (and after 1929 of Unilever), as owners of Southern Whaling Company and the world's largest consumers of whale oil, have thrown much light on to market conditions and fluctuations in the trade, and I am most grateful to Unilever for allowing me to use them. So far as Salvesen were concerned, Dr. Wray Vamplew had worked through their voluminous papers (deposited in Edinburgh University Library) ahead of me for his *Salvesen of Leith* (1975), and he most generously gave me his manuscript to save me the work of duplication. I am greatly indebted to his detailed and lucid account of Salvesen's whaling activities. On a more general level, a magnificent collection of statistics, and information on market conditions and whaling fleets, is contained in the papers of David Geddes & Son, Ltd., the leading whale oil brokers, and I am most grateful to Mr. David Geddes for drawing them to my notice and for lengthy discussions during which I benefited from his immense knowledge of whaling in the modern period.

I should also like to acknowledge my debt to the many institutions and individuals who have made my work possible: to the officers and staff of the Public Record Office, the Scottish Record Office and the British Museum Department of Manuscripts; the Local History Library and Wilberforce House Library, Hull; the Custom House, Hull; and the Mitchell Library, Glasgow. My passage through the mass of Unilever papers was greatly eased by the hospitality and advice of Mr. J.D. Keir, Mr. H. Boyd and Miss M. O'Neil of the Legal Department, Miss M. Staniforth of the Information Library, and Mr. T. Turner of Palm Line, United Africa Company, Dr. P.N. Davies kindly drew my attention to Southern Whaling Company material in the papers of Henry Tyrer & Son of Liverpool, to whom I am indebted for their use. The trustees of the Houblon-Norman Fund generously supported a project of research of which my Scottish whaling material formed part. As usually happens, my work has benefited from the chance remarks or detailed advice of many friends and colleagues, including Frank Broeze, John Butt, Robin Craig, Peter Davies, Tom Devine, John Hume, Joan Lythe and Hamish Whyte. In particular I owe a great debt to Ralph Davis, David Geddes, Edgar Lythe and John Ward, who have read and made valuable criticisms of the manuscript, which owes a great deal to their wide and constructive advice.

Finally, but not least, I should like to thank my wife for her help in the preparation of the manuscript, and Miss Catherine Summerhill, Miss Carolyn Maclean and Mrs. Elziabeth Thrippleton, who did the typing.

In one matter I must crave the indulgence of the zoologist. The whale was *not* a fish, but in the past it was often so regarded and invariably so described, both in whaling parlance and in Acts of Parliament. I have followed this inaccurate terminology because of the difficulties that would have arisen in quotations and legal definitions.

GORDON JACKSON
University of Strathclyde
August 1976

Chapter 1
Northern Adventures and the
Spitsbergen Trade, c. 1604-1670

I

The origins of whaling are hidden in the mists of mythology and are, perhaps, best left there. When and where man first realised the economic potential of the world's largest animals, and how he was first able to catch them, is a matter for speculation based on inadequate texts.[1] So far as Europe is concerned, medieval commentators, including King Alfred, wrote about a Norwegian whale fishery. Icelanders were reputed to have eaten the whale, and Norman-French gastronomes appreciated its tongue. On both sides of the Channel, and in Scotland, whales were accorded the status of "royal fish" and made the subject of grants and charters assigning the benefits to be had from their stranded carcasses. They were viewed with awe and wonderment, especially from the decks of ships that were smaller than they were, but determined efforts were nevertheless being made to catch them in early modern times in both northern and southern Europe. In the north it had been discovered that certain types of small pilot whales which passed in schools through coastal waters could be encouraged to beach themselves by fishermen raising a din and thrashing the water - as happened in the Norwegian, Icelandic, Orkney and Shetland "fisheries." In the south the Basques had by the fifteenth century developed something approaching a modern "industry," as local fishermen went out to attack whales breeding in the Bay of Biscay. It was this Basque fishery, rather than that in the north, which led directly to the modern whaling trade. It was thought for a long time, and recorded by Scoresby,[2] that the whale involved - long since vanished from Biscay - was a type of small fin whale called *Balaena rostrata*, but modern cetologists believe it to have been a type of medium to large black whale called, as if to prove the point, *Balaena biscayensis*. The significance of this lies in the fact that, whatever the zoological differences, *Balaena biscayensis* was simply a smaller version of the great *Balaena mysticetus* which was to become the chief quarry of the European whaling trade over the next two centuries. In other

---

[1]See, for example, the survey of early references in L.H. Matthews, *et al.*, *The Whale* (London, 1968), chapter 1.

[2]W. Scoresby, *An Account of the Arctic Regions, with a History and Description of the Northern Whale Fishery* (2 vols., Edinburgh, 1820), II, 3.

words, the skills developed over generations in the traditional peasant employment of the Basques could be transferred with a minimum of trouble to the commercial whaling trade.[3]

Early European whaling was concerned only with those sorts of whales that were easily caught, and only those sorts that came within home waters, but already, before commercial whaling started, *Balaena biscayensis* was growing rare through constant fishing in the breeding ground. The whaling trade had therefore to await the creation of the true ocean-going ship and the development of oceanic navigation in order to extend the search, either for new stocks of *Balaena biscayensis* or for alternative sorts of whales with similar characteristics. In this respect the founding of the whaling trade was as much part of the "Expansion of Europe" as the discovery of America, and as important, in its own way, as the more publicised Newfoundland cod fishery. Expeditions searching for whales followed hard on the heels of the explorers, but it was not the Basques, despite early visits to the Icelandic seas, who were destined to enjoy the benefits of new discoveries. The initiative passed quickly to the English and the Dutch, who were far more enterprising in their northern explorations. While the Spanish and Portuguese consolidated their transatlantic empires, and the Portuguese acquired the Asiatic spice trade, the English and Dutch sought the north-east passage to the fabled riches of the Indies. In 1553 the "Mystery and Company of the Merchant Adventurers for the Discovery of Regions, Dominions, Islands and Places Unknown," of which old Sebastian Cabot was governor, sent off Hugh Willoughby to find China, and though two of the three ships were lost, the third, under Richard Chancellor, "found" Russia and established the possibility of a regular trade with that vast and unknown country through the port of Archangel, there being no direct access through the Baltic at this time, partly because Russia had no secure outlet to the sea, and partly because the Hanse merchants dominated Baltic trade. Two years later the adventurers regrouped as the first of the great joint stock companies, usually known as the Muscovy Company, and established their trade round the North Cape which introduced the English to the hazards of Arctic weather and to seas in which whales were a constant sight. In 1577, having secured the services of Basque whalemen, the Muscovy Company was granted a twenty-year monopoly on whaling "within any seas whatsoever," though it appears at first to have been interested only in the fin whales around Iceland.[4]

---

[3]For a brief account of the Basque fishery, see J.T. Jenkins, *A History of the Whale Fisheries* (London, 1921).

[4]For the activities of the Muscovy Company, see T. S. Willan, *The Early History of the Russia Company, 1553-1603* (Manchester, 1956), *passim*.

The prospect of a national whaling industry was consistent with aspirations of the embryo mercantilists of Elizabethan England, and with the growing urge to attain self-sufficiency against those countries which appeared to benefit from a more indulgent environment. In 1580 Richard Hakluyt advised the Muscovy Company's explorers to record the existence of whales and fish "to the end we may turn our Newfoundland fishing or Iceland fishing, or our whalefishing that way, for the aid and comfort of our new trades to the Northeast to the coasts of Asia,"[5] and in the same year, in one of those treatises outlining the economic potential of the world that was opening up to the Elizabethans, Robert Hitchcock urged Englishmen to see profit in northern waters: "The whale is upon the coasts of Russia towards Muscovy and St. Nicholas. The killing of the whale is both pleasant and profitable, and without great charges, yielding great plenty of oil, the tun whereof is worth ten pounds."[6] It was, in reality, easier said than done, and not until the end of the century were regular voyages undertaken from England, chiefly, it would seem, by interlopers from the port of Hull, which had established an oil trade with Vardo and Kola in 1579, and had long had traditional connexions with Iceland to which whaling voyages were undertaken in 1598 in the wake of the Basques.

The opening up of Arctic whaling followed a series of exploratory voyages launched by the Muscovy Company in the decade beginning in 1604.[7] In that year Jonas Poole charted the route to Bear Island (then called Cherrie Island in honour of the Company's governor), and came back with reports of foxes, fowls and walrus - the latter most difficult to kill, though a few of their tusks were brought home to encourage the Company.[8] In 1605, 1606 and 1608 Poole returned to Bear Island, exploring its cold and inhospitable landscape - "Mount Misery" was thought an appropriate placename - and increasing the efficiency of walrus hunting until, with luck, 1000 were killed in seven hours in

---

[5]R.H. Tawney and E. Power (eds.), *Tudor Economic Documents* (3 vols, London, 1924-1951), III, 233.

[6]*Ibid.*, III, 246.

[7]The following account is drawn from the writings of participants reprinted in W.M. Conway, *Early Dutch and English Voyages to Spitsbergen in the Seventeenth Century* (London, 1904); and S. Purchas, *Hakluytus Posthumus, or Purchas His Pilgrimes* (20 vols., Glasgow, 1905-1907), XIII and XIV; and from extensive references in the *Calendars of State Papers (Domestic)*. Most histories of the early trade rely on these sources (and on each other); the best of them is probably still M. Conway, *No Man's Land: A History of Spitsbergen* (Cambridge, 1906).

[8]Jonas Poole, "Divers Voyages to Cherie Iland, in the Years 1604...1609," in Purchas, *Hakluytus Posthumus*, XIII, 269.

1608, yielding thirty-one tuns of oil from their blubber.[9] In 1609 he was ordered to explore Lapland with a view to establishing regular purchases of fish, but having failed in his prime object he once more returned to Bear Island, where he was surprised to discover a Hull ship already engaged in walrus hunting, "I went thither," Poole wrote later, "and told him we had taken possession there... He answered, that if the beasts came on shore, he would kill them if he could; and that there were as good men which ventured in that ship, as the Company's. I told him he durst not answer these words in England, and so departed and got some fowl."[10] The tone of this first meeting of English captains in the Arctic – which was rather like Livingstone telling Stanley he had no business to be in Africa – bode ill for the future, and can best be understood in terms of the jealousy with which the early explorers guarded the benefits to be derived from their discoveries, when rivals were never far behind and when those benefits, in this case walrus, were not sufficiently numerous for men to share with good grace.

According to Thomas Edge, another of the Company's early captains, it was the growing scarcity of walrus that "made the Company look out for further Discoveries,"[11] though in fact all the Company's expeditions, at least until 1611, were interested in finding the route to the east, and even after whaling became the prime objective, captains occasionally prejudiced the fishing by spending too long "exploring." While Poole was still investigating Bear Island, Henry Hudson was sent northwards in 1607 and 1608, and in failing to find the North-east passage came upon Spitsbergen, noting "whales, porpoises and the sea full of fowls" around latitude 74-75°. His men also saw a "mermaid" – long-haired, white and human-breasted at one end, and mackerel-speckled at the other – but it was the whales that excited most interest.[12] They had found what they were looking for: an abundance of whales that looked like *Balaena biscayensis* and turned out to be *Balaena mysticetus*, the Greenland Right whale. The whales were, however, in the open sea and consequently beyond the reach of contemporary whalermen. It was not, therefore, Hudson's explorations that were crucial for whaling, but those of Poole in 1610 when, sent in the sixty-ton *Elizabeth* towards the north pole to find a polar route to the east (seventeenth-

---

[9]*Ibid.*, 276.

[10]*Ibid.*, 284.

[11]Thomas Edge, "A Briefe Discoverie of the Northerne Discoveries of Seas, Coasts and Countries...," in Purchas, *Hakluytus Posthumus*, XIII, 11.

[12]"A Second Voyage...of Master Henry Hudson for Finding a Passage to the East Indies by the North East, written by himself," in Purchas, *Hakluytus Posthumus*, XIII, 318.

century charts did not plot the polar ice cap!), he thoroughly explored the seas around Spitsbergen. He not only reported on the abundance of whales, but also marked and named Whale Bay, which could provide the shore base without which Biscay-type whaling could not function.[13] As a result his commission for 1611[14] included leading the first whaler, the 160-ton *Margaret*, in the charge of Edge, to Spitsbergen:

> for as much as by your own report of the great store of whales in those seas, we are at an extraordinary charge this year, of setting out a shop and men for that purpose...And God sending you to the said place, we would have you to stay there the killing of a whale, or two or three, for your better experience hereafter to expedite that business, if through extremity of the ice you should be put from your discoveries...

To this expedition, in 1611, fell the distinction of killing the first Greenland whale and thereby founding the modern whaling trade.

II

The Right whale – so called to distinguish it from the wrong whales to catch – was the most suitable of all the whales on which to found a trade at that time. Some indication of its advantages, and of the difficulties and dangers of whaling, might best be conveyed in a description of the whale itself, and of the methods employed in its capture, which changed little in the next two hundred and fifty years. It must, however, be emphasized that *Balaena mysticetus* has never been scientifically investigated and, in view of its size and scarcity, probably never will be, so that much about it remains a mystery.

As with all the large whales, the Right whale was a passive feeder, that is to say, it supported its huge bulk – some sixty feet in length and weighing a hundred tons or more – with the minimum effort and maximum intake by swimming slowly with its mouth open through the superabundance of plankton to be found in Arctic (and Antarctic) waters. As it expelled the water the plankton, chiefly krill (a sort of shrimp), was caught in the plates of hairy "whalebone" (baleen) that hung from its upper jaw in the nature of a sieve. No other whale had so much bone, the largest pieces of which, in a good-sized animal, might be fifteen feet long and fifteen inches wide. Altogether there were around five

---

[13]For Poole's 1610 voyage, see Purchas, *Hakluytus Posthumus*, XIII, 11-12, and XIV, 1-23.

[14]*Ibid.*, XIV, 24-25.

hundred pieces, weighing around a ton and, in most periods, worth at least as much as the oil.

The animal's feeding habits had a direct practical advantage that was as important as the indirect financial advantage. The krill were to be found with the mass of plankton that was generated where warm water from the south met cold water from the north. Here, not far distant from the ice, the whalers eventually discovered that they would find their quarry in the feeding season, its likely presence indicated by the discolouration of the water caused by the plankton. The first expeditions, and those that followed them for the next half-century, met the whales further south, for though such vast creatures could only survive because of the Arctic foodstore they were impelled southwards, either by necessity or by some primeval influence, to do their breeding. living off their fat until they moved north again. So they could be found as regularly as clockwork in their breeding bays, or the bays in which they rested en route, and before long the old whaling hands could forecast their movements as countrymen look at the sky and sniff the air and know when the ducks will go or the geese will come. Compared with some whales, *Balaena mysticetus* had a rather short migration and spent much of its time in relatively cold conditions, and this may have been the reason why its blubber – at between twelve and eighteen inches – was the thickest of any whale.

Balaena mysticetus was not the right whale simply because its was plump and well endowed with whalebone, or even because it was relatively easily found in the bays of Spitsbergen. The chief characteristic that sealed its fate was the relative ease with which it could be caught. The Right whale had all the docility of a grazing animal and none of its timidity. With no natural enemies it had no adequate mechanism of fear to warn it of impending danger, and for all its intelligence it never learned to suspect man. William Scoresby, reflecting on the relative strength of whales and of the men who overcome them, could attribute success only to the "Great first Cause." "The Providence of God," he wrote in 1820, "is manifested in the tameness and timidity of many of the largest inhabitants of the earth and sea, whereby they fall victims to the prowess of man, and are rendered subservient to his convenience in life. And this was the design of the lower animals in their creation."[15] Unfortunately the Great first Cause inflicted tameness on only two sorts of "commercial" whales, and men needed every ounce of prowess and a great deal of skill to catch even the most docile of them.

Both *Balaena biscayensis* and *Balaena mysticetus* were slow movers, and could therefore be hunted in the double-ended, six-man rowing boats that persisted till the First World War. When whales were seen – or heard – from the shore, the boats were rowed at speed to the approximate vicinity, and then

---

[15]Scoresby, *Account of the Arctic Regions*, II, 240.

manoeuvred stealthily by the expert steersman.[16] If he was lucky the whales remained on the surface, but they were just as likely to be "sounding" – for up to twenty minutes – and coming up only for short breathing spaces. In the latter case it was experience that guided the boat to the spot where the whale was next likely to rise and "blow." It was a matter of constant, back-breaking rowing – "the religion of rowing," as Melville called it – that could go on for hours before the boat was positioned for the harpooner, standing in the front, to throw his hand harpoon into the creature's back. It was then that the battle really began.

The whale was taken, as a fish is taken, by playing it on the end of al line. The harpoon was no more than a hook which could do no serious or lasting damage to a whale. As it sounded it took with it the heavy ropes coiled in the bottom of the boat, sometimes with such speed that the line-manager stood by to wet the rope against firing and to add further ropes if the dive should be a deep one, lest the whale took the boat down with it. Whenever possible a "fast boat" – that is, one fast to a whale – summoned assistance, and more ropes could be added until the whale was dragging a vast sea anchor consisting of several miles of rope and three or four heavy boats. If a second harpoon could be fixed when the whale came up to blow, the operation might be speeded up; but it rarely took less than four hours and could take as much as forty to exhaust a powerful full-grown whale. When at last it came to the surface, tamed, it was despatched with long lances, though this again was easier said than done; it was difficult to penetrate a vital organ, and most whales probably died from exhaustion and loss of blood. Thus the Right whales were penalised by the very qualities that endeared them to their hunters: their huge head (a third of their total bulk) and their vast store of blubber probably had an adverse affect on their relative speed and strength. Certainly the majority of whales cannot be caught in this fashion: only *Balaena biscayensis* and *Balaena mysticetus* (and later the sperm whale) can be "fished." Even in death these hapless creatures had a "favourable" characteristic: they floated, whereas most whales sink, and cannot therefore be towed back to the beach by rowing boats.

The final victory, after the whale was struck, was by no means easy and far from certain, and to make it appear so would be unjust to the men who risked life and limb in a most dangerous trade. As a stricken fish sounded, its tail could turn the toughest shallop to matchwood, while any rapid change of direction not spotted by the boat-steerer could upset the boat and drown the men. At the least they would suffer from exposure, and any delay in returning to base might bring on frostbite, the dreaded curse of the whaling trade. More often the whale escaped, through the harpoon drawing or the rope breaking.

---

[16]One of the earliest detailed accounts of the fishery methods is that of Edge, "Briefe Discoverie," in Purchas, *Hakluytus Posthumus*, xiii, 26-30.

It was an essential part of primitive whaling that the animal should be winched onto a beach for processing. The flensers made deep and expert cuts in the blubber with their curved, razor-sharp knives as they moved over the carcass in their spiked boots, and the blubber was torn away in strips by winch or brute force, undercut by long blubber spades after the manner of lifting turfs. Once free, the blubber was chopped into small pieces – whales' tails serving as chopping blocks – and fed into the iron pots called try-works where it was boiled for many hours until the maximum oil had been extracted. In order to clean it, the oil was poured into a shallop partially filled with water so that the oil floated and the impurities sank, and then sometimes into a second shallop before being casked and rowed out to the vessel which, in these circumstances, was a transport rather than a whaler in the later sense of the word. The residue from the try-works – the fenks – were fed into the boiler and so helped to solve the difficult problem of fuel shortage in Spitsbergen. Oil produced in this way would have been edible had anyone desired to consume it, or reasonable care been taken in handling it. The flesh, too, was edible, though there is no evidence that Europeans ever used more than the tongue. So much has been written about the filth and stench of whaling that it is important to emphasise that oil produced in the manner outlined above had no offensive taste or smell. It was the decomposition of the carcass, not the boiling of fresh blubber, that turned the stomachs of even the most hardened whalermen. Fresh oil could be substituted for vegetable oil for many purposes, and though the Europeans did not easily overcome their prejudice against its use in food, they readily adopted it for soap-making, and were ready to try it in the processing of textiles and in other trades for which oils are essential.

III

The first Spitsbergen whaling season was a failure, through a crippling mixture of back-luck and inexperience.[17] The fishing itself was moderately successful. The six harpooners recruited from the Basque town of San Jean de Luz managed to catch thirteen whales, assisted by Englishmen who were enthusiastically – and incorrectly – reported as rapidly learning the trade. Their efforts were brought to nought, however, by the loss of both vessels. Thomas Edge, unaware of the danger of ice drifting into bays, allowed his whaler to be destroyed at its supposedly safe anchorage; and Poole, coming to the rescue, allowed his ship to capsize while taking on cargo. The whole expedition was only saved from disaster by the fortunate proximity of the *Hopewell* of Hull which, with doubtful legality, was hunting for walrus.

---

[17]*Ibid.*, XIII, 13-15.

For the Muscovy Company this was the third hunting expedition led by Edge which had resulted in loss,[18] but at least the abundance of whales and the suitability of the bays had been proved. The evidence was certainly strong enough to ensure the continuance of Spitsbergen whaling though the region explored and first used by Poole and Edge, between the mainland and Edge's Island, was soon abandoned in favour of the natural harbours of the west coast, which were as easy of access and were more commonly frequented by whales during their migration.

Spitsbergen was clearly a valuable asset to be exploited by its discoverers, who were dismayed to learn that their next expedition, consisting of the aptly named *Whale* and *Seahorse*, had been joined in the fishery by the *Hopewell*, which had turned to whaling, by an independent vessel from London, and, more seriously for the future, by the first whaler to come from Holland, piloted by one Allen Sallowes, twenty years in the Company's service and now forced to flee abroad for debt. There was also a Basque vessel, from San Sebastian, piloted by another former employee, Nicholas Woodcock, who on his return home spent sixteen months in the Tower for his temerity in leading foreigners into an English preserve.[19]

The jealousy and subsequent violence in the Spitsbergen fishery sprang as much from the nature of early whaling as from straightforward international animosities. There were only a few places in which whales were known to congregate within reach of the shore bases that were essential for a rapid transference of skills from the Biscay fishery to the Arctic fishery; so the various nationalities congregated with the whales and shadowed each other in their anxiety that none should enjoy an exclusive success. As rival boats competed for whales within the bays, and lines were tangled or deliberately cut, the dangers of whaling were magnified and the chance of success diminished. Already there were – or were thought to be – too many boats after too few whales. One of the Muscovy Company's captains summed up the situation in a bay where the Dutch were pressing too hard: "With theirs and ours there is 30 shallops in the Bay, too many for us to make a voyage."[20]

Undoubtedly the Muscovy Company was over-sensitive about its rights and about the potential damage to be done by rivals – as, for instance, when it complained to the Privy Council about an interloper ruining the fishing in a "bay" that turned out to be thirty miles across. Nevertheless, a very real problem did exist on the beaches, where try-works and storehouses were established

---

[18]See Edge's 1611 Commission, in *ibid.*, XIV, 30.

[19]Conway, *Early Dutch and English Voyages*, 304.

[20]Robert Salmon, in Purchas, *Hakluytus Posthumus*, XIV, 94.

and where the men lived, first in tents and later in wooden and brick structures. Permanent camps reinforced the advantages accruing to those who secured the best initial sites, and with land and property at stake the Company naturally desired a national possession to guarantee both camps and stores from one season to the next. So began the legal tussles and warlike turmoil that characterised the first half-century of European whaling in the Arctic: Spitsbergen came very near to being a second Amboyna. Exclusiveness was thought to be essential for securing adequate profit, and adequate profit, the Company implied in a petition to James I, might be £500 for every £100 invested! In an age in which adventurers expected such a huge (and speedy) return, and their captains were no less eager for riches, there were two courses open to the Company and its servants: they could keep out rivals, whether English interlopers or foreigners, or they could appropriate their catches. Both courses were pursued with such vigour that the first phase of whaling was disastrous for a Company with neither the capital nor the power to support a policy of aggressive monopoly. In the end it was ruined, but not before it had, in its decline, effectively stifled England's participation in Arctic whaling.

It was Woodcock's success, rather than the activities of the Muscovy Company, that encouraged a burst of whaling preparations in Holland and Biscay in the winter of 1612-1613, and persuaded the Company to seek royal support for its claims, based on Willoughby's supposed discovery of Spitsbergen, now officially called King James' New Land. In March 1613 the Company received confirmation of its "liberties"[21] – including the sole right to trade with Greenland (as Spitsbergen was then popularly called) – and with such a clear token of royal support prepared to enforce those liberties with seven large and heavily-armed vessels, captained by veterans of the north such as Edge, Marmaduke (the Hull captain who was now forced by the monopoly to take employment with the Company) and William Baffin, who three years later discovered – and praised the whaling potential of – Baffin Bay, the last exploited and least accessible of the Atlantic whaling areas. It was the first of a series of battle fleets rather than whaling fleets, and it made short work of a score of foreign vessels (several piloted by renegade Englishmen), driving most of them away clean (as whaling men very appropriately called an unsuccessful ship) but allowing the Basques to remain, and retain a portion of their catches, in return for boiling blubber for the Company.

The appeal to force had apparently succeeded, but it was a victory dearly purchased. The cost of hunting foreigners greatly exceeded the cost of hunting whales, and the Company ended the season with a loss of between three and four thousand pounds. It was, moreover, a lesson easily learned and speedily copied. In 1614 the English faced a larger Dutch fleet supported by four

---

[21]Great Britain, *Calendar of State Papers* (*Domestic*) (*CSP*), 30 March 1613.

warships and a monopoly charter granted to the Noordsche Campagnie by Count Maurice, reciting its claim to regions explored by Barents in 1596, including Spitsbergen. The Company's admiral, while rejecting the Dutch claims, nevertheless recognised that discretion was the better part, and came to terms whereby the fishing was shared, to the exclusion of third parties. The English monopoly of Arctic whaling had been brief indeed.[22]

In the years that followed, a scarcely-veiled hostility that spoiled the fishing and sometimes erupted in violence, brought the Muscovy Company to its knees; and at the most inopportune movement it also faced an invasion of its position at home. James I of England very properly maintained the rights of the Muscovy Company, but as James VI of Scotland was under no such obligation, and in 1618 incorporated the Scottish East India and Greenland Company. The English Companies were less concerned about the threatened Scottish rivalry than about the possibility – which later materialised (see page 19 below) – that the Scottish Company would simply sell licences to English interlopers. When the English Companies protested the unfairness of the situation, James acquiesced and offered to cancel the charter on payment of compensation to the Scots, which, one suspects, was the original object of the exercise. Unfortunately the Muscovy Company, despite having just enjoyed its most productive year in 1617, could not pay (though the sum involved was only £925), and its direct and sole control over the whaling trade ceased when it was forced to accept the offer of the East India Company to cover its various and extensive debts in return for the potentially lucrative Spitsbergen trade being handed over to a joint undertaking of the two companies.

The first joint enterprise, with a nominal capital of £30,000, raised thirteen armed whalers for the 1618 season and sailed straight into trouble. The Dutch, smarting from the English seizure of one of their catches in the previous year, went out in force, with nineteen ships patrolling off Jan Mayen Island, and twenty-three distributed along the Spitsbergen bays. "Where is your Dragon now?" the Dutch are reputed to have asked the outnumbered English before driving them away without their catches. If the Company wished to develop the trade, one anguished captain wrote home, "they must send better ships that must beat these knaves out of this Country, but as far as I can understand by them, they mean to make a trade of continuance of it..."[23]

When the Company came to count the cost of its 1613 resolution to defend Spitsbergen by force, its total losses were set at £66,437. At a later date the sum was reduced to £50,000, of which £22,000 was for English goods taken

---

[22]Edge, in Purchas, *Hakluytus Posthumus*, XIII, 16-17.

[23]Salmon, in *ibid.*, XIV, 94.

and the remainder for whale oil and bone and for damage to shipping,[24] but the actual sum is less important than the clear fact that to conduct whaling under conditions of war was economic suicide. The fiasco of 1618 was unfortunately followed by the disaster of 1619, when, compared with the success of the Dutch, the Company's nine ships and two pinnaces returned with a poor cargo and then lost money on the little oil they had, "in that the Hollanders did as then bring over great quantity of whale oil, and sold it at under rates, so that the Company was forced to keep theirs on their hands 12 months, and sell it afterwards at a very small price..."[25] Chiefly because of the competition of the apparently superior Dutch, the entire joint capital had been lost in two years, and even allowing for stores in hand there was a deficiency of around £11,000. As a result the joint whaling account was abandoned, and the Muscovy Company, which had no permanent capital and therefore no reserve fund, went into liquidation, selling its rights, assets and liabilities to a new Muscovy Company for £12,000.[26] Almost immediately the new Company endeavoured to raise capital and cover debts by auctioning off the whaling side to four of its members, including Thomas Edge, who, "pitying the downfall of so worthy a traffic," agreed to pay half the Company's debt charges, or £520 per annum, for their privilege. In future the Muscovy merchants trading to Greenland, or Greenland Company as it was sometimes called, was a semi-independent subsidiary of the Muscovy Company, though fortunately its internal politics – which are far from clear – need not concern us.

Neither the new Greenland Company, observing the mistakes of its predecessor, nor the Dutch company, seeking to preserve the lead it had gained by 1618, had any intention of ruining profits by whaling with battle-fleets, and the two sides tacitly agreed to separate, as they had done in 1614. The Greenland Company, encouraged to surrender its supposed rights in the expectation of receiving £22,000 compensation for the depredations of 1618 (which appears, in fact, never to have been paid), was allowed unhindered possession of its original fishing grounds in the south of Spitsbergen, while the Dutch moved northward into regions recently investigated around Amsterdam Island. The arrangement involved considerable sacrifice on the part of the Dutch, who entered a relatively unknown area where ice and fog was generally worse. They also surrendered a number of shore bases such as that in Van Keulens Bay in Bell Sound,

---

[24]*CSP*, James I, CXIX, September 1618; and Charles I, 28 September 1629.

[25]Edge, in Purchas, *Hakluytus Posthumus*, XIII, 24.

[26]W.R. Scott, *The Constitution and Finance of English, Scottish and Irish Joint-Stock Companies to 1720* (3 vols., Cambridge, 1910-1912), II, 57.

where they had a cooperage some eighty by fifty feet, a dormitory and a brick and timber boiling house, which the English subsequently used and which were, in fact, substantial enough to see a small group of marooned Englishmen through the winter of 1630-1631.[27]

Other national groups acquired bases as they arrived, again outside the English area, so that the north-western tip of Spitsbergen had Hamburghers Bay, Danes Island, Norways and Biscayers Hook, besides a number of less obviously named places and the chief Dutch base on Amsterdam Island. The Dutch, in order to establish themselves in the north and protect their permanent camp, endeavoured to found a colony at Smeerenberg ("Blubber Town"). The Journal of those left behind, written by J.S. Van der Brugge,[28] was one of the first of such books to recount the horrors of an Arctic winter which bore heavily on a number of such expeditions and killed most men who were brave enough to volunteer or unfortunate enough to get left behind. The Greenland Company even had difficulty in recruiting criminals offered a reprieve in exchange for wintering on Spitsbergen, and a small group taken out chose to return and face the consequences when they saw the conditions in which they were expected to survive.[29] In the end the Arctic winter ensured that Spitsbergen became a colony of neither the British nor the Dutch, but remained a summer no-man's-land which could, for a time, yield a reasonable profit.

From 1618 the fortunes of the Dutch and English in the Arctic diverged. The Dutch were indisputably the masters of European trade, with immense markets and vast fleets, the latter maintained by efficient ships and underpaid crews.[30] For years they had completely dominated the North Sea herring fishery, the "chiefest trade and principle goldmine,"[31] and operated a policy of *Mare Liberum*, publicised by Grotius in 1608, inside English territorial waters. Now they moved with increasing vigour to serve the European oil market, with such success that the English company was constantly bemoaning the competition, and the French company organised by Fouquet ended up buying its oil and

---

[27]Edward Pelham, in A. White (ed.), *A Collection of Documents on Spitsbergen and Greenland* (London, 1855), 251-283, recounts that their nine months' ordeal.

[28]Printed in Conway, *Early Dutch and English Voyages*, 81-168.

[29]Scoresby, *Account of the Arctic Regions*, II, 47-48.

[30]C.R. Boxer, *The Dutch Seaborne Empire, 1600-1800* (London, 1965), 67. For general fishing rivalry, see D.J. Starkey, C. Reid and N. Ashcroft (eds.), *England's Sea Fisheries: The Commercial Sea Fisheries of England and Wales since 1300* (London, 2000).

[31]*Ibid.*, 43.

bone in Amsterdam.[32] The capital which made this expansion possible was read-ily available in a country rich in trade and poor in land. The original Noordsche Campagnie of 1614, though half its capital came from a single Amsterdam house, drew members from the various provinces of the Netherlands, and the renewal of its charter in 1617 widened membership still further.[33] To draw in the ships and capital required to make Amsterdam the oil capital of Europe, new provincial "Chambers" were admitted to the monopoly, and finally, in 1642, the trade was opened to all-comers. As a result the number of Dutch whalers grew rapidly from thirty to 300, and Smeerenberg became during the whaling season a town of some 18,000 people, with its inns, bakeries, shops and chapels.[34] On average, ninety-nine ships per annum sailed from Holland between 1669 and 1678, and 193 between 1679 and 1688.[35]

By contrast the Greenland Company used every means in its power to confine the trade, and when it was forced to give up fighting the Dutch it turned to fighting Englishmen who dared to adventure their capital in the Company's preserve. During the 1620s the Company equipped a series of small expeditions of between seven and twelve vessels whose limited financial success owed less to the quantity of oil (between 1000 and 2000 tuns) than to its ability to restrict the market. The Company periodically pleaded that it had had a hard year, was short of funds, and ought to be protected against the importation of Dutch oil and bone, especially when the price of bone fell from its early level of two shillings to two pence per pound by 1624.[36] Unfortunately for the Company the government's limited sympathy for its case was diluted by the desire to receive customs duties on foreign-caught oil, though the importation of bone was forbid-den in 1613 and again in 1619, and the importation of oil was forbidden in 1628.[37] It may well be the case that the Company as organised was unable to afford larger expeditions, and certainly any substantial decline from monopoly level profits discouraged investment; yet the Company generally restricted the investment by the simple process of excluding willing potential investors, in-

---

[32]Violet Barbour, *Capitalism in Amsterdam in the Seventeenth Century* (Baltimore, 1950), 21.

[33]*Ibid.*, 28.

[34]Scoresby, *Account of the Arctic Regions*, II, 143; and Conway, *Early Dutch and English Voyages*, 81-168.

[35]Scoresby, *Account of the Arctic Regions*, II, 151.

[36]*CSP*, 21 September 1624.

[37]*Ibid.*, 11 September 1614, 18 May 1619 and 25 January 1628.

cluding members of its own parent body, the Muscovy Company.[38] The Company was said at its fullest extent to have around fifty subscribers, but its poor performance and the enthusiasm of its competitors indicate that the number was too small, or at least that the investment was too small.

The Company's monopoly would have been more damaging had it been more effective. Although both the Privy Council and the later Commonwealth Council of State upheld the theory of the Greenland monopoly, in practice neither gave it their consistent support and acted reluctantly in its favour only when goaded, and even then denied the Company the full support for which is petitioned. The men of Hull may well have been right in their claim to have fished the Arctic before the Company, and the men of Yarmouth had early established a *de facto* position in the trade. Neither port could be entirely ignored by government, and while paying lip service to monopoly the State generally accepted a responsibility also towards others who might establish a "fair" claim.

The first major crisis in the Company's fortunes came in 1626, when its fleet of twelve ships arrived at their whaling station to find that nine ships of Hull and York had got there first and had taken away their shallops, burned their casks and damaged the equipment left there over the winter.[39] Although the Company asked for warrants against Hull men, the Attorney-General and Solicitor-General were ordered to mediate between the two parties, and in the end the Company was forced to accept that 3000 tons of shipping should be fitted out in 1627, of which York and Hull men should supply fifth.[40] While the Company petitioned against the tenor of the agreement on the accurate grounds that Yarmouth would be encouraged to copy Hull, the Corporation of the latter took the matter to Parliament in 1628, and though the great Sir Edward Coke was unsure of the justice of Hull's case, Parliament supported the division made by the Privy Council, and when the Committee on the Greenland patent reported on 25 June 1628 it was resolved "Upon question, the Muscovia Company's barring any Englishmen from fishing in Greenland, is a grievance."[41] Fortunately for the Company a Parliament given to discussing petitions of rights soon had troubles of its own, and though in future Hull was wisely left alone, Yarmouth faced intense hostility whenever she attempted to follow the example of her more fortunate rival.

---

[38]Scott, *Constitution and Finance*, II, 71.

[39]*CSP*, 15 November 1626.

[40]*Ibid.*, 9 January and 30 March 1627.

[41]Great Britain, Parliament, House of Commons, *Journal, Vol. 1 (1547-1628)*, 25 June 1628, 919.

Hull had a case which, if not strictly legal, was at least reasonable in so far as her fishery (it was claimed) had existed before the Company's monopoly was confirmed. Yarmouth, on the other hand, had a claim that was neither legal nor, in many people's view, proper. Despite the Company's protest, a licence was granted in July 1625 to Nathaniel Udwart (or Edwards), a prominent Scottish monopolist, enabling him to trade with Greenland to provide oil *for Scotland* and in particular for his own soapworks in Leith. He promptly justified the Company's apprehension by handing over his patent to a group of Yarmouth fish and coal merchants led by Thomas Hoarth. Their technical adviser was Nathaniel Wright, one of the original directors of the Muscovy Company's fishing who was a young man had spent fourteen years in Biscay, and who was instrumental in bringing over the Basques who taught the trade to the Company. Now, as part of the exclusion policy, he was no longer acceptable as a subscriber and so, together with the Company's chief harpooner, he deserted to this new and promising venture.[42]

For the next quarter of a century there were to be arguments, fights and petitions over the right of Englishmen living in Yarmouth to breach the English monopoly in order to service Scotland, and even greater bitterness over the sheer impracticality of determining whether or not the oil eventually reached Scotland. Matters came to a head in 1634, when the Company ships attacked the Yarmouth ships and tried to seize their catches, only to be driven off by small arms and case shot. Both sides appealed to their respective Privy Councils, and having created a minor international incident – "the question now stands between the two nations," Udwart wrote in a petition to the king – the Yarmouth people got their way. They might legally fish for the Scottish market, though there was nothing save the wavering diligence of the Greenland Company to ensure that that was all they did. Indeed, Hoarth secured a contract for supplying the Soapers of Westminster, who had obtained a monopoly in the soap trade in 1632, and was sufficiently confident of his position when the Soapers Company collapsed to ask the Privy Council to force its successor to honour the contract! Although Hoarth did not get his way, Parliament was a little more willing to come down on the side of interlopers during the Civil War, and in 1643 allowed Yarmouth ships to go whaling. Two years later they were formally admitted to the Spitsbergen fishery, except in certain bays which were supposed to be exclusively for the Company, but where Yarmouth vessels were to be found by 1649. The Yarmouth people had successfully followed the example of Hull in enjoying the fishing and leaving the law to look after itself, happy in the knowledge that each practical – if surreptitious – advance in Spitsbergen was worth half-a-dozen decisions in council.

---

[42]*CSP*, 29 January 1631; and "Petition (n.d.)" Charles I, LXXIX, No. 16, 493.

The changes in the soap industry which upset Hoarth's calculations in 1632 had a serious impact on the English whaling trade as a whole during a crucial period of intense competition from the Dutch. Imported whale oil had been used for soapmaking since the sixteenth century, and despite the opposition of vested interests to "corrupt oils" the Greenland Company reckoned that ninety-five percent of its annual sales were to the soapers,[43] while in Scotland the shortage of soap in 1631 was put down to the restriction on whale oil imports imposed by the Greenland Company.[44] Unfortunately, technical developments in the late 1620s were towards a new white soap made from native ingredients, and in 1632 a monopoly in soapmaking was granted to the Society of Soapers of Westminster, who upset the Greenland Company firstly by contracting to take whale oil from Hoarth, and secondly by planning to phase out the use of whale oil altogether and replace it by native-crushed rape. In London the Greenland Company forecast the end of whaling, which was currently employing around 2500 tons of shipping and 1000 men, and in Hull the whalermen and soapers joined forces in refusing to deliver up to the old soap or sell the new, which was condemned as useless.[45] Useless it was, and in 1637, with the transfer of the monopoly back to the old whale-oil soapboilers, the Greenland Company was, for a time, reprieved. The situation for Hull was less promising, for the soapboilers now tried to restrict soapmaking to London, and would only reopen the York soapery when it was agreed to supply oil at 10*s.* per tun less than was paid to the Greenland Company in London.[46]

The condition of the whaling industry on the eve of the Civil War was not, then, such as might excite much enthusiasm. There had been no expansion since the 1620s, and the market for whale oil appears to have settled at around 2000 tuns per annum. Any further sales, on which an expansion of whaling depended, could only be made by persuading people to use more soap, by finding new uses for whale oil, or by moving out into foreign markets. The latter course was almost impossible in view of the Dutch position in international trade and shipping, and the cloth industry stuck resolutely to rape or Seville oil despite their greater cost. In any case, expansion on a large scale would have run counter to the general economic depression that was a feature of England for a quarter of a century and was, indirectly, one of the causes of the Civil War. The

---

[43]*Ibid.*, Charles I, CCLXXIX, No. 71, 392, "Statement of Evils Likely to Ensue to the Greenland Company from New Regulations as to Soap," n.d.

[44]*Ibid.*, 19 February 1631.

[45]*Ibid.*, 8 July 1634 and 16 April 1639.

[46]*Ibid.*, 3 July 1639.

Greenland Company paid dear for its activities against the Dutch, while its monopoly position was threatened by the limited success of Hull and Yarmouth. Whaling from Yarmouth was almost certainly held back by the fines – amounting to many thousands of pounds – following legal objections of the Greenland Company, while the whalers of Hull suffered more than those of the Greenland Company from the troubles surrounding the soap monopoly.

So far as the Greenland Company was concerned, the ending of the Civil War was the signal for a final all-out attack on its external and internal enemies. The Company was among those pressing strongly for the trade sanctions against the Dutch which were embodied in the Navigation Act of 1651, though the most obvious result was not the exclusion of Dutch whale oil (which could be excluded by Order-in-Council anyway) but the rise in the cost of whaling voyages following a general rise in shipping costs resulting from the exclusion of Dutch vessels at a time when there were insufficient English vessels to take their place.[47] Against their internal enemies the Company launched a series of petitions which resulted in the whole question of whaling being aired before the Commonwealth's Committee for Trade and Council of State between 1652 and 1654, and which produced the unwelcome decision that the parties were to arrange their fishing so as not to interfere with each other, and that fishing might be carried on fully in all places and the oil imported without hindrance either for domestic use or for re-export. It was estimated that twelve vessels of 3000 tons were adequate to maintain the fishing at its present level, and that of this total the Greenland Company had provided and should continue to provide 1600 tons, the Hull and York people 400 tons, Hoarth 500 tons, and the London interlopers 500 tons.[48] No account was taken of expansion, but it mattered little, for the 1654 season was disastrous for everyone involved in it. The Greenland Company continued to make losses and by 1656 found it difficult to set out three vessels – compared with five independent vessels from London alone – and by 1657 had lost two complete "subscriptions" since the war. To make matters worse, the Commonwealth, eager to resume friendly relations with the Dutch after the war of 1652-1654, admitted oil to the country, despite the provisions of the Navigation Act, so that "our navigation is prejudiced and that of foreigners improved."[49] The Company had oil on its hands which it could not sell because of the cheaper Dutch product, so that "without help we must give up the fishing trade, and it must fall into the hands of the Dutch and others." The situation was

---

[47]Charles Wilson, *Profit and Power: A Study of England and the Dutch Wars* (London, 1957), 55; and Scott, *Constitution and Finance*, I, 252.

[48]*CSP*, 24 February 1654.

[49]*Ibid.*, 15 February 1656, 7 March 1656 and 17 February 1657.

hardly any better in Hull, where, in 1654, at least a dozen ships had arrived from Amsterdam carrying whale oil and bone, to the chagrin of the local whalermen.[50]

The decline of the whaling trade was accelerated during the unsettled years of the late 1650s, when whaling seamen were ruthlessly press-ganged into the Commonwealth navy. Whereas in 1656 protections had been granted to all whalers, in 1658, following a Trade Committee decision in favour of encouraging the Greenland Company rather than interlopers, only Company ships received protections. In Yarmouth the adventurers cut their losses by selling their provisions to the navy. With continuing troubles in the 1660s very few whaling expeditions were equipped, and most of these were failures. By 1671, when George Turfry and Company fitted out the first English vessel to fish in the West Ice, the trade was on its last legs, and in 1673 the House of Commons appointed a committee to enquire into its decay. The eventual outcome was an Act opening the trade freely to all English subjects, but there was no rush of people to enjoy their new liberty, and attempts to re-establish the trade in London by Sir Laurence Disbusty in 1674 and by Sir Thomas Allen in 1681 were failures, as was an attempt to re-establish Hull's trade by using bigger and cheaper Dutch "fly-boats."

The flurry – to use the whalers' term – appears to have come in 1682-1683 in Leith, with a company organised by James and George Campbell and Robert Douglas, merchants and soapboilers. Twelve partners invested some £1700 sterling in fitting out a vessel which brought back oil worth £525. Undismayed, they fitted out two vessels in 1683, one with Dutch harpooners and one with Scottish, "so that they think it both their concerns to do their utmost," one of the owners was informed.[51] George Campbell was full of enthusiasm that was shared by whalermen and gamblers: "The going of both vessels makes me have good hopes of this year's adventure and with God's Blessing I trust it shall make up our last year's loss." In the final reckoning there was no mention of the vessel with Dutch harpooners, and the other made a profit of £50 sterling, which was swallowed up in fitting out the ship for its return to European treading in 1684. This partnership organised by soapboilers would seem at first sight to be more sensible than partnerships of London capitalists who had to search for customers, but in the end it was no more successful.

---

[50]*Ibid.*, 31 January 1654.

[51]Scottish Record Office, Clerke of Penicuik Papers, GD 18/2568, George Campbell to Sir John Clerke, Edinburgh, 30 April 1683; and various accounts and receipts related to whaling expeditions.

IV

Many factors contributed to the complete collapse of a trade which had shown so much promise in the early decades of the century. Some of them have already been touched on, since they were inherent in the type of organisation adopted by the English and rejected by the Dutch. Others spring from changing conditions within the fishery to which the English could not adapt. The attempt to maintain a monopoly in one company was clearly a disastrous policy. When operated against the Dutch it had serious repercussions on the Muscovy Company itself, and when operated against English and Scottish interlopers it effectively stifled both enterprise and enthusiasm. On the other hand it might be argued that any significant growth in the trade, with or without monopoly, would have been impossible in view of the small market enjoyed by the English compared with the huge European market open to the Dutch. There is no clear evidence of economies of scale, yet the Dutch were always able to undercut the English in their home market, and the imposition of an import duty of £9 per tun in 1672 appears to have had little effect. Despite differential duties, the price of whale oil on the English market could not be forced up to a level regarded as remunerative in England or Scotland. Perhaps the sort of men involved in squeezing monopoly profits out of trade were not the sort to engage in competition with the thriving merchants of Amsterdam, but it certainly seems that prices had slipped to an absurdly low level as the Dutch, French and Germans pushed more vessels into the trade. In the 1570s Robert Hitchcock had expected Englishmen to fit out expeditions for oil worth only £10 a tun, but this was no adequate inducement and whaling did not become "popular" until the price was moving nearer £20. In the 1630s, when prices were declining under Dutch pressure, Hoarth of Yarmouth claimed that at least £16 was essential to give an adequate profit when costs were running at £600 per ship per month, and the Greenland Company claimed that it cost them £12,000 per annum to bring home an average catch of 1100 tuns of oil. Any fall below £16 a tun was likely to have an inhibiting effect on the trade, yet for many years after the Civil War the price was barely two-thirds of this, and when in 1696 the Inspector General of Customs adjusted the ancient Book of Rates to take into account prevailing prices, whale oil was reduced from the traditional £10 to as little as £8 8s. a tun, so that the duty on foreign oil must have been more or less equal to its value. There was a further complication so far as price was concerned: the abundance of Dutch whale oil caused a decline in the international price of seed oil, so that there was a tendency to substitute the preferred rape oil for whale oil. Short of a complete prohibition on foreign oils, which neither monarchy nor protectorate was willing to impose, there was little the English interests could do to prevent the price from slipping below the break-even point even if their fishing had been successful.

Unfortunately the English fishing was generally unsuccessful compared with the Dutch, though precisely why it should have been so is not clear. Much would seem to hinge on technical ability and here the Dutch, with their considerable fund of experience in the herring fishery, were at an advantage. It is generally accepted that their ships were better, though how far this was important during the Spitsbergen phase of whaling is open to doubt. The most important factor, perhaps, was the degree of success in the transference of whaling skills. The Dutch rapidly learned the techniques of their Basque tutors; the English did not, or, if they learned them in the first place, soon forgot them. Henry Elking, one of the first commentators on English whaling, attributed the troubles of the late seventeenth century to the fact that whalers were commanded by persons unacquainted with the finer points of whaling, who interfered with the fishing instead of leaving it to the harpooners. This may be an exaggeration, but certainly by the 1670s there were few Englishmen of any rank who could show expertise in the trade. In 1672 a vessel called the *Mary* could only be got to Spitsbergen by employing forty foreigners in her crew (the Navigation laws had to be waive to allow for such national incompetence) and Dibusty's attempt to revive the trade in 1674 was based entirely on the employment of six ships and crews from Bayonne which were necessary, he said, because "they understand that kind of fishing better than our Englishmen do."[52] The implication was that at a time when the Dutch were approaching the peak of their whaling effort, the English could not find men enough for six ships. In such circumstances the relative price of whale oil ceases to be very meaningful.

The basic reason for this failure on the part of the English may well have been a change in the fishery itself, which quite fortuitously worked in favour of the Dutch and against the English. While the English bays in the south of Spitsbergen may not in themselves have suffered from over-fishing, they certainly suffered from extensive fishing outside them, especially towards the north where the Dutch were established across the path of migrating whales. At first the English had prided themselves on forcing the Dutch towards the inhospitable north, but as early as 1620 the Company's captains were complaining that their fishing was suffering because of Dutch activity there. As more Dutch vessels arrived they extended their searches round the northern tip of Spitsbergen into the area known as the Waigat, which was their area by right of exploration. This fishery was only successful, however, in mild summers when the ice broke up and drifted southwards, and such "south ice years" were relatively rare. In what might be regarded as "normal" years the Dutch took to the sea, exploring northwards and westwards in their ships and returning periodically to Smeerenberg to process blubber. (For the change in fishing techniques

---

[52]*CSP*, 30 April 1672 and ? August 1674 ("Sir Laurence Dibusty's Case").

involved, see below, p. 26). They found their way to the "West ice" – that is, the pack ice along the coast of Greenland – with the minimum of charts and navigational aids, by the simple process of sailing north to around 79° and then allowing themselves to drift southwards in the ice-bearing current to be found in normal years.

Thus while the English remained mesmerised by the supposed yet declining advantages of their bay fisheries, which even at the best of times were only visited by whales between October and April, the Dutch had tapped the vastly greater stocks of whales that moved in conjunction with the ice. That the Spitsbergen bay fishing phase of European whaling must give way to the Greenland pelagic phase should have been obvious to the English by the middle of the seventeenth century. Unfortunately they failed to recognize the fact until it was too late.

Chapter 2
Lost Hopes and Expensive Failures,
c. 1670-1750

I

For almost a century English whaling was a dismal affair conducted on a level akin to an Englishman with a thimble emptying the same tun as a Dutchman with a bucket: the latter's good fortune was the former's despair. Nothing, it seemed, could generate the kind of success enjoyed in the Netherlands or guarantee the profits required to revive the trade. The most notable thing, perhaps, was the want of English interest in the Arctic during the Commercial Revolution of the late seventeenth and early eighteenth centuries as merchants turned their attention to the East and West Indies and to North America, where more profitable outlets for investment were found. Most of the raw materials required in England could be obtained from Europe or America, and whale oil was, after all, only one of many such materials. It could be obtained so easily and so cheaply that there was little incentive for Englishmen to trouble themselves with re-learning the Arctic trade when there were so many other things to divert them.[1]

The root of the withered trade was fixed firmly in an arid domestic market, and no amount of pruning or grafting could produce decent fruit. Occasionally the Muscovy Company and its rivals had brought home over 2000 tuns of oil; almost invariably they regretted their good fortune and complained of having oil on their hands. In good years the price obtained in London was lower than that in Amsterdam; in bad years Dutch-caught oil flooded in at a price to ruin the English adventurers. If import figures are anything to go by, the demand in Britain in the early eighteenth century was actually lower than it had been in the early seventeenth century. Only three times in the first quarter of the century did imports exceed 2000 tuns, and on six occasions they were less than 1000 tuns (see table 1).

This blatantly discouraging background explains in large measure why the British neglected to follow the Dutch from the Spitsbergen to the Greenland

---

[1]There are many vivid accounts of the process of Arctic ice fishing, but undoubtedly the best is that of W. Scoresby, *An Account of the Arctic Regions, with a History and Description of the Northern Whale Fishery* (2 vols., Edinburgh, 1820), II, *passim*, on which this account is based.

fishery, and so lost the advantages to be gained from early experimental voyages in what was, in effect, a novel Arctic experience. Undoubtedly Greenland had disadvantages compared with Spitsbergen, not least of which was the greater cost of stouter ships and additional stores, but these were soon outweighed by the advantages. There was a marked increase in the productivity of whalers, for though ice fishing could not compare with the initial slaughter in the bays, it was infinitely better than the later stages of bay whaling. Intensive fishing had decimated the stocks of whales resorting to particular breeding bays within a quarter of a century, but whales did not disappear at anything like the same rate from the migration lanes or feeding places in the open sea. Not only were there more whales available; there was also a longer season in which to catch them. It is generally believed that the Right whale moved south for the winter and north for the summer, so that the bay fishing which could not start until March – because conditions that suited whales were still too bad for whalers – was over by late April. Now that whales could be attacked in more northerly regions, or on the migration routes, the season could be extended from six weeks to almost as many months, should such an awful prospect become an economic necessity.

II

Once the British had lost the initiative there was a great deal of ground to be made up. Ice fishing was technically quite different from bay fishing. The whaler was the base of operations and the home of forty or fifty men for a voyage of anything up to four or five months. Few vessels have ever been subjected to the immense physical and psychological strains that were frequently the lot of whalers and whalermen. Whalers could be strengthened with internal beams, double planking and an assortment of projections intended to fend off or break up ice pressing on the sides; but no whaler could withstand unrelenting ice pressure for long. A superb seamanship was required of the generations of master mariners who took their vessels into the ice from which all other ships fled – and caught whales in the process. In bay fishing there was little for them to do; in ice fishing they were the star performers. "Not a little depends, in the fishery," wrote Scoresby,[2]

> on the confidence the sailors have in the skill of their captain,
> and in the efficiency of the personal talents and exertions of
> their officers. If the officers are frequently unfortunate, they
> are apt to lose confidence in them, and proceed, even when

---

[2]*Ibid.*, II, 339-340.

good opportunities occur, without spirit in the attack. The
greater their spirits and confidence, the better is the chance
they have of success. Hence the crew of a ship which has met
with success, can generally fish better, and more advanta-
geously, under the same circumstances, than the people of a
clean ship. Men, discouraged by the failure of their exertions,
lose their spirits, and, with them their activity. Their judge-
ments even are clouded by the depression of their minds, so
that they become inferior, in every respect, to successful fish-
ers, of the same natural talent. Hence it is of great importance, that the ardour and confidence of the crew of a whaler
should be encouraged and stimulated: for, on their exertions,
when plenty of whales are in view, success almost entirely
depends. But for the regulation of the ship's movements, – for
the choice of a situation, – for direction in difficulties, – for a
stimulus when discouraged, – for encouragement when weary,
– and for a variety of other important matters, the master
alone must be looked to, on whom, indeed, almost every considerable effort of judgement or forethought devolves.

A failure in masters alone might well be the key to English failure in the Arctic
in the seventeenth and early eighteenth centuries.

Once a whaler reached the ice, the ease of the actual fishing process
was often a matter of fortune, determined by the weather and the ice itself. In
some places it floated southwards in huge solid fields; in others it came in broken packs full of channels and holes. Occasionally the forward ice advanced
rapidly and clear water opened up behind it to produce an "open season" which
was no good for whaling; more usually the ice was fairly solid, producing the
"close season" that whalermen preferred because the whales were more narrowly confined. The danger to whalers sprang from the constant movement of
the ice, often with no discernable pattern. Within hours an unfortunate or care-
less ship in relatively open water might be struck by passing floes or beset in an
impenetrable pack of ice from which only a fresh movement of the ice could
save it.

Waters close to a good solid field of ice were best for fishing. There
the whaler might cruise in as much safety as could be expected in Arctic waters,
sheltered to some extent from the worst gales and ice movement, though snow
and fog were more common. Whenever a whale was seen, all the six boats were
sent out in a "loose fall," and the whaler hove to. Alternatively the whaler was
fixed with ice anchors, sometimes in a specially sawn ice dock, and a couple of
boats set on watch all the time, to be reinforced by the others as necessary.

Gordon Jackson

Whales struck on the edge of field ice were almost always caught because though they usually fled below the ice they had eventually to return to breathe at some point along the edge within the rope's length from the "fast" boat where, with any luck, further boats would be waiting.

Fishing in the more common pack ice was infinitely more difficult – not least because of the danger from the ice itself – and called for all the skill of both master and men. Whales were not always easily approached through ice-strewn water, and a stricken whale might have many opportunities to rise for breath beyond the immediate reach of its hunters. Even if it was easily killed – sometimes by being pursued on foot to holes in the ice – it was not easily recovered unless the whaler could force its way through the ice. Sometimes whales were sunk with weights and winched out under the ice, and occasionally they were flensed and their blubber dragged over the ice – an incredibly hard and dangerous operation.

In normal circumstances the whales were towed back to the whaler and flensed alongside. There was no way in which the whales could be lifted aboard, and until the 1920s the flensers danced precariously on the floating carcass in their spiked boots, or hacked away with blubber-knives and blubber-spades from the equally precarious flensing boat tied up alongside. In heavy weather flensing was impossible because the tackle used for pulling the blubber aboard could not take the strain as the whale rose and fell; and even in a slight swell it required a combination and co-ordination of great skills that were hard to come by. Flensing also called for the worst job in whaling: that of the lad who, periodically drenched to the skin and frozen with cold, looked after the boat during the two to six hours it took to slice and tear off the blubber. His consolation lay in the fact that, as an apprentice, he was learning by repeated observation where and when to make the cuts in what was probably the most difficult task performed by whaling officers.

The remaining task of making off the blubber – chopping it into pieces small enough to go through the bung-hole of casks – occupied most of the crew for half a day or more, again depending on the weather. If a "run of fish" was spotted, flensing and making off might be delayed while they were hunted, and then, with several carcasses tied up alongside, the whole crew would set to in an orgy of clearing up that in some log books lasted for forty-eight hours without proper rest. The natural desire to catch whales whenever they appeared had at some stage to be counterbalanced by the useful "life" of the carcass, or by the mountains of blubber piling up to be made off. An unflensed whale decomposed so rapidly that the blubber might be tainted after a couple of days and flensing become more difficult than usual; after four days the gasses generated inside the whale might well blow up and cause it to sink. Even in freezing conditions the temperature inside an unflensed whale could cook the meat, and modern whalermen, who saw the animals out of water, sometimes spoke of a "charred whale" when referring to an "old" carcass.

This process of decay had a serious affect on whaling insofar as it limited the usefulness of pelagic whale oil. Without rapid flensing and the most careful making off, blubber was contaminated by decaying particles of flesh and blood, while the blubber itself contained a certain amount of blood and fibre which also decayed on the journey home. As a result, whale oil became less popular as it was associated with an unpleasant smell, and the soapmakers began to lose interest in it some years before town planners recognised its virtues as a cheap street-lighting oil. Why, then, did the whalers not carry shipboard try-works as the later sperm whalers did? The answer lies in available technology. The small try-works installed on sperm whalers in the eighteenth century could not cope with the blubber of the Right whale, not least because of the relative yield of the two whales: the sperm whale might produce a little over two tuns of blubber, the Right whale up to twenty tuns (see p. 41 below). There was no ship-board cooker until the twentieth century capable of rendering large quantities of fresh blubber economically. Fresh blubber is hard and fibrous, and the oil is not easily extracted at low temperature; the soft blubber, oozing oil, which was fed into the boilers of the Greenland Yards that sprang up in British ports to service the trade was blubber in a fairly advanced state of decay. With one or two experimental – and unsuccessful – exceptions, Greenland whalers never carried try-works, and their oil, in consequence, was always stale.

The operations outlined above sound elementary enough, given the required skills; and so they would have been had whales always turned up when and where they were expected, and had weather conditions always been perfect. In reality the fishing was hampered by ice in good weather and by gales, blizzards and fog in bad weather. Surviving whaling logs are full of the conflicting problems of catching the whale and escaping the ice: of all hands making fast to the ice or sawing docks for safety or flensing operations; of the "heavy blows" and "nips" that smashed planking and rudders and turned ships over; of men from beset ships out on the ice, warping and sawing their way to clear water; of major repairs as ships were keeled over by brute force and judicious ballasting. Some logs read like pleasure cruises, with little to do save bask in the Arctic sun between catches that could fill a ship in a month or six weeks. Others – perhaps the majority – lurch from crisis to crisis, with fog descending while the boats are out, gales upsetting flensing, ice nipping during making off, and few people enjoying the niceties of a regular watch. In a state of permanent daylight, a ship in crisis or at work ignored time: when whales and ice could not wait, the men did not sleep.

It was a hard life compared with bay fishing, and was infinitely more complex. Above all, it required a new set of skills on the part of the harpooners, steersmen and line-managers who controlled the catching, the flensing and the making off. These skills were learned the hard way by the first adventurers, and those who came after them were unlikely to be economically successful in competition with the experts. With so little incentive from their home market, the English were unlikely to master the techniques of ice fishing which the Dutch (like the Norwegians at a later time in a different fishery) were forbidden to teach them.

III

English whaling would eventually revive as rising prices reflected a growing domestic demand for both oil and whalebone, but in the meantime there were still occasionally men who, misguidedly, saw the whaling industry as a prospect for rapid profit-taking. They are remembered not for the glory of their achievement but for the magnificence of their failure.

The first of the grand designs was that of Sir William Scaven, who recognised the unprecedented opportunity for reviving the English industry offered by the grave political and military troubles of the Dutch in the late 1680s and early 1690s. After reaching a peak in 1682, the importation of oil into the Netherlands, which averaged 46,788 puncheons in 1680-1684, dropped rapidly to only 10,120 puncheons by 1689. A brief recovery in 1690 was followed by the complete abandonment of the trade in 1691, and imports in 1692-1694 averaged a mere 6263 puncheons.[3] With prices responding to such a huge cut-back in supply, circumstances were more favourable for import substitution in England than at any time since the Dutch seized control of the trade, while the disruption of normal trade patterns through war encouraged merchants to think that they might be able to invade markets previously dominated by their rivals. Forty-two men joined Scaven in persuading Parliament to grant joint-stock privileges to "The Company of Merchants of London trading into Greenland," which received its charter in 1692, and some £40,000 was raised to equip the biggest fleet to sail from England to the Arctic for fifty years.

If our assessment of the economic potential of whaling is correct, the catastrophic failure of the new Greenland Company was inevitable. To invest £40,000 when national oil sales were less than 2000 tuns per annum was unwise, and to increase the nominal capital to £82,000 was little short of madness.[4] The Company had no grounds for believing that the troubles facing the

[3]*Ibid.*, 155-156.

[4]*Ibid.*, 59-60 and 104-105.

Dutch would not also apply to it, and in fact it had the greatest difficulty in putting ships to sea during the closing years of the war with France before the treaty of Ryswick in 1697. In order to operate at all the Company had had to secure exemption from the Navigation Acts' requirement that two-thirds of the seamen must be English, but though it was entitled to make up crews with two-thirds foreigners, it found that the Dutch government, which prevented its entire fleet from sailing in 1691, also used every endeavour to ensure that its skilled men did not take service in English whalers. At the same time the English government made no exception for Greenlandmen, who were mopped up for naval service, a fact which was specifically mentioned when the Company secured an Act enabling it to defer calling up its full nominal capital until peace came. Long before peace came the Dutch industry revived, with imports of oil reaching 42,281 puncheons in 1697 and 55,985 in 1698. Faced once more with overwhelming competition, the failure of the English became merely a matter of time. With an unhappy mixture of war conditions, Dutch competition, and plain bad management, the Greenland Company made not a single "saving" voyage, and its capital was lost long before its fourteen-year charter period was up.

The inevitability of decline conceals a number of factors which, if changed, might just have enabled a less ambitious company to serve its protected domestic market (though whether this would have been in the interest of consumers is another matter). Henry Elking, from whose work comes most of our knowledge of the elusive Greenland Company (about which even the learned Scott is reticent), was particularly eager to stress these factors in an attempt to show that there were no sound economic reasons why England should not make a success of whaling, though he did this, paradoxically, by arguing that English whaling was a failure because it was run by Englishmen. More accurately, perhaps, he insisted that it had been run in the wrong way or by the wrong Englishmen:[5]

> Nor is it any just objection to the practicableness of this trade,
> to say, that it has been often attempted without success; since
> the reasons of that want of success, which are fully examined
> in these sheets will appear to arise, not from any deficiency in
> the trade, but from the evident mismanagement of the under-

---

[5]Henry Elking, *A View of the Greenland Trade and Whale Fishery, with the National and Private Advantages Thereof* (London, 1722), edition printed in J.R. McCulloch, *A Select Collection of Scarce and Valuable Economical Tracts* (London, 1859), 71-72.

takers; proceeding either from ignorance, want of stock, want
of conduct, or of honesty.

The Greenland Company was, in Elking's view, a bunch of ignorant
dabblers who imagined that capital could do anything, and that the correct way
to run a joint stock was to spend the maximum amount of money. Its members
were, he said, "wanting due informations of the proper methods of managing
that whole affair." Worse still, they were "ill served by almost all the people
they employed, both at home and abroad, pushing them into extravagant and
unnecessary expenses, and irregular measures in every thing..."[6] The Company's most grievous mistake was in its choice of commanders, and the powers
given to them. In the general ignorance of initiation, the Muscovy Company had
employed chief harpooners who took charge of the whaling, captains who
looked after navigation and discipline, and factors who looked after the Company's interest. The whole fleet was under the command of a "General," at least
in the days when hostilities were to be expected. Such a complicated chain of
command was unsatisfactory, and the Greenland Company quite properly decided to adopt the more usual and successful system of putting the captain in
charge of both ship and fishery, and making him responsible for the Company's
interest. Unfortunately, since England had not progressed beyond the initiation
stages of whaling, the men chosen as captains had little Arctic experience, and
though foreign harpooners were employed, the ships were manoeuvred so badly
around the whaling grounds that "for want of right conduct, they got no whales,
or but few, even when others made a good voyage."[7] The ability of the captain
would not have been a serious handicap in the days of Spitsbergen whaling,
when all he had to do was get the ship to anchorage in the appointed bay and let
the harpooners get on with the "bay fishery." Now the captain had to look for
whales in the West Ice, and the inexperienced Englishmen simply did not know
where to look or what signs to follow. It was only a matter of time, of course,
but time was not on the side of joint stocks given to heavy expenditure.

The issue was complicated somewhat by the Company's decision to
employ captains on fixed salaries. With no pecuniary interest in their own success they were, it was alleged, rather tardy in pursuing the Company's matters,
and their lack of success along the alien territory of the ice was too often followed by a retreat to the better-known bays of Spitsbergen where they hoped to
find the odd whales surviving the slaughter of the past century. There, it was

---

[6]*Ibid.*, 89.

[7]*Ibid.*, 90.

said, they went off hunting for deer which, as perquisites, made more profit for them than whales did: they "left the shallops to look for whales, where few or none were to be found; and thus they ruined the voyages, consumed the provisions, and brought the Company's stock in debt upon every voyage..."[8] The shortcomings of the officers may have owed more to inexperience than to dishonesty, but the results were indisputable: in straight competition with the Dutch, English captains were found wanting, though this does not mean that they would remain inferior for very long once they began to have men "bred in the trade," men who went after the whales rather than waiting for the whales to come to them. Nevertheless, it would be wrong to place too much emphasis on the deficiencies of the captains. The nature of whaling was changing under the pressure of extensive fishing, and as whalers entered the ice-fields the chances of destruction or of a "losing voyage" increased. F. Marten in his *Voyage to Spitsbergen*, published in 1671, explained the difficulties of ice fishing:[9]

> if we do not find whales in one place, we must seek them in others; for the fortune in catching of whales is like the chances of gaming, and there is no great understanding required to find them: some see and catch more than they desire, and others but at a half mile distance from them see not one, which is very common.

Onslow Burrish took up the same theme when writing of the Dutch in 1728: "This trade...is thought to be a kind of lottery, and is therefore undertaken by persons of overgrown fortunes, who, if they fail this year, expect better luck the next, and do not feel the disappointment..."[10]

Whaling may have become more of a gamble – though the more successful captains seemed to win every year – but the Company could have done far more to help itself. When losses and competition were severe it would have been sensible to restrain expenditure, yet the Company continued to equip its vessels in a more elaborate and expensive manner than the Dutch. It victualled extravagantly, paid an exorbitant price for shallops and equipment, and, accord-

---

[8]*Ibid.*

[9]F. Marten, *Voyage to Spitsbergen* (London, 1671), reprinted in A. White, *Collection of Documents on Spitsbergen and Greenland* (London, 1855), 33.

[10]Quoted in C. Boxer, *The Dutch Seaborne Empire, 1600-1800* (London, 1965), 273.

ing to Elking, the ships "were at so many unnecessary expenses for incidents, both at their setting out and coming in." Moreover, the Company failed to make adequate provisions for storing equipment between seasons, so that many items decayed and others were stolen; cordage and lines, for instance, had to be regularly replaced. Finally, the Company paid scant attention to the final stages of the operation – the boiling of the blubber and the preparation of whale fins, both of which were so badly done that they could not compete with the quality of the imported sorts.[11]

Table 1
Whale Oil and Whale Bone Imports, 1700-1704 to 1720-1724

(five-yearly averages)

	Whale Oil	Whale Bone
	tuns	cwt
1700-1704	1402	3706
1705-1709	879	1614
1710-1714	1102	2229
1715-1719	1172	3026
1720-1724	1840	3035

Source: E.B. Schumpeter, *English Overseas Trade Statistics, 1697-1808* (Oxford, 1960).

No serious attempt at whaling was made for a quarter of a century after the collapse of the Greenland Company. Whale oil prices reached their lowest point, and both oil and bone were secured from Holland (appendix 1), though in quantities that were hardly encouraging.

The oil trade suffered from the disruption of the French wars and – more seriously – from the growing seed oil trade and industry. Oilseeds were grown in increasing quantities in Lincolnshire and East Anglia in the late seventeenth century, and seedcrushing mills sprang up, several of them in Hull, which, as we have seen, had long had an interest in the oil trade. In 1709 Robert Pease of Rotterdam, a leading oil merchant and miller, sent one of his sons to Ireland, one to England and one to Amsterdam to organise an international oil business. Joseph Pease, sent to England, eventually rejected London in favour of Hull as the most suitable centre for operations, a point which is of great significance in the later history of whaling. For the time being, however, Eng-

---

[11]Elking, *View of the Greenland Trade*, 74-79.

land could do without any very substantial increase in whale oil imports and, consequently, without her own whaling trade.

The same is largely true of whalebone. In the early days it had been of sufficient value to make the difference between profit and loss, but this was no longer the case, and despite the growing popularity of improved "rounder-look" stays which had become part of every lady's toilette by about 1670,[12] and of which the great hoop petticoats of c. 1710 against which both the *Spectator* and *The Tatler* directed their scorn, the direct importation of bone was hardly more encouraging than that of oil. When the "Trial of the Petticoat" was held before Mr. Bickerstaff,[13] the third argument in its favour was founded "upon a petition of the Greenland trade, which...represented the great consumption of whalebone which would be occasioned by the present fashion, and the benefit which would thereby accrue to that branch of the British trade," but had Sir Richard Steele enquired further he would have learned that there was no Greenland trade, and that the bone, like the oil, came from Holland.

IV

Interest in many unlikely schemes arose during the South Sea Bubble, and a new attempt at whaling was one of the few that survived the crash. The prime mover appears to have been Henry Elking, who gathered a number of prospective partners around him before approaching Sir John Eyles early in 1721. Eyles, at first sceptical because of the total superiority of foreigners and the dismal failure of recent attempts to recover the trade, was gradually convinced by Elking's arguments that a hundred vessels might safely be employed in the trade to the glory of the partners and the profit of the nation.[14] So enthusiastic did Eyles become that his vision grew beyond even that of Elking, who was asked to forego his grand adventure so that Eyles could lay the whole matter before the South Sea Company, of which he was sub-governor and one of those responsible for rescuing the Company's finances after the bubble burst. The General Court of the Company accepted Eyles's proposals in principle in September 1721, and in the following May the Court of Directors proceeded to institute the trade by agreeing to appoint a supervisor, and ordering the building or purchase of twelve suitable ships and the leasing of Blackwall dock, "or any other proper

---

[12]Norah Waugh, *Corsets and Crinolines* (London, 1954), 37.

[13]Richard Steele, *The Tatler* (London, 1953), 158-159.

[14]Elking, *View of the Greenland Trade*, 67-68.

place for the Company's carrying on the said Trade."[15] At this stage, however, an unexpected reticence appeared among certain of the more influential directors, who reverted to the sort of objections already raised by Eyles, and doubted the validity of some of Elking's answers. It was argued, quite rightly as things turned out, that Elking's proposals were unrealistic, over-optimistic, and misleading, if not exactly dishonest. When one considers the type of thoughtless investment in nonsensical schemes that had so recently brought the whole financial structure of the nation to the point of ruin, the caution now expressed might seem commendable. To counter it, Eyles appealed to Elking to present his case in writing before the Directors, and Elking, who felt his honour at stake, "having been supposed to mislead your judgement by false allegations," responded with his *View of the Greenland Trade and Whale Fishery, with the National and Private Advantages Thereof,* the only substantial work on English whaling before Scoresby.

Elking was the sort of patriotic visionary that every country needs from time to time. England had consistently failed in the whaling trade; Elking's was the voice in the wilderness crying that it need not always be so. His object in publishing (apart from vindicating himself) was, he wrote, "that the nation in general may see, that this trade may be carried on from hence, equally at least, if not better, than from other nations; who, by the supineness of this Kingdom, have it wholly in their hands..."[16]

Since the value of the trade as a source of wealth and power was not at issue, Elking's arguments were necessarily directed towards proving that England might enjoy her share of it. "Though it has been generally supposed," he wrote,[17]

> it will be found upon examination a very great mistake, that
> the English cannot manage this trade, which the Hollanders,
> Hamburgers, Bremers, French and Spaniards all carry on to
> advantage, and by which means they are made rich, even out
> of our pockets, who sit still and buy those goods of them, for

---

[15]British Museum (BM), Add. Ms. 25,500, Minutes of the Court of Directors of the South Sea Company, 24 May 1722. The following account of the Company's whaling activities is based largely on the Minute Books. Unfortunately, the minutes of the Whaling Committee are not among the papers lodged in the BM.

[16]Elking, *View of the Greeland Trade*, 64.

[17]*Ibid.*, 71.

our ready money, which the English are every way better qualified to furnish to themselves, and even for export to other nations...

Earlier failures resulted from the incompetence of the adventurers, not the inferiority of English shipping. It was a "vulgar error" that the Dutch could build or sail ships better or cheaper than the English could. The Dutch had no timber, iron, tar or hemp of their own, and no home-grown provisions to victual their ships, whereas the English had all these things either at home or in the Plantations. Where precisely these things were to be found in England was not discussed: it was assumed, just as the greater cost of Plantation produce over Baltic produce was ignored. To a man well versed in mercantilism, colonial produce "cost" nothing at all compared with stuff imported from foreigners; but to a company trying to make profits at whaling it mattered a great deal if Dutch Baltic freights were lower than English Baltic freights.

Elking was obviously right in supposing that the Dutch trading superiority could not last now that the English were so clearly forging ahead, but he was wrong in supposing that a Dutch collapse was imminent. He produced a long account of the Dutch whaling trade to show what prosperity could result from whaling, yet assumed that it would collapse like a pack of cards when English monied men chose to equip their ships and send them to the Arctic manned by the same men as had previously manned the Dutch vessels.

Had this been the sum of Elking's views he could have been dismissed as yet another misguided mercantilist more interested in production than consumption. In fact he was well aware that nothing could be done without adequate markets, and was one of those forward-looking men who argued that England's prosperity lay in harnessing her trade potential for an all-out attack on foreign markets held by the Dutch:[18]

> It is a great mistake to say...we have oil enough, and that there will be no vent for what is imported from Greenland; when we know how many other parts of Europe want the train oil, and the soap boiled of the same. And if our own markets should be over-stocked, and we send the oil to foreign markets, we shall be able to sell as cheap, nay, even cheaper than the Dutch...The gain by exportations is what will increase our wealth and riches.

---

[18]*Ibid.*, 101.

There were two basic requirements for success: capital, which the readers of Elking's book would be encouraged to subscribe; and adequate leadership which Elking himself proposed to give. Much of the blame for the Greenland Company's failure was laid at the feet of its captains. The New adventure must have

> ingenious and experienced commanders, who by their observations are able to judge upon what degrees of latitude to enter the ice, where and to what places of the ice to fasten the ship, where to stay or to remove, and where it is likely that whales will appear, if not discovered immediately; and where 'tis proper to change places to avoid being surrounded with ice; and how to preserve the ship from being lost and crushed to pieces between the great islands of ice: which are accidents that sometimes happen by carelessness or ignorance.[19]

A similar faith in the ability of captains to overcome national disabilities was shown in Scotland, where the short-lived Glasgow Whale Fishery Company was founded chiefly by the Bogle family of tobacco merchants with Dutch connexions. "Allowing that the Greenland Fishery, is but a very precarious Trade," wrote one of them from Leiden,

> yet there is more probability of the Company's succeeding in it when they use right means than if they should not allow the captains (who are certainly the best judges of their own abilities) all the requisites for the carrying on the trade for which the Company called them from their native company [country?], in short the encouraging of foreigners to settle in Scotland, and to learn us many arts and mysteries we are still ignorant of would tend much to our temporal happiness, and the allowing strangers as well as subjects a liberty in every thing that is neither sinful, nor, tending to the ruin of the public good, is one great means, whereby any nation does flourish as may be seen by the surprising condition the Dutch are now in [.] I need not say any more up on this subject only, by mismanagement or other ways it plainly appears that Scotland (tho' the most ancient of most kingdom[s] in Europe) is at

---

[19]*Ibid.*, 75.

least a hundred years behind many of them in their improvements.[20]

Given such experienced commanders, backed up by foreigners hired for the fishery, there was supposedly no reason why success should continue to elude British merchants who now enjoyed cheaper ships (prime costs were more, but they lasted longer), cheaper victuals, lower port charges and lower wages than their Dutch rivals; merchants, moreover, who were now acquainted with the dangers inherent in extravagant and bad management, and for whom Elking had produced a complete guide to success. "A treasure taken out of the sea," Elking said, "is a treasure gained: It must be so; it cannot be otherwise."[21]

To Elking's great surprise and annoyance, his closely argued pages did not have the required effect on the directors when the matter was debated in August 1722. They called in another expert witness from the trade, and in the end rejected Elking's proposals by thirteen votes to ten: there would be no trade to Greenland. Eyles did not give up easily, and by the time Elking requested consideration for lost time and pains, the Court was prepared to re-examine the question, deferring judgement until the following March. Finally, in May 1724, the directors voted unanimously in favour of the whaling trade, and the greatest single adventure ever undertaken from this country to the Greenland seas began. Elking received his reward with his appointment as Agent and Superintendent for the Greenland Fishery at a Salary of £100 per annum plus 1½ percent of gross sales,[22] and at last was able to conduct his experiment on a grand scale, to prove that Britain could face the world. The irony of his life and work was that she could not, and Elking had the heartbreaking task of directing what was also the biggest single failure in Britain's long history of involvement with the Arctic.

The South Sea Company's whaling disaster can be described briefly. The company as a whole was not particularly interested in the Greenland Fishery, which rarely appears in the Minute Books of the Court of Directors, beyond regular bald statements that sums of £1000 to £7000 had been paid for the use of the Fishery. The day-to-day administration was in the hands of the Green-

---

[20]Mitchell Library, Glasgow (MLG), Bogle Papers (BP), George Gogle, Leyden, to Robert Bogle, Glasgow, 16 February 1727. The Glasgow Company appears to have operated only in the 1727 season, and was wound up in 1730.

[21]Elking, *View of the Greenland Trade*, 97.

[22]BM, Add. Ms. 25,202, Minutes of the South Sea Company, 11 June 1724.

land Committee, whose Minute Books were regrettably not among the company's papers deposited in the British Museum. How well this committee knew and was able to control what went on is not clear. There is no evidence that the directors ever questioned the use of the large sums of money they poured into the trade, and it was not until 17 March 1731 that they ordered that the clerk of the Greenland Committee "do forthwith prepare and keep a Journal and Ledger of the Greenland Trade."[23] When, finally, the directors tried to get accounts from Elking, all they received was "An accompt consisting partly of disbursements and partly of pretensions of various kinds."[24] The company certainly seems to have broken Elking's cardinal rule about extravagance, partly through necessity and partly, no doubt, because a company with a capital of millions was never the best institution to guard the pennies. For instance, instead of hiring good but cheap merchantmen and fitting them out for a few hundred pounds, the company laid down a dozen superb 300-tonners for the 1725 season and a further dozen for 1726. Instead of fitting out in the Thames, they hired the Howland dock at Blackwall, a connexion with whaling still commemorated in the name of "Greenland" dock on the same site. Instead of making do with existing buildings, they built boiling-houses, warehouses, and houses for their staff, including Elking. Instead of getting the cheap labour promised by Elking, the 152 men from Fohrde in Holstein hired as fishery officers cost no less than £3057 in the first year, bringing the total wages bill to £6209 for twelve ships, compared with £5040 by Elking's estimate. Of the officers, only the captains were English, and that, perhaps, was unfortunate. Attempts to hire Dutch captains were apparently frustrated by the vigilance with which Dutch magistrates operated the law against their countrymen taking part in foreign whaling – with one South Sea captain going to prison for a time for attempting to recruit Dutchmen for the Company's service.[25]

Such a huge business enterprise, with massive overheads including dock workers and marine superintendents, would no doubt have been justified if everything had gone well: Elking would have gone down in history as one of the greatest business figures of the eighteenth century. Unfortunately it did not go well. By Elking's estimates, it would have taken twelve whales to pay the wages bill alone; and the total catch in the first year was only 25½. A loss might be expected as inexperienced captains explored the Arctic, and a loss in the second

[23]*Ibid.*, Add. Ms. 25,505, 17 March 1731.

[24]*Ibid.*, Add. Ms. 25,506, 4 May 1733.

[25]MLG, BP, George Bogle, Leyden, to Robert Bogle, 11 March 1727.

year, when twenty-four vessels brought home only 16½ whales, might be toler-
ated; but loss followed loss, and in eight years, 172 ships brought home a total
of 160½ whales. Even the staunchest of Elking's supporters grew cold as the
company was forced to seek government help in 1731;[26] and when that help was
not forthcoming and Dutch competition did not diminish, the company resolved
on 27 October 1731 "that without further encouragements, the Greenland trade
be not longer carried on."

Elking and some of his friends made a valiant effort to save the enterprise, and the company responded by offering to hire them sixteen ships for the
1733 season for a mere £1600, an indication of how little it valued the trade.
Ten days later the decision was reversed, and orders were given for the sale of
the ships and stores.[27] Twenty of the ships sold at auction for £26,225;[28] nobody
bothered to record in the minutes how much was received for the remaining ship
or the stores. Elking was a broken man. "His whole being," he wrote in a petition to the company, "depended upon the success thereof, so that his zeal and
hearty endeavours could not be doubted; that in regard his commissions were
very much below his expectation, and that by putting an end to the fishery, his
future hopes are quite frustrated, and he is left to seek a livelyhood."[29] Any
sympathy the directors may have had for his "deplorable circumstances" was
dispelled by the revelation that he owed them money and had no adequate accounts; he was dismissed, ordered from his house, and finally sued. The Greenland adventure was over, the final break coming with the sale of the dock lease
to Sir Joseph Eyles in September 1733. In the same year whaler owners were
offered twenty shillings per ton subsidy as part of Walpole's general policy of
reducing duties and introducing bounties to encourage English trade, but by then
it was too late. In the final accounting, the company had poured £62,172 into
eight Greenland seasons; its total returns, including the sale of ships and stores,
amounted to only £84,390, leaving a net loss of £177,782, roughly £1000 per
ship per annum.

The South Sea Company had immense assets with which to cover its
losses, but the London business community had learned its lesson. If the Muscovy, Greenland and South Sea Companies could not make a go of whaling,

---

[26]BM, Add. Ms. 25,505, 10 May 1731.

[27]*Ibid.*, 14 and 24 November 1732.

[28]*Ibid.*, 5 January 1733.

[29]*Ibid.*, 26 January 1733.

there would be no more attempts by joint stock companies. In future, whaling adventures would be initiated not by the owners of capital, but by merchants directly interested in oil, or by master mariners: by men, above all, who knew their trade. There were very few of them in the 1730s and 1740s, and on average they fitted out only three ships per annum between 1733 and 1749. Unfortunately nothing at all is known about the activities of these firms which must have acted in some small way as a reservoir of entrepreneurial and technical expertise. The raising of the bounty to thirty shillings per ton in 1740 (for the duration of the war) made no difference whatever to the trade, which barely survived the war. Presumably the people involved were able to make some sort of profit – at least enough for them to persevere – but any advance was inhibited as always by inadequate markets, and by a new and growing rivalry.

V

It is important to contrast the failure of the South Sea Company's efforts with the success of whaling in the New England colonies. Black Right whales (*Balaena glacialis*) – the same as, or similar to, the Biscay whales – were in abundance off the coast of North America, and, since the Arctic drift ice comes further south there than on the eastern side of the Atlantic, there may also have been Greenland Right whales. Bay whaling, following traditional Indian methods and employing Indian harpooners, began almost with the Founding Fathers. The taking of whales ranked with mining for gold and silver in the plans of Captain Smith in 1614, and though for some time the catching of whales was a piece of accidental and occasional good fortune, an organised prosecution of the trade was beginning in the middle of the century.[30] First the people of Long Island, then Martha's Vineyard, Cape Cod and finally Nantucket, set out for patrols along the coast lasting for two or three weeks, stopping on shore at night, and bay-whaling wherever possible. Eventually the trips became longer as whales were pursued further from the shore, and the profits earned in whaling boats were used to fit out whaling ships. Something approaching a "whale fishery" had developed by about 1730, when Nantucket, the leading port, had twenty-five vessels of forty-fifty tons engaged in long-distance whaling.

This move onto the high seas sprang partly from the thinning out of inshore whales, and partly from a completely new development that was to have far-reaching effects on whaling in both America and Europe. In 1712 a Nan-

---

[30]Alexander Starbuck, *History of the American Whale Fishery* (Waltham, MA, 1878), chapter 1, *passim*. This is still probably the best account of early American whaling; most subsequent books follow it.

tucket boat blown offshore in a gale came across, and killed, the first specimen of the oceanic sperm whale, *Physeter catodon*, which was destined to become the chief quarry of American whalers and provided the lighting and lubricating oil for the top end of the international market.

The sperm whale, which was quite different from the Greenland and black Right whales, had characteristics that made a sea-voyage worth while. Unlike the larger baleen whales, it had teeth, and fed chiefly on squid and cuttlefish, with the result that it was not tied to polar regions. It could be found almost anywhere in the world in temperate or tropical waters, and the possibility of extending the fishery was therefore boundless compared with the narrowly circumscribed Arctic or Sub-Arctic fishery. The absence of the valuable baleen was compensated for by the value of the oil, which was commonly worth several times as much as ordinary whale oil. Presumably because of differences in diet and habitat the blubber of the sperm whale produced a paler oil of better quality than that produced from baleen whales; but the prize was the liquid wax – the pure spermaceti – contained in the "case," the cavity in the huge "nose" which distinguished this whale from all others. A fair-sized animal might produce a tun of this "head matter" and perhaps two or three tuns of blubber oil; a very large whale as much as five tuns and seven tuns respectively. Although some merchants distinguished between sperm oil and head matter (which was about twenty-five percent dearer), the two were usually mixed and imported as sperm oil to compete with whale oil.

The chief advantage of sperm oil sprang from its waxy quality. It was chemically different from ordinary whale oil, having almost three-quarters of its component fatty acids falling in the wax rather than the oil range, with the result that on cooling the blubber oil was a thick liquid and the spermaceti was a semi-solid, very soft wax. It was quickly discovered that after prolonged exposure to cold weather – as during a New England winter – the waxy and oil parts tended to separate, and by a careful and elaborate pressing process the latter could be expelled, leaving a dry and brittle wax which in the trade was known as pure spermaceti.[31] Its potential as a candle-making material was soon recognised, and those who made them advertised their superiority:[32]

> Sperma Ceti Candles, exceeding all others for Beauty, Sweetness of Scent when extinguished; Duration being more than double Tallow Candles of equal size; Dimensions of Flame, nearly four Times more, emitting a soft easy expanding Light, bringing the Objects close to the Sight, rather than causing the Eye to trace after them, as all Tallow Candles do, from a constant Dimness which they produce. One of these Candles serves the Use and Purpose of three Tallow Ones, and upon the whole are much pleasanter and cheaper.

By 1761 the American spermaceti chandlers were sufficiently established to form one of the first inter-colonial trade associations,[33] and the spermaceti candle was firmly ensconced in the drawing rooms of London.

Quite apart from its greater relative value, the unique qualities of the sperm whale facilitated pelagic operations. As noted above, the head-matter was a liquid when warm, and could be transferred from "case" to cask by bucket; there was no immediate processing required, and no degeneration of the head-matter through contact with putrefying blubber. The blubber, on the other hand, was more likely to decay than Arctic blubber (because of the higher temperature), and had to be dealt with on board ship. This was a feasible proposition because of the small amount involved, compared with the twenty tuns of a large Right whale, and colonial whalers soon began to carry small try-works that would have been impracticable in the Arctic.

---

[31]The process is described in L. Holmes, *The Arctic Whaleman, or Winter in the Arctic Ocean, being a Narrative of the Wreck of the Whale Ship Citizen, of New Bedford, qith a Brief History of Whaling* (Boston, 1857), reprinted in E.P. Hohman, *The American Whaleman: A Study of Life and Labor in the Whaling Industry* (New York, 1928), 334-335.

[32]Advertisement in the Boston *Newsletter*, 30 March 1748, quoted in G. Wills, *Candlesticks* (Newton Abbot, 1974), 107. (I owe this reference to Joan Lythe). The spermaceti candle weighting one-sixth of a pound became the standard unit of "candlepower" in photometry in the nineteenth century.

[33]A.M. Schlesinger, *The Birth of the Nation: A Portrait of the American People of the Eve of Independence* (New York, 1968), 48.

Thus, at a time when the English were failing to develop the rather difficult Arctic ice fishery, the colonists were ranging further afield from their highly productive bay fisheries in pursuit of Right whales as far north as Davis Straits, and of sperm whales as far south as Bermuda. An aptitude born of peasant fishing became a flourishing industry in the hands of men who knew instinctively what they were about. Indeed, for the men of Martha's Vineyard, Cape Cod or Nantucket, whaling was not so much a way of making profits as a way of living in an inhospitable land. Their incentive to persevere was great, and their tastes were simple. Having learned from Indians and men brought over from Biscay, they taught their craft to their children in a way as yet unknown in England. Many years later J.H. St. John de Crèvecoeur described the training of Nantucket whalermen in his *Letters from an American Farmer:*[34]

> ...at fourteen they are sent to sea, where in their leisure hours their companions teach them the art of navigation, which they have an opportunity of practising on the spot. They learn the great and useful art of working a ship in all the different situations which the sea and wind so often require; and surely there cannot be a better or more useful school of that kind in the world. Then they go gradually through every station of rowers, steersmen, and harpooners; thus they learn to attack, to pursue, to overtake, to cut, to dress their huge game: and after having performed several such voyages, and perfected themselves in this business, they are fit either for the counting house or the chase.

By such standards the directors and captains of the South Sea Company were fit for very little, a point which is perhaps borne out by the failure of the only "Company" attempt to establish whaling in America: that of the Hudson Bay Company which experimented with whaling from Fort York in the 1690s.[35]

The progress of colonial whaling was to be a crucial influence on British whaling. Imports of oil from Holland, paying £9 per tun duty since 1673, withered away under the impact not of English-caught oil but of colonial-caught

---

[34]J.H. St. John de Crèvecoeur, *Letters from an American Farmer* (Philadelphia, 1782; reprint, London, 1962), 114-115.

[35]Instructions to Governor of York Fort, 1693, printed in J. Thirsk and J.P. Cooper (eds.), *Seventeenth Century Economic Documents* (Oxford, 1972), 558. (I owe this reference to Edgar Lythe.)

oil paying three shillings a tun, and by the time the South Sea Company ventured into the trade in the late 1720s almost the entire volume of imported oil
came from the colonies, which alone could more than satisfy the English market. The price of sperm oil fell to as little as £7 a tun in the late 1720s with
colonial over-production, and there was little opportunity for South Sea Company rejoicing. Moreover, the Americans were ready poised to respond when
prices doubled in the 1740s. Along the New England coast whaling developed in
the towns and villages: in Boston, Salem, Chatham, Sag Harbour, Southampton
and, in 1755, in Dartmouth, Massachusetts which, under its more common
name of New Bedford, can justly claim to have fostered more whalers than any
other port in the world. As a result of their activities, though periodically disrupted by war, imports of non-Greenland oil into England rose from 2419 tuns
per annum in 1725-1729 to 3067 tuns in 1745-1749 and 6494 tuns in 1765-
1769.[36]

There was a confusion within colonial oil statistics that reduces their
value to some extent. They were, according to the usual Customs classification,
train oil figures, and therefore contain an indeterminate quantity of Newfoundland fish oil. Nevertheless, it seems fair to follow the customs of both officials
and merchants who, when arguing about the whaling trade, always referred to
train oil without further definition. So far as they were concerned, *all* train oil
was in actual competition with any oil that might be brought direct from Greenland. Certainly the rise of the colonial fishery diverted the attention of English
oil merchants away from both Greenland and Holland. As transatlantic trade
developed, ships became readily available for the carriage of oil from the northern ports, and by the 1730s ships commonly went to Nantucket for their cargoes, collecting them directly from the whalers while they were still at sea. The
Nantucket people did not bring the oil to England themselves, as all the old
whalers had done, for two very positive reasons. Firstly, specialist whalers
could be kept at sea for longer periods, thus becoming primitive factory ships
and increasing their earning power, so long as ordinary English merchantmen
could be used to carry the oil. Secondly, for the English importer such an arrangement was financially advantageous because the Customs duty was six
shillings per tun on oil caught and imported by colonial vessels, but only three
shillings on oil caught by colonial and imported by English vessels.

The consequence of this division of labour was, in the long run, good
for English whaling. Master mariners fetching oil from Holland learned nothing

[36]Calculated from Great Britain, Public Record Office (PRO), Board of Trade
(BT) 6/93/116, An Account of Train or Animal Oil Imported and Exported, 1701-1785.
See also appendix 1.

of its catching. The young men growing up in the Nantucket trade – men such as Samuel Standidge of Hull – found themselves in a community that lived for whaling, and on occasions collected their cargoes on the whaling grounds where they could observe the business of fishing. These men, and the oil and transatlantic merchants who employed them, were a core around which the English trade could develop when other favourable factors emerged in the middle of the eighteenth century.

Chapter 3
The Rise of the Greenland
Trade, 1750-1783

I

By the mid-eighteenth century politicians were well accustomed to arguments about the advantages derived from trade. Pitt's famous dictum, "When trade is at stake you must defend it or perish," echoed views that had inspired the Navigation Laws a century earlier. Since the sum of world trade was limited, trade warfare was necessary to increase the British share of world prosperity, a prosperity which could only come about, according to the "bullionist" theory that still held sway, when Britain imported more gold than she exported. Matthew Decker put the matter succinctly in his *Essay on the Decline of Foreign Trade* in 1739; "if the Imports of Britain exceed its Exports, we must pay foreigners the balance in Treasure, and the Nation grow poor."[1] The basic unsoundness of bullionist theory (gold flows alter the terms of trade and, if left alone, are self-righting) did not detract from its popularity, and from the time of Walpole governments had considered it their duty (encouraged by vested interests), to use protection and bounties to encourage British industry and shipping in their "fight" with foreigners.

Some trades were permanently in the red: bullion *had* to be shipped abroad to pay for the luxuries from the East Indies and the raw materials from Northern Europe. Any savings that could be made elsewhere were therefore particularly welcome, and the Greenland trade seemed a useful trade to defend – or encourage. It was, moreover, a trade which, with the other fisheries, had long been venerated as a "nursery of seamen," hardened to the worst of conditions. The naval inadequacies uncovered by the War of the Austrian Succession (1740-1748), and the likelihood of further world-wide conflicts, persuaded government to invest in fishermen. "Though the tonnage bounties," wrote Adam Smith,

> do not contribute to the opulence of the nation, it may perhaps
> be thought that they contribute to its defence by augmenting
> the number of its sailors and shipping. This, it may be al-
> leged, may sometimes be done by means of such bounties at a

---

[1] Matthew Decker, *Essay on the Decline of the Foreign Trade, Consequently of the Value of the Lands of Britain, and on the Means to Restore Both* (London, 1739), 7.

much smaller expense than by keeping up a great standing navy...[2]

With these factors of wealth and security in mind the bounty on fishing boats was advanced to thirty shillings per ton in 1750, and that on whalers, which had hitherto failed to respond to bounties, to forty shillings per ton. The response was immediate and impressive, so far as whaling was concerned. Two ships had been fitted out in 1749; there were twenty in 1750 and eighty-three (including those from Scotland) by 1756. At first sight the extra ten shilling bounty appears to have been the long-awaited inducement, offering £600 to the owners of an average 300-tonner. As one wit later put it, "a number of ships were fitted out as much certainly in the intention of catching the bounty as of catching fish."[3] The certainty of the former helped to offset the uncertainty of the latter, but with so many variables in whaling it is doubtful if £600 could ever have been more than a marginal inducement, a trigger mechanism that only worked because of a confluence of favourable factors.

The most obvious of these factors was the expanding use of both vegetable and animal oils. The rapidly growing woollen textile industry – which provided the bulk of Britain's exports before the rise of the cotton industry – consumed oil on a grand scale for the cleansing of wool prior to spinning. It took about three gallons of rape oil to make enough yarn for 100 yards of white cloth,[4] and while whale oil could not be substituted for rape in the manufacture of good quality cloths – it discoloured and stiffened them – it was ideal for

---

[2]Adam Smith, *An Inquiry into the Nature and Causes of the Wealth of Nations* (2 vols., London, 1776; reprint, 2 vols., London, 1910), II, 18. The bounty was payable to ships over 200 tons which carried four whaling boats, each with six men. Larger ships were required to carry one boat and six men for every fifty tons. (To qualify, a ship which was not full must remain in the fishery for sixteen weeks.) By contrast with Smith, Pitt the Younger did not regard the Greenland Fishery as a nursery of seamen (Hansard, *The Parliamentary History of England* [London, 1816], XXV, columns 1381-1384).

[3]*Monthly Supplement of the Penny Magazine of the Society for the Diffusion of Useful Knowledge*, No. 74 (1833), quoting "a recent author." Adam Smith said something very similar of the herring bounty (p. 19), and this, in fact, may be the origin of the quotation. The *Monthly Supplement* devoted to the whaling trade is one of the best brief accounts.

[4]Great Britain, Parliament, House of Commons, *Parliamentary Papers (BPP)*, 1816 (272), VI, 161, Select Committee to Examine into the Policy of Imposing an Increased Duty on the Import of Foreign Seeds, 2nd Report, evidence of Jervis Walker.

cheap coarse cloths. It was, for instance, used extensively for the military cloth which was in great demand throughout Europe at least until 1815. Manufacturers might argue that yarn processed with whale oil would not weave easily or produce a fine quality finish, and that it was liable to spontaneous combustion,[5] but in practise they were eager enough to use it because it was cheaper than superior oils, and the coarse cloth trade around Leeds came to rely heavily on it.

Industrialisation in general, and the urbanisation which followed it, increased the demand for oil in a variety of ways. The mills and mines required lubricants for their new machinery. The building going on all over the country required varnish, paint and putty. Above all, a vast market opened up as whale oil was applied to illumination. The city of London had become the best lit city in the world when five thousand street lamps were installed in the 1740s, and street lamps became a common feature of the residential areas to the west. Hull had had street lights from at least 1713 (though whether they used whale oil before mid-century is not clear), and many other ports had them around their docks and warehouses after the middle of the century. The new towns of the eighteenth century did not all dispel nocturnal gloom, but there were many, following Birmingham's example, that did, at least in their better streets. Whale oil found its uses indoors as well. The dark satanic mills owed their long hours and night working at least partially to oil lamps, though the manufacturers of the finest quality cloth would not even have whale oil in their lamps because the slightest splashes produced rust-like staining. At the top of the social scale the diamonds and wit sparkled in the light of spermaceti candles, generally held to be superior to the old fashioned tallow sort.

Whatever its uses, the market for whale oil was growing fast in the middle of the century (as imports in general were rising), and increasing demand had a welcome effect upon prices. In 1742-1744 the average price had been £14 7s. and the quantity imported 2193 tuns; by 1754 the price had risen to £29 and the quantity imported to 4018 tuns.[6] Prices over £20 were considered remunerative alongside a bounty of £2 per ton, and the importation of native- and American-caught oil passed 5000 tuns in 1763, 6000 in 1766, 7000 in 1768 and 8000 in 1771.

---

[5]*Ibid.*, evidence of John Nussey, *passim.*

[6]Prices from W. Scoresby, *An Account of the Arctic Regions, with a History and Description of the Northern Whale Fishery* (2 vols., Edinburgh, 1820), II, 409; quantities from Great Britain, Public Record Office (PRO), Board of Trade (BT) 6/93/116 (England) and 6/93/117 (Scotland).

About the second product of whaling – the bone – little need be said at this point. There had been no fundamental change in female armour since the early part of the century. Hooped skirts supported by whalebone remained in fashion throughout the century and were compulsory for court wear until the 1820s. Pinched waists and straight backs were still produced by heavily-boned bodices, but as materials changed – especially with the introduction of printed cottons – the boning was increasingly consigned to undergarments, although the dresses might also be lightly boned to produce the "off the shoulder" look.[7] By the 1770s staymaking had become a fine art, as it was discovered that carefully cut stays with judicious boning could produce a better and more pliant "figure" than the earlier solid boning, but it seems likely that any reduction in the amount of bone used in a single pair of stays would be taken up in the increasing number of women wearing them.

Bounties and prices were only part of the story, though obviously an important part. Against this generally favourable economic background were a number of more specific encouragements. The first was the gradual decline in Dutch whaling efforts during the second quarter of the century. Threatened by an expanding oilseed-crushing industry on the Continent, and demoralised by low average catches in the Arctic (especially in Davis Straits), Dutch owners withdrew many of their vessels, which declined from an average of 225 per annum in the 1750s. As the number of vessels fell, average catches and profits rose, making the 1740s one of the most lucrative decades for individual owners, and it was in this context of declining competition that British owners felt encouraged to try their hand at securing some of the better catches now to be expected so long as more Dutch vessels were not drawn back into the trade.

A more immediate incentive, however, was to be found in the changing relationship between the British trade and that in the colonies. Another reason, perhaps, for the declining Dutch activity had been the growth of whaling in the western Atlantic and Davis Straits as the eastern area was over-fished, and – as noted above – this fishery was based, for the most part, on the British North American colonies. So long as the colonies remained an excellent source of cheap oil there had been little incentive for heavy investment in long-distance whaling operations from Britain itself. Unfortunately for the colonists the expansion of the metropolitan market came at a time of proliferating obstacles to their fishing. Anglo-French rivalry for the possession of North America led to disputes over fishing rights and, more seriously, to skirmishes along the borders of Canada, which were uncomfortably close to the whaling settlements. In particular the French were trying to assert their claims to Nova Scotia, and blocking

---

[7]N. Waugh, *Corsets and Crinolines* (London, 1954), 41-45.

access to the potentially valuable whaling grounds around the Gulf of St. Lawrence. The outbreak of unofficial warfare in 1754 hit the trade hard, as men and
ships were drawn into government service, ninety whalers being taken for the
famous St. Lawrence campaign that finally ousted the French from Canada. The
increase in the bounty therefore came at a most propitious time, and was taken
up by men in Britain who might have remained aloof had the transatlantic oil
trade continued unmolested, and who would soon be discouraged when the
American trade revived. This episode in British whaling may well have been no
more than another flash in the pan had not the whole future of whaling been
altered by renewed troubles in America in the 1770s.

II

The rise of the British trade after 1750 was novel in its speed, geographical
location and business structure. For the first time whaling spread throughout the
length and breadth of the country as merchants and shipowners, freed from the
inhibiting restrictions of London-based joint-stock monopolies, exercised their
independent initiative and capital wherever they recognised a local market or
distribution system. London, serving its own huge market, and fitting out
seventy-one percent of the English and fifty-one percent of the British whalers in
1753, was indisputably the centre of whaling, and was to remain so for a long
time.[8] But the growing demand for oil and bone in industrial and urban centres
encouraged enterprising men in other places where, to some extent, they were
saved from the competition operating within the London market.

The Scottish outports were particularly favoured, and sent more whalers to the Arctic than did English outports during the first phase of revival during the 1750s. They were, from their northern position, well placed for Arctic
voyages, being saved the long and dangerous run down the English coast; and
their great distance from the London entrepot created in them what was very
nearly a "private" market. Moreover, the "Bubble" Act, which limited partnerships in England, did not apply in Scotland, where co-partneries operated freely.
Thus merchants interested in whaling came together to form whaling companies
which controlled the trade in any particular port, and expansion took place within these companies. As a result the Scottish ports did not suffer from the sort of
competition that could ruin everybody as too many people were drawn into a
limited market. The port of Leith (serving Edinburgh) was first off the mark in
1749 with the Edinburg Whale Fishery Company, which equipped its first

---

[8]Details of whalers, by ports, in PRO, BT 6/93/98 (England) and 6/93/119
(Scotland).

whaler, appropriately called the *Tryall*, in 1750.[9] It was joined in 1751 by companies in Glasgow and Campbeltown, and in 1752 by the East Lothian and Merse Whale Fishery Company operating from Dunbar on the assumption, according to the contract of copartnery, "that the carrying on the whale fishery from the harbour of Dunbar may be of eminent advantage to the trade of this part of the country."[10]

The major expansion in the trade began in 1753, as more whalers were equipped in London and by the Scottish companies, which were joined by new ones in Aberdeen, Dundee, Kirkcaldy and Bo'ness. In the same year the major English outports joined in with vigour: Newcastle and Whitby on the east coast, and Liverpool and Bristol on the west. Hull, which eventually became the leading port, did not enter the trade until 1754, and even then was not notably enthusiastic in pursuing it, chiefly, it would seem, because her merchants were used to importing their oil from America, and continued to do so even when whalers were going direct from Hull to the Arctic.

The spread of whaling round the coast was possible because the very newness of the trade ensured that no particular port or ports enjoyed advantages derived from experience. All the ports were starting more or less from scratch, as ignorant of whaling as the men of Dunbar who put up their £6000 sterling for the East Lothian and Merse Whale Fishing Company. Like the other companies they had their set of rules and regulations, but sensibly added number xx:

> This branch of trade being new in this part of the Country,
> every thing that may be necessary for carrying it on to advan-
> tage cannot be seen, so as to be specially provided for by the
> present articles, but must be discovered by experience.

Some of the ports encouraged by the bounty to believe that anyone could go whaling were, indeed, renowned for no particular trade. Campbeltown, for instance, had no hinterland worth talking about, and could only hope to survive insofar as she could supply Glasgow via the Clyde coastal trade. In fact the *Argyle* of Campbeltown sailed only twice, and the *Campbeltown* was bought by the Edinburg Whale Fishing Company in 1753 and transferred with her captain to Leith. Whaling from Glasgow was hardly more successful, and though two ships owned by substantial Clyde merchants remained "of Glas-

---

[9]Details of Scottish whalers in Scottish Record Office (SRO), E/508, Bounty returns.

[10]Contract of co-partnery, enclosed in SRO, E/508/8/11.

gow," they actually fitted out from and returned to, Bo'ness on the Forth. Indeed, a third "Glasgow" whaler was equipped *ab initio* in Bo'ness in 1755, though she was lost on her maiden voyage. The basic unattractiveness of the west coast for whaling bases soon became apparent, and though Glasgow, Whitehaven, Liverpool, Bristol and Exeter all showed interest in the trade, the early move from Clyde to Forth was an indication of things to come: *all* the major whaling ports were to be on the east coast.

The rapid spread of whaling in the 1750s required the involvement of many small firms in many ports, and this in itself was a most important determinant of future development. Previously whaling had been more or less tied to London by political decisions. Now the trade was free to settle where it would, and each of the outports and each of the firms was a potential point for expansion. Ports would be judged on their merits, or rather on the performance of their entrepreneurs. As a result whaling ports tended to change in relative importance with shifts in markets and the growth in internal transport systems; and there is much to be said for the flexibility which was introduced into the trade's capital structure. The Scottish system of co-partneries undoubtedly had advantages in the early days in small places, insofar as it limited competition. But for a time it may well have inhibited growth while the industry expanded more quickly in England after 1763. Scottish whaling companies existed solely as whaling companies, but in England no such companies could exist in law with more than six partners. A group of men could own a ship, though each of its sixty-four shares was an independent property and there was no ship-owning "company." Thus the men who owned a whaler had no corporate entity and could not buy another, though as individuals they might, by some miraculous chance, end up with approximately the same shares in more than one ship. The point is not worth arguing here; all that matters is that anybody could buy shares in an English whaler, and the men who did the organising, the "managing owners," could draw on new investors for each of their ships if they wished. By and large such managing owners did not accumulate ships in their own name, and it was exceptionally rare to find men with leading interests in more than three or four during the eighteenth century. Moreover, to talk of whaler owners in the early days is not entirely accurate: they were shipowners, who chose to use their ship as a whaler, and this is a completely different thing. It meant, for instance, that owners could put a vessel into the trade and take it out again without in any way upsetting their *raison d'être*, so that whaling was an extremely flexible operation so far as its capital was concerned. Moreover, since whaling was part of shipowning, the vessels were not, as they had been with the South Sea Company, specially built and expensive ones. For the most part they were Plantation built, which meant that they were much cheaper than London-built vessels, and they tended not to be new: whalers, with their reinforced hulls and constant refits, went on forever, though the only piece of original timber might be the cabin door! Such ships were relatively cheap, freely available, and easily manned in ports with plenty of trade or a long involvement in fishing. In general, then, the possibilities for rapid expansion, drawing in the capital of many disparate groups of shipowners, was certainly greater in England than in Scotland until the 1790s, but this fortunately corresponded with the differences in markets, which made greater demands south of the border.

The fact that whaling was more obviously associated with shipowning than with merchanting, at least in England, had a result worth emphasising. Since whaling did not have to be in a place with existing trade, it could develop anywhere where there was, for whatever reason, an easy access to shipping and seamen, and a reasonable coastal trade to places that were major trading ports. Thus Dunbar or Anstruther in Scotland and Whitby in England could become whaling centres on the basis of a shipowning or fishing tradition.

The first phase of revived whaling, between 1750 and 1762, might well have been abandoned after a year or two had there been no bounty to spice the gamble. The results of the fishing, in terms of whales caught, were poor, and though there were notoriously bad years in which everyone did badly in the Arctic, the British did consistently worse than the Dutch in the good years which were supposed to make up the long-term profit. The first non-London ship, the *Tryall* of Leith, can serve as a typical example. Equipped by the Edinburgh Whale Fishery Company in 1750, her catch was four sea elephants; in the following years her catch was four sea elephants; in the following years her catch of whales was 0, 2, 4, 0, 0, 3, 0, 0 and 0. Some of her sister ships did slightly better, to produce an Edinburgh average of 1.8 whales per ship per annum, but some did much worse, and the number of whales is not a totally adequate guide because some of them were very small, to judge from the number of casks required to hold their blubber; for example, the *Edinburgh* brought home sixty casks containing the blubber of three whales in 1753, fifty-eight casks from one whale in 1754, and seventy-six from two whales in 1755. Taken over the country as a whole, the years 1750-1754 and 1756 were relatively successful, but the rest of the period was as disastrous as anything that had beset the South Sea Company in the 1730s, with nothing but the bounty to make ends meet.[11]

---

[11]For a discussion of the performance of the Scottish whalers, see Gordon Jackson, "Government Bounties and the Establishment of the Scottish Whaling Trade, 1750-1800," in J. Butt and J.T. Ward (eds.), *Scottish Themes: Essays in Honour of Professor S.G.E. Lythe* (Edinburgh, 1976), 54 ff.

The trouble was not, as we noted, entirely owing to Arctic conditions (though weather conditions were particularly bad in 1757 and 1758, for instance, and the Dutch also had relatively unsuccessful years). The truth, to judge from the certificates signed by masters on their return to claim the bounty, was that the British had not yet fully mastered the art of whaling. Many of the whalers carried foreign harpooners, and those that could afford it had foreign line-managers and steersmen. While foreigners on board did not guarantee a good catch – or any catch at all – it is generally true that ships manned only by Englishmen or Scotsmen rarely had good catches (the Glasgow and Hull ships being notable exceptions). It was an unwise economy to dispense with Dutch harpooners.

An equally devastating problem for the trade was the war which broke out in Europe in 1756, with results similar to those already apparent in America. Whatever the law might say about press-gangs, the fact is that they acted first and asked questions afterwards, relying on force and *fait accompli*. There were occasions in which men were taken off whalers which had already cleared out and were proceeding on their voyage, so that they had to return, or make up their crew in northern ports. Less damaging to the voyage was the press-gang habit of waiting "in ambush" for returning whalers, which were attractive because they had five times the normal ship's complement, made up for the most part of excellent seamen. The men countered by deserting the ships before they reached port, Edinburgh men at Crail, Hull men off Cleethorpes, Londoners at the mouth of the Thames. For short periods of active service this sort of thing may not matter, but any lengthy impressment took away the most valued seamen from the ensuing season's fishing. More serious still for the trade, though not for the owners, was the use of whalers for war purposes, chiefly as transports. The most ambitious of such occasions, though not one which detracted from the fishing, was the hiring by the government of the London whaling fleet after the 1757 season for a projected invasion of France which did not in the end materialise.

A run of poor results, and troubles exacerbated by war, coming at a time when prices were not particularly good, threatened the continuation of the whaling trade at the level it had reached in 1756. By 1759 the number of whalers had dropped from eighty-three to forty-nine, and when war ended in 1763 there were only forty. The oil, once again, was supplied by the Americans. As early as 1757, for example, the Hull whaler *Bosville* had been returned to the transatlantic run after her brief experience as a whaler. Seven vessels were fitted out from that port in 1755 and 1756, four in 1757 and only two in 1758, when shares in whalers were selling at a twenty percent discount.[12] For the next decade British whaling was in the doldrums as men lost heart and withdrew their ships. Both Whitby and Hull abandoned whaling altogether for a time, and the chief Scottish ports retracted their efforts as catches and profits failed to match expectations. Of the outports only Newcastle, Liverpool and Leith carried on to any great extent, and only one new port – Exeter – appeared among the list of adventures. Not until 1766 was there any sign of improvement, when Whitby and Hull came back into the trade. Indeed, viewed in perspective the revival of interest in Hull was the most significant event of the decade, since it initiated a train of progress leading to that port's complete domination of the trade within two decades. In 1766 – a bad season for Newcastle, the leading outport which now began to decline – Samuel Standidge, sometime master in the transatlantic trade and lately shipowner and merchant, took the old Hull Whale Fishery Company's *Berry* to the Arctic. Though he had but slight success, capturing only one whale and a few hundred seals (their skins, worth five shillings each, being the first brought home to Hull in any quantity in the eighteenth century), he was not deterred, and in the following year equipped two further vessels, the *British Queen* and *Britannia*. In typical fashion for England, Standidge's success encouraged other shipowners, backed by oil merchants, to try their luck; by 1770 there were seven whalers operating from the port, and twelve by 1775, just before the American Revolutionary war had revolutionary effects on the whaling trade.

The revival of whaling in Hull in the late 1760s reflected the condition in England as a whole – though *not* that in Scotland, where complete stagnation produced identical official returns for the years 1766-1772 which might seem to imply fraudulent statistics were the bounty certificates for every vessel not available for inspection. Between 1762 and 1770 the number of English whalers rose from twenty-eight to fifty, a number exceeded in the past in only five years (1754-1758). It is necessary, however, to view the trade in perspective, and that can only be done by setting it in the context of the total national trade in whale oil, and particularly by paying attention to oil-producing areas other than Greenland

III

While the British trade fell into decline after 1763, the colonists in New England and Newfoundland threw themselves with fresh vigour into their own trade as

---

[12]For Hull whaling, see Gordon Jackson, *Hull in the Eighteenth Century. A Study in Economic and Social History* (London, 1972), chapter 7.

soon as hostilities ceased. Once the French were no longer a threat, the British colonists could range freely along the whole northern coastline and Canada was drawn in as a new, though relatively small, source of oil. The Americans were, in particular, encouraged in 1764 when a revision of regulations relating to American trade included an Act (4 Geo III, c. 29) removing duties previously payable on American-caught whalebone. According to Macpherson, the removal of this duty of £31 10s. per ton (which was around ten percent of the value of the bone at that time) resulted in a doubling of the American colonial whaling fleet, though the relationship between these two facts may not have been so close as Macpherson supposed.[13] Nevertheless, George Grenville recorded at the time that the Act was fully expected in government circles to have a serious effect on the British Greenland trade, but was looked on as a useful imperial measure: "Though we resign a valuable Branch of Trade in their favour...yet the Preference is given upon truly national Considerations, when the Inhabitants of *America* and of *Europe* are looked upon as one People."[14] Grenville was, of course, right. In mercantilist theory colonial raw materials were the same as home-produced, and men who wished to develop the empire pointed to the natural advantages enjoyed by the colonists, especially now a new fishery had been opened up off the Gulf of St. Lawrence. The colonists had also enjoyed, since 1750, the same bounty as that paid in Britain, though there is little evidence to show that they went to Greenland in order to secure it. While the British whalermen had a series of poor years around the Greenland seas, where they were still second fiddle to the Dutch, the colonists exploited their own relatively unspoiled fishery with comparative ease. Among those mightily impressed was Edmund Burke, who referred at length to the colonists' enterprise in a famous purple passage in his great speech "On Conciliation with the Colonies" (22 March 1775):[15]

> Whilst we follow them among the tumbling mountains of ice,
> and behold them penetrating into the deepest frozen recesses
> of Hudson's Bay and Davis's Straits, whilst we are looking

---

[13]D. Macpherson, *Annals of Commerce, Manufacturers, Fisheries and Navigation* (4 vols., London, 1805), III, 567-568.

[14]Quoted in G.L. Beer, *British Colonial Policy 1754-1765* (New York, 1907; reprint, New York, 1933), 221.

[15]H. Law (ed.), *Burke's Speeches and Letters on American Affairs* (London, 1908), 88-89.

for them beneath the arctic circle, we hear that they have pierced into the opposite region of polar cold, that they are at the antipodes, and engaged under the frozen serpent of the south. Falkland Island, which seemed too remote and romantic an object for the grasp of national ambition, is but a stage and resting-place in the progress of their victorious industry. Nor is the equinoctial heat more discouraging to them than the accumulated winter of both the poles. We know than the accumulated winter of both the poles. We know that whilst some of them draw the line and strike the harpoon on the coast of Africa, others run the longitude and pursue their gigantic game along the coast of Brazil. No sea but what is vexed by their fisheries. No climate that is not witness to their toils. Neither the perseverance of Holland, nor the activity of France, nor the dexterous and firm sagacity of English enterprise ever carried this most perilous mode of hard industry to the extent to which it has been pushed by this recent people – a people who are still, as it were, but in the gristle, and not yet hardened into the bone of manhood.

Burke spoke at the height of the British American fishery. In the years 1772-1775 the average oil imports from the colonies were, at 7219 tuns, almost four times as great as the 1908 tuns brought home from Greenland by the British fleet,[16] and a pessimistic observer might well have forecast the complete collapse of the British based trade, especially since the bounty was due for reduction to thirty shillings per ton in 1776. However, the troubles distressing Burke were a godsend to the British whaler owners. The fate of British whaling was, in fact, being decided not in Britain, but in America.

The trade regulations and commercial chaos in the northern states which led ultimately to the outbreak of violence at Concord, in April 1775, had a serious effect on North American whaling. The British attempt to close the port of Boston, and the retaliatory non-intercourse measures of the colonists, threatened to cut off at least the supplies of oil from New England, and British shipowners were wise enough to anticipate trouble by equipping 10,000 tons of new whalers for the 1775 season. The government actually tried to encourage

---

[16]These colonial figures include imports from Newfoundland, and come from PRO, Customs 17, *passim*. For the New England colonies alone the figures are somewhat smaller, being 3696 tuns per annum for 1764-1775 compared with 1168 tuns brought home by the British-based whalers (PRO, BT 6/93/122).

them, and the Newfoundland whalermen, by granting a special bounty to ships that fished in the Gulf of St. Lawrence or along the coasts of Labrador and Newfoundland, an area technically outside the limits (59° 30') of the Greenland fishery.[17] As a consequence, the Newfoundland trade remained remarkably steady during the ensuing war, and was only seriously upset during the seasons 1781-1782.

By contrast, the New England whalermen of Nantucket and Rhode Island were soon in a most difficult situation, insofar as they were completely dependent on the British market. They could only sail regularly from New England if they swore that they were as rebellious as their fellow New Englanders; and if they did, the British would seize their vessels as rebels. Some of the whalermen moved to Newfoundland or Canada in an effort to remain British loyalists while continuing to exploit the northern fishery. Others escaped to the Falkland Islands and pursued the recently discovered fishery there for the English market without bothering to go home to face the rebels. Yet others took their chance of crossing from New England to old England in the expectation that the rebel "navy" would not be sufficiently numerous to find them or strong enough to stop them. One such "blockade runner" was taken in 1776 by Paul Jones, who reported that "she appeared...to be the property of rank Tories who ordered their oil to be carried to the London market..."[18] She did not arrive there; nor for that matter did the fifty whalers taken by the British for military use at the outbreak of the war. Under such pressures, the New England trade collapsed and supplies reaching England dropped catastrophically from 4093 tuns in 1775 to fifty-two tuns in 1776.[19] New England whaling was, for the time being, ruined, the Nantucket men alone having lost ships estimated to be worth £200,000 by the time the war ended.[20] In this case America's loss was – sometimes quite literally – Britain's gain.

Although British shipowners were eager to fill the gap left by the rebels, immediate war conditions made life almost as difficult for them as for their late rivals, and the whaling fleet shrank noticeably after 1777. Privateers – including John Paul Jones – were active on the east coast when France joined in

---

[17]Macpherson, *Annals*, III, 576.

[18]Quoted in E.A. Stackpole, *The Sea Hunters: The New England Whalemen During Two Centuries, 1635-1835* (Philadelphia, 1943), 82.

[19]PRO, Customs 17, *passim*. See appendix 6.

[20]PRO, BT 6/95, "History of the Nantucket Fishery," by Mr. Roach, 51-53.

on the side of the rebels, and impressment by the royal navy seems to have had a more disastrous effect during this war than during earlier ones because the press-gang was more ruthless in taking "protected" men. In 1779, for instance, the *North Star* of Dunbar lost two harpooners, four steersmen and four line-managers, and the *Blessed Endeavour* lost two harpooners (including her mate), five steersmen and all six of her line managers. In the English ports, where Greenland protections were better organised and violently supported, such a loss of vital men was less common, but wages rose, and many owners took the "easy" way out and hired their whalers to the government at the encouraging rate of £1 per ton per month. "The number of transports necessary for the trans-portation and supply of the army and navy in America," it was said in a Com-mittee of Trade office memorandum, "afforded the owners of the vessels usually employed in the Greenland Fishery an opportunity of employing them in the service of Government, at a certain and very considerable advantage, more than equal to the uncertainty of a Fishing voyage, if unsuccessful, even aided with the Bounty, and perhaps equal to the advantages of a successful voyage."[21] There is a proverbial story of one such vessel, Samuel Standidge's 350-ton *British Queen*, sent to New York with supplies in 1775 and from there to Lisbon. Seven years and £17,000 later, when Standidge made enquiries about her state of repair, since she was overdue for refitting, the navy eventually "found" her – still in Lisbon. A diligent search of admiralty records may dis-prove the story, but the point remains: by comparison, risking ships in the Arc-tic was a fool's game. Nothing much could be done until peace returned.

---

[21]PRO, BT 6/93/115.

Chapter 4
The Boom in the Northern Fishery,
1783-c. 1808

I

However humiliating for the politicians and soldiers, the peace of 1783 was the signal for an immense expansion of the British economy and a consequent rise in the demand for all manner of raw materials. So far as the oil trade was concerned, the peace terms removed at a stroke the most damaging competitors. "We are surprised," said John Adams, the America minister in London, "that you prefer darkness and consequent robberies, burglaries and murders in your streets, to the receiving, as a remittance, our spermaceti oil."[1] It was many years before the Americans were reconciled to the fact that they were either colonists or foreigners; and despite many valiant efforts at compromise, foreigners they remained. (It was an ironic touch that the first British ambassador to the USA, George Hammond, was the son of an English whaler-owner.) Imports from America, which now bore heavy duty, were running at about a tenth of prewar levels, and ceased altogether by 1793. The American trade was, for a time, suspended, but the street lamps stayed alight. British oil merchants and shipowners, realising the implication that Adams missed, raced to serve their own market. Oil was now provided by a rapid expansion of the British fishery in the Arctic – with the number of Greenland whalers rising from forty-four in 1782 to 102 in 1784 – and by the exciting novelty of a new British initiative in whaling to the south of the traditional Northern Fishery zone. Fore the sake of clarity the former fishery will be dealt with in the present chapter, and the latter fishery in the following chapter.

The exceptional growth in the number of Arctic whalers operating from English ports after 1783 was encouraged in other ways when war ended. The largest vessels employed in the trade consisted of many "sold by the Commissioners of HM Navy, others that have been transports, armed ships and privateers, most of them fit for no other trade or employment but the Greenland Fishery being sharp ships and not burthensome."[2] Nor was it simply a case of

---

[1]Quoted in E.A. Stackpole, *The Sea-Hunters: The New England Whalemen during Two Centuries, 1635-1835* (Philadelphia, 1943), 122.

[2]Great Britain, Public Record Office (PRO), Board of Trade (BT) 6/93/88, J. Lucas to Lord Hawkesbury, April 1786.

the navy selling redundant ships. The run down of the transatlantic carrying trade released seamen (forcing down Greenland wages from thirty to less than twenty-seven shillings a month) and redundant merchantmen "above what could be engaged in Commerce,"[3] and many of the east coast whalers fitted out after 1783 were large vessels built in the colonies and originally registered in Glasgow, Liverpool or Bristol. Presumably, in the circumstances, they were cheap, and they were certainly substantial enough for Arctic conditions. At the same time the purchasing and equipping of vessels by British owners was deliberately encouraged by the government. According to the provisions of the last Bounty Act, the bounty should have been reduced from thirty shillings per ton to twenty shillings per ton on 25 December 1781, and was due to end completely five years later. Such a reduction, during the troubled war period, wold have been extremely serious for the trade and would certainly have inhibited growth after the war. The Corporation of Hull was only one of the interested parties petitioning in favour of a more generous policy on the part of the government:[4]

> your petitioners cannot conceal their apprehensions, that if the said bounty of thirty shillings per ton, should be permitted to cease at the time limited by the said Act, it would render ineffectual the views of the Legislature, in making the salutary provisions, for the encouragement of the whale fishery, and as a necessary consequence would greatly prejudice so important and useful a branch of trade...Your petitioners having cause to fear that, since the rupture between Great Britain and the United Provinces, the navigation to the Greenland seas and Davis's straits, will be attended with more peril than heretofore, and will consequently require a longer continuance of the bounty of thirty shillings per ton, than is provided for by the said act.

So difficult, in fact, were conditions in the trade expected to become at the end of war, that the Corporation of Hull petitioned again shortly afterwards for an *increase* in the level of the bounty to forty shillings; and so persuasive were they and others interested in the trade that their petition was granted. It was therefore with a valuable subsidy that the British owners went adventuring after the war.

---

[3]*Ibid.*, BT 6/93/89; and 6/94/89.

[4]*Ibid.*, BT 6/93/75.

There were two other encouragements which were, perhaps, less obvious. The first was the very difficult political and economic situation in which the Dutch found themselves at the end of the American war, in which they had joined the Americans and the French in the contest with the British. Despite its earlier decline, the Dutch whaling fleet was still superior to that of Britain in the 1770s, but after the war it could barely muster sixty vessels per annum and was noticeably inferior to the British. Competition was therefore reduced in the Arctic, which allowed average catches to increase; and competition was similarly reduced in the European market, so that British exports were able to quadruple in the mid-1780s, when the British whaling fleet was double that of the rest of Europe.[5]

The second encouragement came through cost-saving changes in the operation of whalers. The war sw the end of the more expensive Dutch specialists on whalers. In future the harpooners, steersmen and line managers were British, who finally proved themselves to be just as capable as Dutchmen. Another result of the war was the discovery that whalers could function with far fewer first-class seamen than had been supposed possible. Partly to foster the "nursery of seamen," whalers claiming bounty had been required to carry two apprentices per hundred tons, and in the mid-1780s a quarter of the non-specialists on board were apprentices, whose cost to the owner was minimal. At the same time it became common for whalers to recruit "Greenmen," a term which had nothing to do with Greenland, but indicated that they were new to the job – and therefore cheaper. Such moves are perhaps best illustrated by the *Robert* of Peterhead (though admittedly one of the smallest whalers), which in 1795 had only two "sailors" among its crew of twenty-three.[6] The final stage, which emerged in the Napoleonic war period, came when even the cheapest native crews were swelled by half-starved wretches picked up for a song in the Shetlands and heartily despised by their more fortunate shipmates.[7]

---

[5]*Ibid.*, BT 6/94/29, Account of foreign whalers, 1786.

[6]Scottish Record Office (SRO), E/508/95/8/10.

[7]It was illegal, under 26 George III, c. 41, s. 1, to take on men in the Shetlands because whalers wishing to qualify for bounty had to muster crews before leaving their home ports. As late as 1793 the Board of Trade refused to allow Shetlanders aboard whalers: BT 5/8, Minutes of Board of Trade, 13 February and 22 March 1793. Vessels were allowed to take on Shetlanders up to three per fifty tons by 46 Geo. III, c. 9. Although initially for the duration of the war, the indulgence was extended until, with the ending of the bounty, it ceased to be meaningful.

Expansion brought Greenland whaling to a peak in 1787-1788 so far as the commitment of resources was concerned (appendix 4). Some 250 vessels were involved in each of these years, employing around 10,000 men. They represented between £0.9m and £1.1m in capital (ignoring shore-based capital) and by any standard were a major economic adventure: an average whaler was worth as much as David Dale's New Lanark mills in 1786.[8] Together they expressed the enterprise and initiative of no fewer than twenty-three ports in 1788, thirteen of them in England and ten in Scotland. London, fitting out ninety-one whalers in that year, was still the leading port by far, followed by Hull, which had become deeply involved in the trade and now had thirty-six whalers. Liverpool, the only important whaling port on the west coast, equipped twenty-one, and Newcastle and Whitby twenty each, which was about the maximum involvement in these places; thereafter they tended to decline as whaling ports, noticeably so in the case of Liverpool. A general enthusiasm pervaded the other ports, large and small alike. Sunderland equipped eight vessels and Stockton two; Yarmouth, after a long relapse, came back into whaling with eight vessels, and Lynn provided six – an involvement which was never to be important by national standards, but was sufficiently memorable locally for the Lynn whaling shanties to provide the basis for Vaughan Williams' collection. Ipswich (with five vessels), Whitehaven (two), Exeter (two) and Scarborough (one) were the other ports involved, but none of them in the end persevered.

In Scotland the activity after 1783 was disappointing considering the earlier interest shown, and by 1788 the number of vessels equipped by Hull alone was greater than that from all the Scottish ports. The Edinburgh complex of ports – Leith, Bo'ness, Grangemouth and Queensferry – equipped twelve, Dunbar five, Aberdeen four, Glasgow and Greenock six, Monstrose three and Dundee three. Glasgow and Greenock, like Liverpool, were making use of ex-American traders and soon lost interest, though the difference between the two sides of the country would appear to be partly the result of the Clyde's traditional specialization on an entrepôt trade with the middle American colonies, and partly the result of the concentration of the coarse linen industry, a major consumer of oil, in the eastern countries.

II

Perhaps the Scots were the wiser men, for the massive surge forward in the number of whalers could not possibly last. As oil from the Northern Fishery

---

[8]S.D. Chapman , *The Early Factory Masters* (Newton Abbot, 1967), 128. New Lanark was valued at £4800 for insurance purposes.

rose from an average of 1791 tuns in 1775-1779 to 3148 in 1780-1784 and 7732 in 1785-1789, the average price dropped from a high point of £345 per ton in 1782 to £200 in 1787 (appendices 5, 6 and 7). Not only did prices decline: the general principle remained true that an increase in the number of whalers led to a reduction in average cargoes, and inevitably to a decline in profitability. One of the consequent problems can be illustrated simply. By 1787 whalers were sometimes having difficulty in securing enough bone (thirty cwt.) to qualify for the bounty,[9] largely because excessive fishing was possible only with the catching of immature whales with a low bone to oil ratio; and a low ratio automatically reduced the value of the catch without reducing the difficulties involved in catching it! The trade drifted rapidly into a state of dismay, and then panic, as the economic consequences of "good harvests" were realised. In 1785 there were considerable losses throughout the trade, and 1788, the year of greatest activity, brought disaster. London owners alone lost £40,000, and national losses were put at £199,371 by the Committee of Owners when they bemoaned their fate to the Committee of Trade.[10] Though they had fitted out ships at a cost of £700,000 "experience during the last two years, has convinced them of the impossibility of carrying it on, without evident ruin to the adventurers; who are now reduced to the alternative of fitting out their ships at an almost certain loss or to lay them by totally useless."

The financial problems of the owners were aggravated to some small extent by the government's decision to reduce the bounty in 1786. On the one hand the owners and other interested parties in the whaling ports petitioned for a forty shilling bounty as the only real encouragement to the trade, pointing to their losses and forecasting the inevitable decay of the industry without this assistance. The Board of Customs, on the other hand, opposed *any* bounty, with the assertion that "this trade is now in so flourishing a state, as not to stand in need of the aid of bounties."[11] They wished, as guardians of the revenue and the public interest, to see whaling "left to stand upon its own bottom...That it may well do so, there is no reason to doubt, from the successful voyages these ships now almost constantly make." There was something to be said for the Customs view; after all, bounties supposed to encourage a new trade had now been oper-

---

[9]PRO, BT 6/94/5, Memorial concerning whalebone.

[10]*Ibid.*, BT 5/3, Minutes, 21 March 1786; and BT 6/94/87-91, Memorial of merchants.

[11]*Ibid.*, BT 6/93/132, Report of Board of Customs, 23 March 1786; and BT 5/3, Minutes, 21 March 1786.

ating for sixty-five years! But there was a lot the Customs did not know about trade – as they showed when they described imports of oil as excessive because they exceeded the prewar average. The Board of Trade was more realistic, and finally recommended a bounty of thirty shillings, but this was certainly not enough to make up for falling prices. Vessels left the trade as fast as they had previously entered it, and the fleet was halved by 1790, when exports to Revolutionary France were seriously affected. Three years later Britain was once more at war, and as press-gangs ravaged the ports, and costs – particularly of seamen – rose, the number of whalers slumped until in 1795 it was, briefly, lower th an at any time since 1767, with the exception of the most troubled war years of 1781-1782. Despite the Customs optimism that the trade could "stand upon its own bottom," it appeared that internal competition was as ruinous as foreign competition; that by its very nature, the trade would never balance supply and demand in its own favour. Owners still relied heavily – too heavily – on the bounties, and one major reason for the decline in whaling in the early 1790s was the reduction of the bounty to twenty-five shillings per ton in 1792 and twenty shillings per ton in 1795. The bounty might still act as a safety net for clean whalers, but nobody in future would go fishing for the bounty.

The general importance of the whaling bounties is worth emphasising. In supporting a trade in which individual entrepreneurs rarely made large profits for any length of time, and clean ships were not uncommon, the bounty achieved its object of encouraging ships to enter the trade, though whether it actually added ships to the British Register is open to serious question. What it did do was provide a most important subsidy to the shipping industry in general, since most whaler-owners were shipowners and most whalers were modified merchant-men. The whalers made heavy demands on port facilities, ship-repairing, ship-chandling and victualling, and their crews were among the better paid seamen. The ports certainly benefited through the multiplier effects of a huge sum of government money made available to them through the whaling trade. Between 1733 and 1800 no less than £1,975,089 was paid out in bounties[12] and not until the 1780s was the cost to the state of a tun of whale oil less than its market value. The cost of national self-sufficiency was considerable.

To put the matter into perspective: the average whaler received an annual subsidy worth almost a third of the insurance value of Arkwright's second, third or fourth cotton mills (excluding stock).[13]

---

[12]*Ibid.*, BT 6/230/92.

[13]Chapman, *Early Factory Masters*, 128. The mills and machinery were valued at £2000 at Cromford (Lower), Bakewell and Belper.

Table 2
Cost to the State of Subsidised Whale Oil, 1733-1800
(per tun)

1733-1749	£21	1787-1792	£13
1750-1776	33	1793-1795	7.3
1777-1881	21	1796-1800	3.3
1782-1786	16		

Source: Great Britain, Public Record Office (PRO), Board of Trade (BT) 6/230/92.

III

The reduction of the bounty and the troubles of the Revolutionary War finally separated the men from the boys in whaling, the professionals from the amateurs. Those who persevered probably reaped a greater reward than ever before. There was always a tendency for average cargoes – and values – to increase during wartime, when fewer British and foreign whalers were active, but there had never been quite such a long-term increase in oil imports coinciding with a declining number of vessels. Between 1790 and 1794, for instance, an average of ninety-seven whalers brought home 3309 tuns of oil from the Arctic, whereas in the second half of the decade sixty-one whalers brought home 4872 tuns. Moreover, because of expanding domestic consumption in industry and lighting, the increasing quantities of oil did not have an adverse effect upon its price, which continued to rise more or less steadily from 1788, to £22 in 1790, £31 in 1795, and £38 10s in 1800 (appendix 7). Fortunately for the industry, this rise in prices did not encourage an indiscriminate rush of new owners, for marginal investment in whaling was by no means as productive as marginal investment in the fixed capital of the textile industry or any other land-based industry. For a number of years during the war the benefits and profits of the trade went to experienced men, and this in turn helped to concentrate the future expansion of the nineteenth century in what might with justice be regarded as "professional" hands, in specialist ports.

The most prosperous period of whaling began, then, around 1795, and its most obvious witness was the large number of "tails" drawn in the log books to denote a kill. Previously the size of a whaler had not been of great significance, because anything larger than was required for navigational purposes was more or less waste space except in most propitious circumstances. A full ship was a novelty in Britain before the 1790s: clean ships were far more common. George Young emphasised the changes that were taking place in his contemporary *History of Whitby* (1817):

> The success of the whale fishery at its first commencement,
> and for many years after, bore no proportion to that of later
> years. In former times, a ship was reckoned well fished with 4
> or 5 whales, and it was counted a great matter that Mr. Banks
> ...brought home 65 fish in 10 years; but, about the year 1795,
> or soon after, a new era in the whale fishery began, and
> through the growing experience of our captains and seamen,
> the success of former times has been far surpassed. In 10 suc-
> cessive voyages, beginning with 1803, the *Resolution*, Scores-
> by, obtained no less than 249 whales, yielding 2034 tons of
> oil...

Young lists other examples of huge cargoes, culminating in the twenty-eight whales, making 230 tuns of oil, brought home by the *Resolution* (under a different captain) in 1814.

This growth in productivity was, for the remaining owners, the road to prosperity, though it was an increasingly long and hazardous road. Average catches did not rise simply because fewer whalers were active, whether British or Dutch; they were the result of wider-ranging activity, and particularly of a move towards Davis Straits. Here a new fishery was opened which, though in theory and law was merely an extension of the traditional Greenland ground, was sufficiently different in a number of ways for the whaling fraternity always to make a clear distinction between the two.

IV

Vessels engaged in the Greenland fishery usually left home in March and April and sailed northwards until they met the ice around Sptisbergen, and then drifted westwards searching for migrating whales among the pack ice off the Greenland coast. If they found none, or too few, they sailed eastwards and tried again, until winter closed in and drove them south, or until the migration of the whales made their stay useless. The season generally lasted four or at the most five months, though a happy run of good fortune in the fishing could reduce it to perhaps six weeks. By contrast, vessels engaged in the Davis Straits fishery sailed westwards in late February, battling their way through Atlantic storms to arrive in April or May in the darkness, fog, and icy sea off Labrador.[14] Here they waited, or moved slowly northward until the ice barrier, usually around

---

[14]W. Scoresby, *An Account of the Arctic Regions, with a History and Description of the Northern Whale Fishery* (2 vols., Edinburgh, 1820), II, chapter 5.

66°-68°, opened to allow an abundance of whales through in their progress to their feeding grounds in and beyond Baffin Bay. The great advantage of the Straits fishery in the early days lay in the fact that whales tended to congregate or rest in specific areas of open water where they were easily found, around 65°-66°, 68°-69°, and again around a second ice barrier usually located at 71°. Thereafter, as the ice receded the whales moved northwards at a leisurely pace with the whalers in pursuit, until they disappeared in the impenetrable icy wastes of the north and west of Baffin Bay. If the whalers were unfortunate they had a second chance as the whales returned southwards again, but very few ships needed such a chance. In the open water on the east side of the Straits, where weather conditions were very much better than in the Greenland fishery, whales were so common that every ship, barring accident, could expect to be well fished. In the Greenland fishery whales were sufficiently scarce by the end of the century for ships to go for weeks without seeing one (or, indeed, another ship), and the best way to increase the total yield of oil was to increase the number of whalers. In the Davis Straits ships tended to hunt in packs, and because of their greater productivity the total supplies of oil and bone increased much faster than the number of ships. Log book entries talk of "runs of fish," and look-outs counted them fifty together. Sometimes in the early days when ships went into new areas within the Straits it was dangerous to even lower the boats because so many whales were pressing through narrow channels in broken ice, or disporting in fjords along the coast.

The opening of the Davis Straits fishery was a wholesale slaughter for the sake of quick returns on a buoyant market. Within a few years whales were less common in the easily fished grounds at the entrance to the Straits, and vessels were compelled to follow them further and further into the eastern part of Baffin Bay, then the western side, leaving a trail of desolation behind them. In 1823, for instance, when the Davis Straits fishery was well developed, the *Cumbrian* of Hull noted in her log a passage through the recently explored Lancaster Sound, which was one of the channels through which whales migrated to and from the Hudson's Bayarea.[15] There she witnessed the success of those who had preceded her:

> Here and there along the floe edge lay the dead bodies of hundreds of flenched whales, and the air for miles around was tainted with the faetor [stench] which arose from such massess of putridity. Towards evening, the numbers come across were

---

[15]For extracts from *Cumbrian's* log, see T. Sheppard and J. Suddaby, "Hull Whaling History and Miscellaneous Material," *Hull Museums Publications*, No. 31 (1906).

even increasing, and the effluvia which then assailed our
olfactories became almost intolerable.

It was easy, in such circumstances, to make money if the market could
bear it, and the *Cumbrian* herself was hardly guiltless: she arrived home with
245 tuns of blubber stripped from the bodies of twenty-three whales which she
also left to rot in the Arctic summer. There was, however, a severe price to be
paid. The Straits themselves were relatively pleasant on the eastern side, but
Baffin Bay and the west side of the Straits were areas of fickle climate, with
gales, ice, snow and fog conspiring to make life difficult and navigation impossible. In theory the season was longer than in Greenland; in practice it was
unwise to spend too long in Baffin Bay, for the ice closed quickly and often
without warning, as many over-zealous vessels found to their infinite cost.

These, however, were difficulties that would arise in the future. In the
1790s Davis Straits was a "new" fishery that provided good catches "under the
most favourable circumstances."[16] At the same time this movement westwards
relieved some of the pressure on the Greenland fishery and enabled vessels there
to increase their catches as well. Indeed, in some years during the experimental
period, c. 1795-1805, ships which went to Greenland did better than those
which had left the field open to them by going into the poorer conditions (despite Scoresby's optimism) of Davis Straits.

The success of the Davis Straits Fishery was not simply a matter of the
number of whales, any more than of the number of whalers. It was generally
agreed that the whales in the Davis Straits, which had not yet suffered from
over-fishing, were much better specimens than the remnants to the east of
Greenland. Because the whales were bigger, full cargoes could be assembled
with greater ease and in a shorter time. Scoresby, who did some work on the
comparative yields of the Greenland and Davis Straits fisheries, reckoned that
the average Greenland whale yielded 9½ tuns of oil and the Davis Straits whale
fourteen tuns of oil in the years immediately after the Napoleonic war, and this
is certainly borne out by evidence of individual ships. At an earlier date the
difference seems to have been greater, which one would normally expect; over
any period there was a tendency for the average size of whales to decline, even
though extra-large individuals might still be caught. In 1804, for instance, when
the Hull fleet was roughly divided between Greenland and Davis Straits, the
Molly's forty-four Greenland whales yielded only 190 tuns of oil, whereas the
Thomas' thirteen Davis Straits whales boiled down to 195 tuns.

---

[16]Scoresby, *Account of the Arctic Regions*, II, 388-389.

There was another important and potentially valuable result of the westward movement of the whalers. Whales were supposed in theory to yield a hundredweight of bone for every tun of oil, and ships qualifying for bounty were supposed not to leave the Arctic before an appointed date unless they had already caught thirty tuns of oil and thirty cwt of bone. In practice the Customs returns show a lower ratio than this, partly, perhaps, because of difficulties in measurement, but largely because whalers in desperate competition were taking whales that were not "sizeable," that is, with immature bone less than six feet in length, and because cargoes were being made up with oil extracted from seals. Quite suddenly, around 1790, the bone to oil ratio began to shift in a manner most agreeable to owners to whom bone was then worth around £250 per ton. In the period 1750-1786, for instance, the Greenland whaling fleet had averaged 0.6 cwt. of bone per tun of oil whereas in the period 1787-1800 the average had risen to 1.2 cwt. per tun.[17] It was partly because the removal of the Dutch left more "sizeable" Greenland whales for the British, but more noticeably because of the greater availability of larger Davis Straits whales, despite the fact that experts thought the larger Davis Strait whale yielded less bone than the larger Greenland whale.

Against the obvious advantages of the Davis Straits fishery must be set one serious disadvantage. The enlarged yields did not always result in enlarged profits. Because a Davis Straits expedition lasted for one or two months longer than a Greenland expedition the wages and victualling costs were higher, and because of poor conditions wear and tear on the vessels was considerably greater. It was Scoresby's considered opinion in 1820 that, all things considered, the balance in favour of Davis Straits was "a very small sum."[18]

V

With the development mentioned above, the total importation of oil and bone from the northern fishery increased slowly but steadily during the French Revolutionary and Napoleonic war period, and the number of whalers began to increase again after reaching a nadir in 1795, though their numbers did not keep pace with the oil imports, which trebled between 1794 and 1804.

In the past an increase of imports on this scale would have ruined the price, if not the entrepreneurs, and such developments were only possible because a huge increase had taken place in the domestic demand for oil, coupled

[17]PRO, BT 6/230/92, "Account of the Greenland Trade."

[18]Scoresby, *Account of the Arctic Regions*, II, 391.

with a healthy and expanding export market. Even at a "low" point of £23 in 1805, oil was still worth far more than it had been half a century earlier, and as demand and inflation grew during the war the price of oil crept up to £60 in the London market in 1813, though this was admittedly a bad year; the average, nevertheless, was c. £37-40 in the years 1810-1817.

Table 3
Average Number and Tonnage of Whalers and Quantity
of Oil and Bone, 1790-1805
(5-yearly averages)

	Whalers		Oil	Bone
	No.	Tons	Tuns	Cwt.
1790-1794	97.2	28,094	3309	3996
1795-1799	60.6	16,922	4872	6394
1800-1804	84.2	24,980	7053	7144

Source: PRO, Customs, 17, *passim*.

The encouragement of advancing prices was offset to some extent by two countervailing factors. The first was war-related inflation, which whittled away some of the apparent advance in profits. Owners had estimated costs for the 300-ton second-hand *Aurora* at £4771 in 1784, and in 1786 £12 twelve shillings per ton was thought reasonable for fitting out a second-hand vessel of 200 to 400 tons, whereas by 1803 the 291-ton *Resolution* of Whitby cost £7791 to put to sea new, and the *Esk* of Whitby cost £14,000 in 1813.[19] The age of the vessel, and building costs, actually accounted for only a small proportion of this increase: the hull of the *Aurora* had been valued at £1500 and the hull of the *Resolution* cost only £2321. Clearly a very considerable advance in the price or the quality of oil was required to make up for increasing costs.

The owners' ability to withstand inflation was damaged by the second adverse factor, the rapid decline in the bone market during the war. Rousseau[20] had pronounced against

---

[19]PRO, BT 6/93/93-94, "Cost of the Ship *Aurora*;" and Scoresby, *Account of the Arctic Regions*, II, 393.

[20]J.J. Rousseau, *Emile* (Paris, 1762; reprint, London, 1911), 330.

those frames of whalebone in which our women distort rather
than display their figures. It seems to me that this abuse,
which is carried to an incredible degree of folly in England,
must sooner or later lead to the production of a degenerate
race. Moreover, I maintain that the charm which these corsets
are supposed to produce is in the worst possible taste; it is not
a pleasant thing to see a woman cut in two like a wasp – it
offends both the eye and the imagination.

He was followed by those, such as Mesdames Tallien and Hamelin, who
preached a very special kind of "liberty" for women during the Revolution, and
long before the Empire replaced the Directory the heavily-boned stays were as
much out of fashion in England as in France. Even in Hull, the centre of the
English whalebone trade, actor-manager Tate Wilkinson was bemoaning by
1794 that there was still one actress "who would not unveil her beauties even to
the chaste Diana; therefore she, with well-bound bone, forbids all access." In
the following year *The Times* noted the transformation that had taken place:
"Corsettes about six inches long, and a slight buffon tucker of two inches high
are now the only defensive paraphernalia of our fashionable belles, between the
necklace and the apron strings."[21] The girls, if not the matrons, had left off their
whalebone and gone "Greek," with figure-hugging muslins and light materials
that attracted the attention of at least one country parson in the metropolis – "the
Ladies wear their dresses so close that the form of the bosom is distinctly
marked"[22] – and earned the praise of Macpherson in 1804 when he noted that
"that rage [stays] has now greatly abated, thanks to the writings of Doctor
Buchan and the good sense of ladies."[23]

---

[21]Quoted in N. Waugh, *Corsets and Crinolines* (London, 1954), 71.

[22]Scunthorpe Museum Library, Diary of Rev. Dr. J. Parkinson, 5 May 1796.

[23]D. Macpherson, *Annals of Commerce, Manufacturers, Fisheries and Navigation*
(4 vols., London, 1805), III, 512n. Dr. Williams Buchan's *Domestic Medicine* (Edinburgh,
1769) ran through many editions in the late eighteenth century. "Even the human shape,"
he wrote (101-102), "is often attempted to be mended by dress, and those who know no
better believe that mankind would be monsters without its assistance. All attempts of this
nature are highly pernicious. The most destructive of them in this country is that of
squeezing the stomach and bowels into as narrow a compass as possible, to procure, what
is falsely called, a fine shape. By this practice the action of the stomach and bowels, the
motion of the heart and lungs, and almost all the vital functions, are obstructed. Hence
proceed indigestions, syncopes, or fainting fits, coughs, consumptions of the lungs, &c."

The "good sense" of the ladies was not, perhaps, such a sensible re-
mark for a historian of commerce, for it dealt a severe blow to the whaling
trade. At a time when they might reasonable have expected demand to grow,
with an expanding population and a growing number of relatively wealthy females, owners suddenly lost a most valuable part of their earnings. While the
total value of imported Greenland oil doubled between 1795 and 1800, the value
of bone was halved. Admittedly there had been a steady downward trend in
bone prices since the 1760s, when it was worth over £400 a ton, but there was
no precedent fo the depth of the decline in 1796-1797.

Table 4
Average Price of Greenland Whalebone 1766-1800
(Per ton, 5-yearly averages)

1766-1769	£398	1785-1789	£186
1770-1774	330	1790-1794	184
1775-1779	295	1795-1799	102
1780-1784	308		

Source: 1766-1785: PRO, BT 6/93/94; and 1786-1799: BT 6/230/95.

Worse was to follow, for prices were unstable in the early years of the
nineteenth century, and sank to a mere £30 for a time towards the end of the
war, though the average was nearer £80.[24] For a well-fished ship, with five to
ten tons of bone in the late 1790s, this decline in price meant a return that was
£1000 to £1500 lower than might have been expected in more favourable circumstances, and for the industry as a whole it represented something of the
order of £1.4m per annum – a severe blow to a trade which had previously
reckoned to obtain around half its income from the bone side.

Although the income from bone was partially lost, the situation was not
so bad as it seems. The lower price was to some extent offset by larger volumes
of bone yielded by larger whales without much greater effort on the part of the
whalers. Moreover, whalers continued to bring home huge quantities of bone, at
the risk of ruining the market, simply because it was an inevitable by-product of
the trade, and short of dumping whalebone over the side there was nothing
owners could do but enjoy the reduced income they still received from bone,
while making their profits out of the inflated price of oil. One immediate result
of the fall in the price of bone was its rapid adaptation to less fashionable uses.
The elasticity and flexibility that endeared whalebone to the staymakers were
attractive in other areas where a combination of great strength and lightness

---

[24]G. Young, *A History of Whitby* (2 vols., Whitby, 1817), II, 569.

were needed. The material was, for instance, ideally suited to the manufacture of umbrellas, and dominated this market until Samuel Fox of Sheffield developed his patent umbrella steel in 1852. The heavier variety of bone made knife handles, carriage springs, fishing rods and framing for portmanteaus, while the lighter, whiter sort made frames for ladies' hats and was a more durable substitute for split cane in upholstery. The hairy fibres along the edges of the plate was also suitable for upholstery as well as for sieves and fine nets. Samuel Crackles of Hull patented a method of making brushes from whalebone in 1808, and they remained in fairly general use for a century or more if remains in museums are anything to go by. At the other end of the scale in semi-luxury market developed around the materials' capacity to retain a shape moulded into it when hot and allowed to cool under pressure, producing twisted handles of various sorts, walking sticks, decorate hair combs and other articles after the fashion of tortoiseshell. However, it was the return of the corset which shortly brought relief to the whaler-owners, if not to their wives and daughters.

VII

Despite the falling value of bone since around 1787, the total real value of the Greenland trade, as calculated by the Board of Trade officials, was very impressive in the last twenty years of the eighteenth century, and amply justified the interest shown in it by merchants (table 5).

So far as individual firms are concerned, profits over time are not easily assessed in the absence of business papers and any very accurate method of calculating costs and earnings. Looking simply at the gross earnings of whalers, an analysis of every Scottish whaler showed them with an average of less than £2 per ship ton in the 1760s and 1770s, something under £5 in 1785-90, but £13.08 in 1801.[25] More important perhaps was the fact that the most successful vessels in 1801, the *Eliza Swan* of Montrose and the *Raith* and *Royal Bounty* of Leith, grossed approximately £5530, £6323 and £5463 respectively (bounties included). Such sums were unheard of only a few years earlier when, for instance, the *Manchester*, one of Hull's most successful whalers, had grossed around £3750 in 1786, and the *Gibralter* of Hull, which cost around

---

[25]G. Jackson, "Government Bounties and the Establishment of the Scottish Whaling Trade, 1750-1800," in J. Butt and J.T. Ward (eds.), *Scottish Themes: Essays in Honour of Professor S.G.E. Lythe* (Edinburgh, 1976), 63-65.

£3000, was lucky to earn £6000 between 1787 and 1796.[26] Yet within a few years fortunate whalers were bringing home cargoes worth around £10,000 per annum, though this was at the height of the war when costs were also considerably inflated. Scoresby quotes the case of the *Resolution* of Whitby, which grossed an average of £6810 over fourteen seasons and made a profit over that period of twenty percent on capital, though she was admittedly a very fortunate ship in a very favourable period.[27] Nevertheless, available evidence suggests that even in the 1780s a vessel with thirty tuns of oil and thirty cwt of bone might expect to make eleven percent on invested capital (including bounty);[28] something of the order of eight to ten percent may well have been usual on those ships that enjoyed a measure of success on the fishing grounds.

Table 5
Numbers of Whalers and Real Value of Greenland Oil and Bone, 1781-1799
(5-yearly averages)

	Whalers	Oil	Bone	Total	Value Per Whaler
1781-1784	57.3	£64,330	£16,790	£81,613	£1,424
1785-1789	204.6	128,909	58,243	190,778	932
1790-1794	100.4	77,932	36,752	116,898	1164
1795-1799	61.8	148,215	30,935	182,301	2950

Note: Total value includes a small amount for sealskins.

Source: PRO, BT 6/230/76.

From almost any view, then, the prospects of the Greenland fishery seemed excellent in the early years of the nineteenth century. The oil market was good; the bone market was soon improving; and the Davis Straits fishing ground was opening up new possibilities of rich rewards. However, the prosperity of the war years was not shared evenly among the old whaling ports. The decline of the trade in the late 1780s had left only six English and five Scottish ports with any substantial share in 1790 (see table 7).

---

[26]G. Jackson, *Hull in the Eighteenth Century. A Study in Economic and Social History* (London, 1972), 169-170.

[27]Scoresby, *Account of the Arctic Regions*, II, 95.

[28]BT 6/93/95, "State of Profits of the *Aurora*."

Most future development took place within these ports, and, in particular, growth was located primarily in the north-eastern ports, where outfitting costs were said to be cheaper.[29] London, which had dominated the trade since its inception, declined until by 1814 her twenty vessels were only fourteen percent of the total operating in that year (143). Liverpool in the same period had been reduced to only two vessels. Whitehaven, Yarmouth and Sunderland had left the trade, and Lynn was reduced to two and Newcastle to five vessels. By contrast the war years were marked by the very heavy concentration of the trade on Hull. Between 1800 and 1802 she almost doubled her involvement, from twenty-two ships to forty-one, and almost every year thereafter saw the launching of one or more vessels designed specifically for the trade. With captains such as Marshall and Sadler renowned for their success, with an assured market in a rapidly expanding industrial hinterland, and with wealthy oil merchants and shipowners such as Eggintons and Gees prepared to invest in whalers at £10,000 a time, there was apparently nothing that could retard Hulls' progress. By 1814 she had fifty-eight whalers, over a third of the British total, and for many years had occupied a major position in the national oil and bone trade.

The rise of the Scottish ports was as dramatic and potentially important as that of Hull. In 1795 and 1800 there had been only ten and eleven whalers equipped from Scottish ports: three/four in Aberdeen, two each in Dunbar, Dundee and Leith. Within a few years the situation was quite different. In Aberdeen, the Aberdeen Whale Fishery Company was joined by the Union Whale Fishery Company as optimism went beyond the bounds set by the traditional co-partnery which had dominated whaling in each of the Scottish ports except Leith (which had two companies for a time). The eventual success of the Aberdeen companies' four whalers led to the fitting out of another twelve in the years 1812-1814 by these and three further companies. "Our whale fishing ships," it was reported in the *Aberdeen Journal* on 10 January 1813,

> are now beginning to prepare for the fishing, and we are proud to say we shall send out 14 Davis Straits' and Greenland whalers – most of them as fine ships as ever put to sea. We wish them success. Within these two years our townsmen have laid out upwards of £100,000 in that speculation, which will, we hope, soon return.

---

[29]British Museum (BM), Add. Ms. 38,356, Liverpool Ms., f. 144, "Information supplied by Mr. Enderby, 1801."

Table 6

Whaler Arriving From Greenland, by Port, 1790

	No.	Tons		No.	Tons		No.	Tons
Hull	22	6265	Whitby	10	3180	Bo'ness	1	321
Liverpool	14	4134	Whitehaven	1	301	Dunbar	3	1001
Lynn	4	1191	Yarmouth	4	1014	Dundee	4	1027
Newcastle	7	2308	London	33	10,177	Glasgow	2	623
Sunderland	4	983	Aberdeen	4	916	Leith	5	1218
						Montrose	3	790

Source: PRO, Customs 17/12.

Aberdeen's success was mirrored in her near neighbour and member-port, Peterhead. She had equipped one diminutive ship, the *Robert*, for a time in the 1790s, and then lost interest, but by 1814-1817 she was equipping an average of 8.25 per annum.

Table 7
Performance of the Major Whaling Ports, 1814-1817
(averages)

Port	No of Whalers	Total Catches		Catches Per Ship	
		Oil (tuns)	Bone (cwt)	Oil (tuns)	Bone (cwt)
Hull	57.25	5223	5320	91.2	92.9
London	19.25	1658	1730	86.1	89.9
Whitby	9.75	1045	1005	107.2	103.1
England	98.00	8956	9030	91.4	92.1
Aberdeen	13.75	1155	1125	84.0	81.8
Leith	10.00	939	850	93.9	85.0
Peterhead	8.25	954	935	115.6	113.3
Dundee	8.00	874	795	109.2	99.4
Scotland	48.5	4671	4455	96.3	91.9

Source: Calculated from table in W. Scoresby, *An Account of the Arctic Regions, with a History and Description of the Northern Whale Fishery* (2 vols., Edinburgh, 1820), II, 131.

Dundee, which had regularly two or three vessels, now had eight, while Leith had at last revived her flagging interest and equipped ten per annum.

The ships of Peterhead and Dundee were particularly successful, sharing with Whitby the top ranking among the major whaling ports so far as average cargoes was concerned. It is not entirely clear why this should have been so. Scoresby writes of the superior fishing skills compared with the past, but the particular variations for the years 1814-1817 may well be accounted for by the differences obtained in the Greenland and Davis Straits fisheries. If, in fact, the larger cargoes came from Davis Straits, they do not necessarily represent a more prosperous voyage since, as was seen above, those voyages were more expensive to equip. Nevertheless, the point remains that Dundee and Peterhead *were* comparatively successful, and this fact, coupled with a buoyant local market for oil in the linen industry, assured their future participation in the industry at a level higher than that to which they had been accustomed.

Chapter 5
Expansion South of the
Arctic Seas, c. 1776-c. 1808

I

For most people in the eighteenth century, and for most British people to this day, the whaling trade was synonymous with the Arctic voyages about which almost all the British whaling histories have been written. It is, however, important to remember that, despite its dramatic potential and home-spun quality, the Northern trade was no more than a subsidiary source of whale oil in the eighteenth century. Before 1770 it was rare for more than a tenth of peace-time imports to come from Greenland, and until the American Revolution the bulk of supplies came from the New England colonies. Imports from there averaged 3696 tuns in the years 1764-1775 compared with only 1168 tuns from Greenland.[1] The Northern Fishery was naturally encouraged by the turmoil of the Revolutionary war, but from the same war sprang another serious rival: the Southern Fishery. They were official designations, the former covering the area north of 59° 30' in which the whaling bounty was payable, and the latter covering the area south of this where only a token subsidy was given in the form of premiums of £500, £400, £300, £200 and £100 for the five best-fished ships. (See pp. 66-67).

Once the mercantile consequences of rebellion were realised, the American whalermen had moved north or south in an attempt to remain loyal. The Nantucket men, it was later reported, "are dispersed over America and Europe – one half of them died during the war."[2] Some moved northward and helped to build up the whaling industry in Newfoundland or settled at Dartmouth in Nova Scotia. Others, while continuing to fish in the ocean between Cape Verde and Brazil in latitudes 31° to 36°S, moved to London and so established the Southern Fishery in England. The chief of the newcomers, and spokesmen for the trade for the rest of the century, was the Enderby family of Boston, Massachusetts. Samuel Enderby and his sons – one bearing his name – arrived in London in 1775, together with Alexander Champion and his son – "a well informed intelligent young man" – and John St. Barbe, a naval lieutenant "of a

---

[1]Great Britain, Public Record Office (PRO), Board of Trade (BT) 6/93/122.

[2]*Ibid.*, BT 5/4, Minutes, 26 December 1787, interview with B. Ray.

very active enterprising adventurous disposition."[3] In the following year, using American vessels and crews, they equipped twelve whalers which returned with 439 tuns of oil and were pronounced a success, Enderbys' three ships alone earning £6676 gross and premiums worth £900.[4] In the following year thirteen vessels were equipped, and nineteen in 1778, before the trade collapsed for a time under a series of political and economic pressures, chief of which was the loss of half the vessels to American and French privateers.[5] (appendix 5)

The unfortunate outcome of the Revolutionary war – so far as Britain was concerned – precipitated interest in the Southern Fishery in both government and commercial circles. It was no longer simply a gratifying expression of loyalist sentiments: firms such as Enderbys' had experienced considerable success, bringing home twenty-nine ships in the years 1776-1780 and 1782-1783, and grossing some £64,358 (together with £6900 in premiums).[6] English investors and shipowners were showing interest, and the Committee of Trade was anxious to attract more Americans to England for the sake of self-sufficiency:[7]

> It is of great importance in the present moment, when the American fishery is declining, and it is doubtful to what countries the people heretofore employed in it may resort, and whether Great Britain or any foreign country may get possession of it, that a proper effort should now be made to secure to this country the advantages of a fishery which was once so lucrative to the Americans.

In the previous month Jenkinson, the leading member of the Committee of Trade, told Parliament that in his opinion the cause of the recent success of the Greenland fishery was "that we got rid of powerful competitors in the fish-

---

[3]*Ibid.*, BT 6/93/4, Board of Trade office memo, March 1786.

[4]*Ibid.*, BT 6/93/136.

[5]British Museum (BM), Add. Ms. 38,367, f. 107, "Case of Whale Ship Owners versus the Gas Companies."

[6]PRO, BT 6/93/136. Figures for 1781 are not recorded.

[7]*Ibid.*, BT 6/93/64, Report on bounties, 3 May 1786.

ery (the Americans) which gave us, as it were, a monopoly of the trade."[8] He was unlikely to do anything to diminish that monopoly or encourage the Americans, and though he was not in favour of rash subsidies it was largely his doing as Lord Hawkesbury, President of the newly formed Board of Trade, that government came to appreciate the value of raw material sources to an industrialising nation, and in particular that the oil interest was indeed the interest of the nation. For many years he pondered the best way to increase British oil supplies, and encouraged a process of expansion that meshed into the general commercial expansion towards the end of the century and played a part in the opening up of the unknown southern oceans to British imperial activity.[9]

II

There were two ways, basically, in which the Southern Fishery could be built up. New recruits to the trade could be enticed to England in a body with their ships and families; or the existing London-based trade could be nurtured and expanded with new recruits. The former course presented itself first for the simple reason that the situation for the remaining Nantucket people was becoming desperate. In July 1785 they sent over a deputation led by a Mr. Roach or Rotch, a man of property and influence in Nantucket and, said a Committee of Trade memorandum, "wherever he goes it's supposed the greatest number of their fishermen will go also."[10] He had an interview with Pitt and with Hawkesbury, and then toured the West Country, with its long associations with the north American fisheries, in search of a base where the Nantucket people might settle as a community. While still awaiting the government's decision on his "terms" (which included removal and housing costs of around £20,000 for thirty whalers, and the naturalisation of the ships and 500 people),[11] Roach met Charles Greville, a minor politician and impecunious nephew of Sir William Hamilton, owner and "improver" of Milford Haven. It took but a short time for them to decide that Milford Haven was an admirable site for a new port for the

---

[8]Hansard, *The Parliamentary History of England* (London, 1816), XXV, column 1377.

[9]This aspect of whaling is well covered in V.T. Harlow, *The Founding of the Second British Empire* (2 vols., London, 1952-1964), II, chapter 5, section 3.

[10]PRO, BT 6/93/10.

[11]*Ibid.*, BT 6/95/41-47, Papers relating to Mr. Roach's proposals.

Nantucket fleet, and so began a barrage of propaganda, entreaties and accusations which Greville directed at the government, privy council and Hawkesbury through into the 1790s.

At first sight the Greville solution to the problem seemed foolproof. Hamilton wished to improve Milford, as other landowners were doing in various places, by erecting a port in one of the best natural harbours in the country. Its position on the west coast was convenient for the trade, and it was adjacent to the West Country with which the people of the far north of the USA had always had the closest relations. It was, moreover, sufficiently isolated for the Nantucket people to be able to rebuild a recognisable community to suit themselves and make them feel "at home." On the other hand Greville and Hamilton had reckoned without the influential opposition of the London-based trade and the implacable hostility of the Customs service.

The London merchants, led by Enderby, Champion and St. Barbe, were eager for Nantucket whalermen to join them in London as naturalised Englishmen able to bring their expertise to the fishery. Indeed, Samuel Enderby, Jr., went to America in 1786 in a vain attempt to recruit Boston and Nantucket men for his family whalers, and Alexander Champion, Jr., was "very desirous it should be carried on from Britain in preference to the colony [Nova Scotia] in America."[12] But they were not eager for a rival "American" community to spring up elsewhere within Britain and flood the market with what would, in effect, be "foreign" oil competing with their "native" oil. It is, of course, a nice point whether Americans who arrived in 1775 were more "English" than those arriving in 1785 who had never desired to be aliens and who had been Loyalists until handed over to the United States at the peace of Paris. But the fact remains that in law the former were loyal British subjects deserving aid, and the latter were indisputably citizens of the United States, whether they liked it or not. Roach probably damaged his own case by asking that his group be allowed to bring to Britain up to thirty-five American ships, manned by Americans, and that in future they should be allowed to man them with further Americans up to half the number of crewmen. Such a request was bound to arouse the Board of Customs, as, indeed, it did.

The chief purpose of the first great Shipping Registration Act, in 1786, was to distinguish between British and American ships so that the latter should be excluded from the privileges enjoyed under the Navigation laws by native ships alone. To allow thirty or more ships and their owners to call themselves British because it was in their economic interest to do so was absolutely at variance with the meaning of the Acts which the Customs service was trying to

---

[12]*Ibid.*, BT 6/93/4, Board of Trade office memo, n.d.

operate. The intent was precisely to penalise those foreigners who would gain by calling themselves British. For the sake of the oil trade, Hawkesbury was prepared to ignore the protests of the Board of Customs, and his Act for the Encouragement of the Southern Whale Fishery in 1786 allowed these foreign vessels to be licensed as British by Order-in-Council until 1790. But he was not prepared to deviate from traditional policy and upset the existing Southern whalers by granting the British premiums to such vessels. The mere access to the British market, for which the Nantucket men begged, was concession and encouragement enough. Nor would he give undue financial assistance to the immigrants. As one Committee of Trade adviser put it, the Americans were coming for their own benefit, and "I know the people of New England too well to imagine that any proposition of theirs can be without some latent view..."[13] Roach, in annoyance, led his people to Dunkirk, where the French government offered a bounty of forty-two shillings a ton (with favourable tonnage measurement) and where the cost of living was cheaper, in an attempt to outdo the London "Americans" in the Southern Whale Fishery. For a time they offered their men a better living than was offered by London owners, but in fact very few Americans chose to go to France. Of those who remained in Nantucket, "some," it was said, "are bigotted, and may not chuse to leave that island; a part of them however would come, but they are very poor and do not know how to remove their families hither; they marry young, and in general have large families."[14] In view of the government's reluctance to offer much in the way of financial inducements, the prospect of a simple transfer from America to England receded rapidly. Any development of the Southern Fishery was therefore sought in the expansion of the London trade, and further attempts to bring over Americans were both sporadic and unimportant.

III

At the same time as Greville had been pressing the claims of Roach and his party, the London merchants had been pressing their own case with slightly more success. Faced with a rapidly growing Greenland trade, whose bounty was due for revision, the Southern whaling interest petitioned in January 1786 for a tonnage bounty to replace the premiums which they said had failed in their purpose. They asked for forty shillings per ton (the same as the Greenland bounty) for three years followed by thirty shillings per ton for a further three

---

[13]*Ibid.*, BT 6/95/33, Grey Elliott to Lord Hawkesbury, 24 July 1786.

[14]*Ibid.*, BT 5/4, Minutes, 26 December 1787, evidence of B. Ray (427).

years, on the grounds that competition and costs were such that "those who have
not been so fortunate as to obtain oil enough to entitle them to one of the largest
premiums, have lost considerably."[15] This, they thought,

> will fully answer the purpose of encouraging the Southern
> Whale Fishery, without imposing on Government, as the
> thirty shillings per ton will be but a small proportion of the
> expense on an unsuccessful voyage; and your memorialists
> have proposed the bounty of forty shillings per ton for 3
> years, as they know it will be an inducement to the Americans
> to settle in England, and it will be a means of establishing the
> fishery here in preference to Nova Scotia, where it will be out
> of the power of Government to prevent American oil from
> coming here free of duty, and from its near situation to the
> Massachusetts, will be a cover to a great deal of American
> property and whaling vessels, besides the disadvantage of the
> nursery of seamen being in America, from whence it will be
> difficult to get them in case of a war.

The request for a tonnage bounty came, in fact, at a most inopportune
time, since the Greenland bounty was itself under strong attack from the Board
of Customs, which regarded it as an unnecessary waste of government money
(see chap. 3, pp. 65-66). Southern owners were told bluntly that there would be
no more blanket subsidies, but that the government would reward enterprise and
initiative by those who carried on the trade "with Spirit." Following interviews
and negotiations between the traders and the Committee of Trade, the latter
agreed, in March 1786, to recommend the quadrupling of the existing premiums, so that the four largest catches received £500 each, and so on.[16] It was a
valuable inducement insofar as the number of premiums was roughly equal to
the largest number of vessels fitted out recently, and only three less than the
number in 1785. It was, in any case, as much as the trade could expect; it was
too lively an infant to attract much sympathy for its ills. "The subjects of Your
Majesty, residing in Great Britain," wrote the Committee of Trade in its final
report on the trade,[17]

---

[15]*Ibid.*, BT 6/93/2, Memorial of Enderby & c., 6 January 1786.

[16]*Ibid.*, BT 5/3, Minutes, 30 March 1786.

[17]*Ibid.*, BT 6/93/64, Report, 3 May 1786.

have been gradually improving in it, and...since the peace, the
number of ships employed in it, under the present encouragement, has annually increased. The Committee cannot think it
necessary therefore to subject the public to the payment of
large bounties on the tonnage of vessels employed in this fishery, as prayed for by the memorialists, nor to a bounty upon
the oil imported, which they have also desired, especially as a
bounty, granted in this way, must necessarily be exposed to
great frauds.

IV

In rejecting tonnage bounties for the Southern Fishery the Committee of Trade
was in fact recognising the fundamental differences between the Northern and
Southern Fisheries. Perhaps the most obvious of them was climatic. The Northern Fishery involved necessarily short forays into the inherently hostile conditions of the Arctic. The Southern Fishery, in contrast, offered immense potential
in relatively warm waters; and, moreover, it offered the sperm whale, which
was more valuable than the Right whale. However, as with the Greenland trade,
excessive and ruthless activity by the Americans was already counter-produc-
tive, and longer voyages to new areas were inevitable. Bay stations were set up
wherever congregating whales were to be found, while sperm whales were also
hunted by pelagic whalers. Already by the Revolution the North Atlantic was
becoming unproductive, and while the South Atlantic became the chief fishing
ground, the London-based operators were already thinking in terms of still
further explorations, as they stated in their petition of January 1786:

> Your memorialists further request they may have permission
> to go round the Cape of Good Hope, where they are credibly
> informed there are great numbers of whales, and as the fishery
> at the Brasils has been carried on about 10 years, the whales
> from the great numbers killed and wounded begin to be
> wilder, which in time will make success more precarious; but
> could they obtain permission to go round the Cape they have
> no doubt of success.

The desire to go beyond the "normal" limits of the old Southern Fishery (viz. 59° 30' North to 36° South) sprang chiefly from reports of whale-
sightings by the masters of East Indiamen, and was supported by naval intelli-

gence and explorers. Admiral Sir Hugh Palliser, called in to advise the Committee, was particularly enthusiastic:[18]

> I think this fishery may be much increased and extended, by encouraging the most adventurous to extend their searches after whales, which I understand, many of them are disposed to do, to Cape Horn, and the Cape of Good Hope, by this means, many fresh places of resort for whales may be discovered, and certain distant seas, and coasts, now very little known, may be explored, and be better known, which may hereafter be of use in other respects.

In other words, whalermen may be as useful in "opening up" the southern oceans as they had once been in opening up the northern seas: "the more they are at liberty to range about the better."

As the fishery moved inexorably southwards the structure of the trade changed. Whereas voyages had been roughly of the same duration as Arctic voyages (and often shorter off the New England coast), trips into the southern hemispheres were time-consuming. Crews on the London-Brazilian run could expect to be away for upwards of a year, and by the mid-1780s owners were talking of expeditions into the deep south lasting for two years. Inevitably costs rose in comparison with similar-sized vessels in the Arctic: a whaler did not produce four cargoes because it was away for four times as long, though in fact a southern whaler did carry relatively more than a northern whaler because its casks contained oil, not blubber. The long-distance Southern Fishery had reverted to the Spitsbergen system. Whalers anchored in convenient places along the South American or African coasts and boiled their oil on the spot. Pelagic whalers after sperm whales towed the whales to land where it was possible and set up simple try-works on board where it was not. Such operations were essential because the blubber could not be carried through tropical waters, but on the other hand they were greatly facilitated by the relatively small blubber yield from a sperm whale – it took a hundred whales to fill a ship – and by the fact that the spermaceti contained in the whale's head was a liquid requiring no immediate processing. It was the great value of the sperm oil and spermaceti that made the longer voyages worthwhile, but it is necessary to emphasise that the higher price was offset to some extent by the higher production costs, and

---

[18]*Ibid.*, BT 6/93/9, Anonymous observations, but almost certainly Palliser, n.d.

that there was no additional income from whalebone as there was in the trade in Right whales.[19]

Quite apart from the proceedings at sea, the Southern Fishery showed its American antecedents in a number of ways. Following North American custom, for instance, the ships – which were smaller than Arctic whalers, averaging 218 tons in 1788[20] – were not the property of shipowners and merchants with interests in whaling – as the Arctic whalers generally were – but the property of specialist whalermen who lived by and for the trade, and who by 1792 had already invested more than £360,000.[21] The leading entrepreneurs were all of American origin, even at the end of the century, and since they remained a close-knit community, and settled almost exclusively in London, there was no general mixing of those engaged in the Northern and Southern Fisheries. Indeed, the Southern owners were entrepreneurs on a scale unknown in the Northern trade. The Enderby family, for instance, had seven ships in 1787, and with the concentration of good fortune the four leading houses in 1802 between them owned thirty-eight whalers, representing an investment of no less than £273,800.[22] Altogether there were thirty-nine owners with eighty-seven vessels worth some £569,300, ranging from the old-established houses such as Enderby, Champion, Mather and Roach, to the newer enterprises such as that of Lord Camelford (owner of *Willding, Cambridge* and *Caerwent*) which was regarded as something of a joke by the "old whalers."[23]

The problems associated with heavy, long-term investment were offset to some small extent by the different system of remuneration adopted in the two

---

[19]*Ibid.*, BT 5/4, 26 December 1787, evidence of B. Ray. Blubber oil refined on board ship was inferior to oil refined in Britain, as the owners admitted, and always fetched a lower price than Greenland oil.

[20]*Ibid.*, BT 5/5/181-182, Account of vessels in the Southern Whale Fishery, 31 December 1788.

[21]*Ibid.*, BT 6/95/275, Account of vessels, 1792.

[22]BM, Add. Ms.. 38,345, ff. 224-225, List of ships in the Southern Whale Fishery, 1802.

[23]Wilberforce House Library, Hull, J. Parker, London, to Captain Borlinder of *Willding*, 7 June 1804. When Camelford was killed in a duel, his whalers passed to Lord Grenville, who sold them on their return to London. Aristocratic investment in whalers was rare. The only other known case was the northern whaler *Lonsdale* of Whitehaven, of which the Earl of Lonsdale was a major owner; PRO, BT 6/93/112.

trades. The Northern owners, whose men were away for a few months, paid
wages plus bonuses. The Southern owners, following American "peasant" tradition, paid only by results. This, according to the owners, was the only way to
ensure that men away for several years actually exerted themselves on their
owner's behalf.[24] At least in the 1780s the captain and crew received seven-
sixteenths of the earnings of a whaler, though this was by no means enough to
attract sufficient good seamen during the boom in the 1790s. As noted above,
Southern whalers were generally smaller than Northern whalers, and they also
saved on crews and equipment. Southern whalers carried four boats compared
with six in the Northern trade, and the crew was correspondingly smaller, at
around thirty instead of fifty. The boats worked two together, their task eased to
some extent by the gregarious habit of the sperm whale, but their risks magnified because whales were, it was thought by the Southern men, more active and
aggressive in tropical than in Arctic waters. Life on a Southern whaler had its
pleasant and relaxing interludes that were better than anything the Arctic whalers had to offer; yet from the point of view of hardened seamen life on a Southern whaler was by no means as superior as might be supposed at first sight, and
most British seamen interested in whaling preferred the north to the south. The
immense boredom of the longer voyages, and the ever-present threat of starva-
tion or scurvy, took a severe toll of the men's morale and health; and they were
increasingly moving into seas where hostile natives were a greater problem than
the hostile elements in the north. Those who suffered most were the apprentices,
who were particularly valuable to Southern owners, "they being the instruments
by which this Fishery must become an English instead of American Fishery."[25]
They were also the means by which owners accumulated money even more
shamelessly than in the Northern Fishery. Southern apprentices received no
benefit from the share system, their shares being split between the owner and
the captain. This might not have been objectionable had the apprentices been in
a lowly, learning situation. In fact they often did the work of officers: "The
higher their stations as officers, the more the owners are benefited," wrote
Samuel Enderby, who had fifty apprentices in nine ships in 1790 and proposed
to raise the number to sixty.[26] In theory the ending of a boy's apprenticeship

---

[24]PRO, BT 6/93/4, Board of Trade office memo concerning Enderby &c, n.d.;
and BT 5/3, evidence of Enderby in Minutes, 22 March 1786.

[25]*Ibid.*, BT 6/95/238, Enderby &c to Hawkesbury, 30 March 1791.

[26]*Ibid.*, BT 6/95/315-316, Enderby &c to Hawkesbury, 4 February 1790.

might lead to a command; in practise it was more likely to finish his career in whaling.

V

There was another, fundamental, difference between the Northern and Southern Fisheries. In the Arctic men were free to fish wherever they wished. But they could not range the southern hemisphere in search of new fisheries, plotting potential trade routes and suggesting naval stations – and perhaps even colonies – without raising the sometimes violent opposition of those who regarded that hemisphere as their commercial or national monopoly. The government was eager to encourage longer voyages, and instead of quadrupling the premiums in the traditional area (7° North to 36° South), as originally proposed, the Act of 1786 only trebled those premiums and reserved the extra five (which were increased in value to £700 down to £300) for vessels proceeding beyond 36° South and returning between eighteen and twenty-eight months after 1 May in the year of their departure.

However, to entice whalermen into the south seas was one thing; to secure their legal right to go there was quite another. Enderby and his friends wished to go round the Cape of Good Hope in search of those whales reported by East Indiamen; but they could not do so because the East India Company's Charter excluded all vessels but its own from the seas to the east of the Cape and – by a logical extension – to the west of Cape Horn. Fortunately for the whalermen the theoretical breach in the monopoly had already been made in 1785. Following the publication in 1784 of Captain Cook's last journal, with its account of the west coast of Canada, the King George's Sound Company was formed in London to establish a North Pacific fur trade between Canada and the Far East; and though their expedition was hedged round with obstacles and fines it was in fact allowed to proceed to King George's Sound, more commonly called Nootka Sound. There, among other things, the Company proposed to search for and import to Britain "whale fins – or oil, the produce of whales, seals, sea horses, or any other fish or creatures to be met with in the said seas."[27]

The East India Company had thus admitted the possibility of whaling and sealing – albeit under licence – within its monopoly zone to the west of Cape Horn. The proposed activity of Enderby and his friends to the east of the Cape of Good Hope was a more damaging intrusion, insofar as whalers might

---

[27]Printed in V.T. Harlow and A.F. Madden (eds.), *British Colonial Developments, 1774-1834. Select Documents* (Oxford, 1953), 22.

rendezvous with the East Indiamen and purchase from them goods for the European and American markets, or sell to them European and American goods for eastern markets. Moreover, the Company based its suspicious on the eminently sensible grounds that so far as it knew there were so few whales around the Cape, and the seas were so bad for whaling, that anybody proposing to spend time and money going there *must* have ulterior motives: and that could only mean illegally trading to the detriment of the Company's monopoly. It took the combined efforts of Hawkesbury, Dundas at the India Board, and Prime Minister Pitt to persuade the East India Company that the whalermen were sincere in their applications, and a compromise was eventually worked out in which the Company sold licences to whalers to operate in "its" waters so long as they did not go beyond carefully prescribed lines of latitude and longitude which would keep them away from trade routes.[28] Initially the limits were set at 15° East of the Cape of Good Hope and 100 leagues west of the Horn, but the principle had been conceded and it was only a matter of time before the whalers' limits were extended, as they were on a number of occasions.

The first instinct of the whalermen – for instinct was as vital as luck in the early days of the Southern Fishery – was not, however, leading them towards the Indian ocean or China seas, but towards the more easily accessible coastline of South America: and here they met a far more serious challenger than the Honourable East India Company. With the exception of Portuguese Brazil and minor enclaves in the north, the whole of South America was claimed by Spain, and the Spaniards were as anxious as the British to preserve a "colonial system" against foreigners. But in sharp contrast with the British, the Spaniards claimed far more than it was in their power to occupy while their domestic economy was quite unable to answer the demands made upon it by the mercantilist system. As a result, South America had for generations been a continent under siege, with governors in the northern states sporadically fighting off the smugglers who were more or less essential for their survival, and with the coastguard in the southern states keeping their eye open for ships that might establish claims to some deserted part of Patagonia. When whaling began off the South American coast the King of Spain forbade it, and patrols were ordered to harass and drive away whalers whether or not they were in "territorial" waters; and though their powers in the Atlantic was no longer respected, the Spanish were still pleased to call the Pacific their own. Clearly there must be a show-down with Spain before the Southern Fishery could develop, and the excuse for it came in two consecutive clashes, one on the east coast and one on the west.

---

[28]PRO, BT 5/3, Minutes, 4 May 1786; and BT 6/93/33. The attitude of the East India Company is revealed in communications in both Minutes and Papers, *passim*.

In April 1789 a Spanish naval patrol caught two London vessels engaged in sealing on Penguin Island, off Puerto Deseado, some 200 miles north of Santa Cruz, in Patagonia. There were ships based at Montevideo, the Spanish commander told the English captains, with orders to patrol the coast "and to persecute any persons that shall be found employed in the whale fishery or killing of seals or other animals that these seas produce."[29] Though the English protested that they had had to put in for repairs and water, they were ordered to be gone within a week, and the seal skins were confiscated. When the news reached London, Enderby led a delegation to the Board of Trade, complaining that "a general prohibition on the part of the King of Spain to fish in those seas would not only be detrimental but destructive to our fisheries."[30] The Board, after hearing their case, and studying the relevant papers in the Spaniard's broken English, suggested to the "Foreign Secretary" that the time had come to make a stand. If the Southern Fishery was not to be abandoned, the government must resist Spanish claims to exclude British vessels, claims which offended against international law and against existing Anglo-Spanish treaties going back to the seventeenth century. The right of sealers to land on uninhabited shores must be protected, though the Spaniards could be placated to some extent by a British denial of any intention to colonise the area.

Long before the Penguin Island matter was settled a far more serious pot had come to the boil at Nootka Sound, which British vessels had been using for a number of years, and where a small settlement was in the process of erection. In May 1789 a Spanish battleship arrived with instructions from the Viceroy of Mexico to clear the English out of Spanish territory, which he fixed as all the coast south of latitude 60° North (i.e., the northern limits of present day British Columbia). The details need not concern us. The points at issue were that at least two British vessels were seized and their crews taken prisoner, that the British flag was replaced by that of Spain, and the rudimentary settlement destroyed. Negotiations in an atmosphere of confusion got nowhere, and on 5 May 1790 Pitt reluctantly asked Parliament for armaments to resist Spain. He used the same sort of arguments as Hawkesbury had used some months before over the Penguin Island affair:[31]

---

[29]*Ibid.*, BT 6/95/256, Translation of Spanish captain's letter. Papers relating to the Penguin island affair are BT 6/95/227-279; and BT 5/5, Minutes, 4 December 1789.

[30]*Ibid.*, BT 5/5, Minutes, 20 October 1789.

[31]Hansard, *Parliamentary History*, XXVIII, column 770.

> If that claim were given way to, it must deprive this country
> of the means of extending its navigation and fishery in the
> southern ocean, and would go towards excluding his majesty's
> subjects from an infant trade, the future extension of which
> could not but be essentially beneficial to the commercial inter-
> ests of Great Britain.

The British did not want to fight, and Spain was unable to fight, so after much wrangling and feinting, the Anglo-Spanish Convention was signed in October, conceding more or less what Britain wanted. So far as the fishery was concerned, British rights in the Pacific and South Seas were recognised. Whalers could operate in "Spanish" waters so long as they did not come within five leagues of the Shore, and their crews might land in "unoccupied territory" and build temporary huts for sealing or bay fishing so long as no attempts at permanent settlement were made. When Fox attacked the Convention on the grounds that limits had now been set to what the whalermen could do, Pitt arrayed its true advantages in a single, lucid, sentence:[32]

> We had before a right to the Southern Whale Fishery, and a
> right to navigate and carry on fisheries in the Pacific Ocean,
> and to trade on the coasts of any part of it north-west of
> America; but that right not only had not been acknowledged
> but disputed and resisted; whereas by the Convention it was
> secured to us – a circumstance which, though no new right,
> was a new advantage.

For many people the Convention was seen as the long awaited opportunity for the Southern Fishery. Alderman Curtis, a whaler-owner who represented London in Parliament, "made no doubt, but the trade would have been long since more flourishing but for the apprehensions which the fishermen had of the Spaniards, who were constantly annoying them."[33] Henry Dundas, who with Hawkesbury was the leading proponent of a "forward" policy in commercial matters, summed up the feeling of euphoria that was beginning to affect the

---

[32]*Ibid.*, XXVIII, column 1002.

[33]*Ibid.*, XXVIII, column 974.

commercial community as the vast opportunities of the southern hemisphere were rapidly revealed. "At Nootka," he said,[34]

> we had obtained a specific right of settlement, to trade and fish, and Spain, by the Convention, had receded from her claim to exclusive right. The fishery had flourished with a rapidity unequalled, when even cramped by restrictions. With what rapidity, then, must it improve, when every impediment to its prosperity was removed! This country would not be limited in its market. Its wealth was founded upon the skill of our manufactures, and the adventures of our merchants. These raised our armaments, and rendered us formidable in the scale of nations. Our prosperity was the admiration and envy of the world. We did not insist on any right to invade the colonial rights of other nations, in order to extend our commerce; but the spirit of commercial adventure in this country was unbounded.

It remained to be seen how far commercial adventure was unbounded, for the paradox of the Convention was that Britain had almost gone to war to force Spain to allow free access to the Pacific for British merchants who were still denied that free access by Britain herself. From the outset in 1786 the merchants had been unhappy with the narrow limits set by the East India Company, namely 15° to the east of the Cape of Good Hope, and 50° West of Cape Horn, and Enderby and his fellows kept up a continual bombardment of the Board of Trade to secure extensions, which the East India Company, with equal vigour, resisted. In 1788 Hawkesbury, prodded by Enderby and eager to use whalers in the opening up of the Pacific, introduced a new Act (28 Geo. III, c. 20) whereby three of the premiums, advanced to £800, £700 and £600, were reserved for vessels that had spent four months west of Cape Horn, and the limits were extended to 180° West. Beyond the Cape of Good Hope the Company would yield little, and though the northern limit was advanced from 30° South to the Equator, the eastern limit was resolutely fixed at 51° East. In fact the Company was being overtaken by events: six months before the Act passed, the first ships had arrived to establish the penal settlement at Botany Bay. The subsequent building of a colony gave the British an official Crown colony in the Pacific against which the East India Company could say little, and provided a much needed base for whalers wishing to operate in the vast and unknown Pacific or Southern

---

[34]*Ibid.*

Oceans. Moreover, the movement of ships between Britain and New South Wales would inexorably open up the sea routes so jealously guarded by the East India Company, while the demand for ships would provide a remunerative outward passage for whalers, several of which paid their way by carrying convicts.

VI

While government activity was preparing the ground for the whalermen, the wide-ranging explorations undertaken by "Country Trade" merchants – who could trade within the East India Company's area so long as they did not try to leave it – were rapidly increasing the European's knowledge of the western Pacific and the animals in it. In January 1789 Samuel Enderby was already taking soundings for a further petition for extension, in an informal letter containing the latest "news." An American whaling captain on a trading voyage to China "had seen more spermaceti whales about the Straights of Sunda and the Island of Java than he had ever seen before, so much so that he could have filled a ship of 300 tons in 3 months."[35] Enderbys had patriotically declined to take shares in an American expedition there, and now found the Americans were going ahead without them:

> It is hard on us we cannot send a ship there, we have 2 ships of 300 tons each of which we are beginning to fit for the Southern Whale Fishery, to sail in March and are undetermined which branch of the Fishery to send them on, we should like to send them to the Straights of Sunda but dare not without permission.

Permission was not forthcoming: the Board of Trade was unwilling to confront the East India Company again so soon.[36] Nevertheless, Enderbys pressed ahead with the fitting out of the *Emilia*, the first British whaler to pass Cape Horn for a ranging voyage in the Pacific, though they shared with other

---

[35]Enderby to G. Chalmers, 17 January 1789, quoted in W.J. Dakin, *Whalemen Adventurers* (Sydney, 1934; rev. ed., Sydney, 1963), xxv. A series of letters which do not appear in the Liverpool Papers or Board of Trade material were taken to New Zealand by Charles Enderby in 1849, and are now preserved in the Mitchell Library, Sydney. They are partially printed in Dakin's book, which is basically concerned with Australian whaling.

[36]PRO, BT 5/5. Minutes, 29 April 1789.

less enterprising owners the apprehension that no sperm whales would be found within the legal limits:[37]

> On the success of our ship depends the Establishment of the Fishery in the South Pacific Ocean, as many owners have de-clared they shall wait till they hear whether our ship is likely to succeed there, if she is successful a large Branch of the Fishery will be carried on in those seas, if unsuccessful we shall pay for the knowledge.

The ship was successful, returning full in 1790, and the move into the Pacific began. Enderbys promptly hired their vessels to the government for the transportation of convicts to Botany Bay, while the Committee for the trade petitioned in January 1791 for permission to go as far north as 15° North, and as far east as New South Wales Colony. "The Adventurers," they said, "would not request this extension of their limits if they did not know that whales were in great plenty within the limits they have requested, and that the French and American whalers will have that Fishery to themselves without the English whalers have the save privilege."[38]

Their optimism was justified when Captain Thomas Mitchell of Ender-by's *Britannia* wrote home in November 1791 from Port Jackson, Botany Bay.[39] In the voyage out, via the Cape of Good Hope, he had spotted two shoals of sperm whales around longitude 76° East, but the greatest surprise came within sight of Port Jackson:

> Within three leagues of the shore we saw Sperm Whales in great plenty. We sailed through different shoals of them from 12 o'clock in the day till sunset, all around the horizon, as far as I could see from the mast head. In fact I saw very great prospects in making our fishery upon this coast and establish-ing a fishery here. Our people was in the highest spirits at so great a sight and I was determined as soon as I got in and got

---

[37]*Ibid.*, BT 6/95/220, Enderby to Chalmers, 25 April 1789; and Enderby to Chalmers, n.d. (but early 1789) quoted in Dakin, *Whalemen Adventurers*, xxvii.

[38]PRO, BT 6/95/395, Enderby &c, 24 January 1791 in reply to Board of Trade enquiries.

[39]Quoted in full in Dakin, *Whalemen Adventurers*, 9-11.

clear of my live lumber, to make all possible despatch on the
Fishery on this Coast.

The new dumping ground for Britain's "live lumber" had turned out,
quite fortuitously, to be one of the ancient breeding grounds of the Southern
whales! Mitchell tried to keep his discoveries a secret from the other whalers in
the fleet, who had arrived a month earlier and missed the migrations, but such
news could not be hidden for long. The whalers were off as fast as they could
provision, and Mitchell noted that "the colony is alive expecting there will be a
rendezvous for the fishermen" – that Port Jackson would become a whaling
port.

Technically the whalers were liable to prosecution by the East India
Company, and Governor Phillips had no business encouraging them as he did,
since the western limits of the Pacific fishery were still set at 180°, clearly
excluding Australasian waters. The inevitable petitions followed the new discoveries, which were even more exasperating than those to the north, around Java,
but nothing could be done. After the Spanish Convention the Board of Trade,
supported by Dundas and Pitt, had endeavoured to cajole the East India Company into opening at least the southern Pacific, but they failed in their intention
and the only concession gained when the Company's charter was renewed in
1793 was the removal of the northern limit of the Pacific fishery to the east of
180°. In the same year Enderbys financed an exploration led by Captain Colnett, one of Captain Cook's men, in search of non-Spanish bases for the sperm
fishery in the eastern Pacific, and at his suggestion the trade concentrated for a
time on the Galapagos Islands where food (including the giant tortoises which
gave them their name) was plentiful, and where the sperm whales – according to
Colnett's supposition – had one of their breeding grounds.[40]

The fairly rapid changes in the areas of activity within the Southern
Whale Fishery can be followed for a few years in detailed shipping lists that
were prepared for the Board of Trade.[41] In 1786 whalers were to be found operating only in the waters between Brazil and West Africa, with a very occasional
trip down to the Falklands. Four years later over half the increased number of
vessels (twenty-five out of forty-three which sailed in 1789 and returned in
1790) still operated off the African coast, four patrolled the Brazilian coast,
three ran between the two coasts, and one went down to the Falklands and one

---

[40]D. Macpherson, *Annals of Commerce, Manufacturers, Fisheries and Navigation*
(4 vols., London, 1805), IV, 329.

[41]PRO, BT 6/95/370-371, ff. 249 and 275.

to Staten Island. On the other hand eight vessels, four of them owned by Ender-bys, ventured into the Pacific, and a single vessel braved the displeasure of the East India Company by doubling the Cape of Good Hope.

When the next list was prepared only two years later, in 1791/2, the situation had altered dramatically. While twenty-four vessels remained on the African station, and nineteen fished elsewhere in the Atlantic, the new spirit of adventure was indicated by ten vessels that now proceeded east of the Cape of Good Hope, eighteen which went west of Cape Horn, three which went up to Nootka Sound, one which went, rather vaguely and probably illegally, to "The East Indies," and five which went to "New South Wales and the Pacific."

As one might expect, the new fishing grounds, despite their geograph-ical disadvantages, were remarkably productive. "The Pacific Ocean abounding with Spermaceti whales," it was said, "all adventurers who can afford to ven-ture the risque of so large a speculation send their vessels into those seas..."[42] The government did its best to encourage them by altering the Southern whale premiums in 1795. The fifteen premiums for vessels going south of the equator were fixed at £300 to £100; five for vessels proceeding beyond 36° South were to be £400; and eight premiums, one of £600 and the rest of £500, were re-served for vessels spending four months in the Pacific. Three years later, Atlan-tic premiums were reduced to sixteen, and the Pacific ones increased to ten, when the East India Company's ban on whaling vessels in the Southern oceans was finally lifted. Thereafter whalers could proceed beyond 51° East so long as they did not go further north than 15° South until they passed 180°. In other words, Australian waters were now open, and the "Pacific" bounty applied anywhere to the east of 105°. Already in the previous year Enderbys had asked Chalmers to put in a good word for them with the people arranging convict transport because they wanted "an opportunity of giving the fishing on the Coast of New South Wales a fair trial as we are very sanguine of success,"[43] though they were still sufficiently cautious as to suggest a Peru voyage in case the Aus-tralian one failed.

By 1800 Enderbys and Champions were convinced of the value of west-Pacific whaling, as they told Hawkesbury (now Lord Liverpool) in yet another informal petition:[44]

---

[42]Enderby to Chalmers, quoted in Dakin, *Whalemen Adventurers*, 18.

[43]*Ibid.*

[44]Letter of 1 August 1800, quoted in *ibid.*, 15.

After many years of fruitless and expensive attempts, we have
at length succeeded in ascertaining that there is a valuable
spermaceti whale fishery on the Coast of New South Wales,
two vessels having returned from that Coast, one with a cargo
of 170 tuns, and the other with 120 tuns of spermaceti oil,
which are sufficient inducement for adventures to send their
vessels direct to that coast for the purpose of whale fishing.

There were, however, problems. The first was the weather, which was
far from good to the east of Australia, where gales lashing up from the Antarctic
turned the seas to fury and hindered pelagic fishing. The second was the old
one, economic viability, and we are back once again to the East India Company
and its accursed monopoly. The colony was delighted with the infant industry –
its first. "Much advantage will arise to this colony," the governor wrote home
in 1800, "not only in the frequent intercourse it will produce between it and
England, but also the advantage of bringing convicts and stores out on lower
terms than have hitherto been paid."[45] In fact, although they could carry convicts and government stores, the whalers could not carry trade goods, unlike
their American rivals who had already secured a head start in the fishery because the East India Company's monopoly applied only to British shipping.
"The Americans," wrote Enderbys to Liverpool,

hearing that New South Wales is considered within the chartered seas of the East India Company, and that no British merchant can send goods to that colony without the risque of seizure, have at times sent small vessels there with investments
of goods on their way to India or the North West Coast of
America, and have benefitted themselves so much thereby,
that there is no doubt if the restrictions are still continued
against British merchants sending goods there, that they will
monopolise all the advantages of the trade to New South
Wales.[46]

It would be to the advantage of both colonists and merchants if goods
could be taken out in whalers, especially since whale-oil had become the principal export. It was one of Colquhoun's reservations, in 1814, that "ships de-

---

[45]Governor King to Duke of Portland, 28 Sept. 1800, quoted in *ibid.*, 16.

[46]See note 44.

signed to carry out merchandize will obtain no freights in return."[47] But Colquhoun was more interested in ending the Australian experiment in favour of South Africa than in providing cargoes for whalers – whose produce he ignored. The situation in the Pacific became much easier after the ending of part of the East India Company's monopoly in 1813, but it was not until 1833 that its China monopoly, with the attendant restrictions in the waters of South East Asia, was finally abolished. By then the Americans were so dominant in Southern whaling that the British never played more than a subsidiary role.

VII

Presented on the one hand with a rapidly growing demand for good quality lamp oil, and on the other with increases in premiums and extensions of fishing limits, there is small wonder that the Southern trade grew enormously in the decade after the American Revolution. The larger premiums offered in 1786 may have had some effect in encouraging adventurers and raising the number of vessels returning home from eighteen in 1785 to forty-two in 1788 and sixty-four in 1791. But a more telling inducement was the relative ease with which the early catches were made, and the high prices obtained for them. Sperm oil was worth two or three times as much as common whale oil, and such was the demand for it that an increase in volume appears to have had little effect in forestalling a spectacular rise in its value in the years 1785-1790, exactly at the time when increases in the volume of Greenland whale oil had ruined its price for a time. Sperm oil fetched on average £40 in 1785, £48 in 1786 and from £57 to £65 in 1787 when owners, worried that such high prices would kill the trade in favour of tallow candles, endeavoured to import American sperm to reduce them.[48]

Looked at from the point of view of individual owners, the Southern trade appeared most attractive. Enderbys' vessels returning in the eight years prior to 1786 earned an average of £2265, plus an average of £226 bounty money, while the average of all whalers returning home rose spectacularly from £1640 in 1785 to £2424 in 1786 and £4471 in 1787.[49] Unfortunately there are no accurate statements of the value of the Southern trade after this date, because the

---

[47]Patrick Colquhoun, *Treatise on the Wealth, Power and Resources of the British Empire* (London, 1814), 413.

[48]PRO, BT 6/95/84, Petition of Enderby &c, 13 November 1878. Prices from BT 5/5, Minutes, 7 March 1788.

[49]Enderby's results in BT 6/93/136; all whalers in BT 5/5, 7 March 1788.

Customs men did not distinguish between whale oil and sperm oil, and used standard valuations of £13 per tun for Greenland oil and £23 per tun for Southern oil in their calculations. It is possible, however, to show the over-all volume of the two trades, and to make an estimate of values using the Board of Trade's price tables and assuming that the whalebone imported from the Southern Fishery was accompanied by whale oil in the usual ratio of 1 cwt to 1 tun. While these values can only be very approximate, they nevertheless give some idea of the orders of magnitude of the two trades, including whale and sperm oil, whalebones and sealskins (table 8).

Already by 1791 the quantity of Southern oil had passed that of Northern oil, though as with the Northern trade the greatest prosperity for owners came with a diminution in their numbers towards the end of the century, when vessels were averaging over £10,000 per voyage. The highest valued cargo known to an informant of Scoresby was no less than £30,000,[50] and though this was undoubtedly an exceptional figure, there is no reason to suppose that the Southern Fishery did not retain its prosperity throughout the French wars.

Table 8
Southern and Northern Fisheries: Whalers, Oil and
Estimated Real Value of Imports, 1791-1800

	Southern			Northern		
	Whalers Arriving	Oil (tuns)	Estimated Value	Whalers Arriving	Oil (tuns)	Estimated Value
1791	64	3551	£122,569	114	3397	£125,949
1792	58	4321	152,066	102	2715	104, 151
1793	52	5917	223,972	88	3354	117,519
1794	45	4059	182,403	61	3041	104,189
1795	28	3102	165,547	47	3475	156,483
1796	24	4398	240,203	52	4468	184,285
1797	35	5552	376,767	65	5486	204,861
1798	18	3679	228,073	69	5295	181,510
1799	25	3182	205,079	70	5637	184,367
1800	25	3374	325,358	62	5572	237,247

Source: Northern Trade: Great Britain, Public Record Office (PRO), Board of Trade (BT) 6/230/76; Southern Trade: PRO, Customs 17, *passim*.

---

[50]W. Scoresby, *An Account of the Arctic Regions, with a History and Description of the Northern Whale Fishery* (2 vols., Edinburgh, 1820), II, 532.

The early 1790s were the great years of activity in the Southern Fishery. By the end of the century the Northern Fishery had once more asserted itself, and after 1797 the quantity of oil from the Arctic once more exceeded that from the south. A massive expansion in the Greenland trade in the early years of the nineteenth century was not shared by the Southern trade and within a decade it was the future of the Southern Fishery that was in question.

There were two basic reasons for the changed relationship. Firstly, as we saw in chapter 4, the Northern Fishery was revitalised by the opening up of the Davis Strait section. Secondly, the costs of Southern fishing rose steeply as voyages went beyond 36° South in the Atlantic, and especially for the Pacific voyages. Southern voyages were remunerative so long as herds of migrating animals could be easily found and easily caught, but as soon as fishing diminished the stock of sperm whales, profits were more doubtful. As a result the Southern Fishery was a constantly moving fishery, seeking out not so much areas where long-term fishing might be possible as breeding grounds where wholesale slaughter might earn quick profits. In the Northern Fishery, for instance, most whalers avoided calves, whereas in the southern breeding grounds it was common for whalers to strike calves because the sperm herd would come to their rescue. The point should not be pushed too far, but the fact remains that the early days of Southern fishing were judged on the produce of what were more or less virgin fishing grounds, and were therefore not likely to be fully representative of future seasons. It was also the case that international competition in the south was more intense than it was in the north. By the end of the eighteenth century Britain was indisputably the chief fishing nation in the Arctic, but in the south she was challenged by a rapidly reviving American trade.

In contrasting the Northern and Southern trades, a word about oil values is appropriate. The Southern trade is often regarded as more valuable than the Northern because sperm oil was so much more valuable than whale oil. That may have been so, and those eager to claim benefits for the Southern trade were not slow to emphasise this fact. When, for instance, the Committee for the trade produced a "Comparative state of the Southern Fishery" in 1788,[51] they claimed to have imported 1714 tuns of oil valued at £57 per tun, which was the price for sperm, in 1787. But they also claimed 789 cwt of bone, and nobody in all the voluminous Board of Trade papers about whaling appears to have commented that sperm whales do not produce bone. Either the southern whalers were killing Right whales for the bone alone (which might, perhaps, have made economic sense), or they were claiming sperm values for southern whale oil which was, because of its inferior quality, actually worth a few pounds a tun *less* than

---

[51]PRO, BT 5/5, Minutes, 7 March 1788.

Greenland oil. Unfortunately there was no official account of how much oil was sperm though there are several lists of price differentials among the Board of Trade papers. On only one occasion, when Sam Enderby submitted a break-down of the trade for 1788, was it admitted that only twenty-two percent of the oil (688 tuns) was sperm worth £60; the rest was black oil worth only £14.[52] The expansion into new regions in the 1790s certainly increased the sperm fish-eries, but the chief catches continued to be Right whales, and the development of bay whaling in the western Pacific in the early nineteenth century merely emphasised the trend. Using the bone:oil ratio as our only guide, it appears from the bone imported that roughly a third to a half of oil imported in the 1790s must have come from the Right whale. This puts an entirely different complexion on the Southern trade, and helps to explain why some owners could bewail their poverty when the price of sperm was so high. Not until 1799 was there any significant drop in the bone:oil ratio, but this reflects a general decline in the fishery rather than an increase in sperm whaling, despite the recent opening-up of the breeding grounds to the east of the Cape of Good Hope, in the western Pacific, and around the Galapagos Islands. The great days of the Pacific sperm fishery were still far off at the turn of the century.

---

[52]*Ibid.*, 27 January 1789.

Chapter 6
Decline in the North in the
Early Nineteenth Century

I

The ending of the Napoleonic war in 1815 was not followed by the same sort of bounding activity as followed the ending of the previous war in 1783, for two very obvious reasons. The sudden expansion after 1783 had resulted chiefly from the changed relationship between Britain and America; and the last few years of the Napoleonic war had themselves witnessed both "recovery" and prosperity in the whaling trade which preceded the normal return to peace-time activities. The year 1808 had been one of appalling depression in overseas trade when, because of restrictions imposed for war purposes, ports all over the country came virtually to a standstill. The whaling trade had suffered with the rest, and the prosperity of the early years of the century was briefly interrupted. Only fifty-six ships sailed for the Northern Fishery in 1808, and only nineteen for the Southern, though the aggregate value of their catches – as usually happened – remained disproportionately high.[1] Whaling revived as other trades revived, and the number of ships going northwards had risen by forty-five percent between 1810-1812 and the end of the war, chiefly because of investment in Hull and the Scottish ports, which continued to expand their efforts while London and the remaining English ports (with the exception of Whitby) rapidly lost interest in whaling. There was, therefore, no major addition to the whaling fleet after the war, and it stood at something of the order of 150 ships aggregating 43,000 to 45,000 tons for seven or eight years before beginning its long physical decline after 1821.

It was not simply the number of vessels that gave the appearance of prosperity, for a large number of vessels was usually associated with low average yields or profits. According to Scoresby, who used figures compiled within the trade, these years of greatest physical activity in the nineteenth century were also years of immense average catches, standing at 91.4 tuns of oil for English and 96.3 tuns for Scottish ships, while both countries averaged 4.6 tons of bone.[2]

---

[1]Great Britain, Public Record Office (PRO), Customs 17/30.

[2]W. Scoresby, *An Account of the Arctic Regions, with a History and Description of the Northern Whale Fishery* (2 vols., Edinburgh, 1820), II, 131.

Table 9
Ships Fitting Out for the Northern Fishery, 1810-1818

	1810	1811	1812	1813	1814	1815	1816	1817	1818
England	75	76	83	94	97	98	97	100	104
Scotland	22	22	27	43	46	49	49	50	53
Total	97	98	110	137	143	147	146	150	157

Source: W. Scoresby, *An Account of the Arctic Regions, with a History and Description of the Northern Whale Fishery* (2 vols., Edinburgh, 1820), II, 120.

Moreover, while bone prices were certainly not as encouraging as they once were, they had already begun to improve, rising to around £65 per ton in 1814-1816, £80 in 1817-1821, and £185 by 1822-1824.[3] Better still for the trade was the failure of oil prices to fall immediately under the pressure of large catches. The average price in 1814 was, according to Scoresby, around £32, whereas the average for the years 1814-1818 was no less than £36 10s. In Hull the local price was around £40 in 1810, 1813, 1814, 1815, 1817 and 1818,[4] the last year being that of greatest activity in the port, with one of the highest importations of oil ever recorded, and average catches worth £4323. Scoresby estimated the gross earnings of the Northern Fishery to be no less than £3m sterling for the years 1814-1818, though the accuracy of his estimate is not certain because it is not clear whether contemporaries based their calculations on the true average price of all the oil sold, or on the median sale price. Nevertheless, there is every reason for accepting Scoresby's assertion that 1814, for instance, was "uncommonly prosperous," and the years immediately following the war were no worse.

II

Unfortunately the long-term prosperity of the trade was soon threatened by changes on both the supply and demand side, and, in particular, by the far-reaching implications of Free Trade. To a trade owing its position largely to the exclusion of cheap foreign oil, it was a serious matter that in the years following

---

[3]Local oil prices are recorded in the tables relating to Hull's trade, in W. Gawtress, *Report of an Enquiry into the Corporation of Hull* (Hull, 1834), 382.

[4]Prices for 1805-1815 are in Great Britain, Parliament, House of Commons, *Parliamentary Papers (BPP)*, 1816 (272), VI, 191, "Select Committee Set Up to Examine into the Policy of Increasing the Duty on the Import of Seeds, 2nd Report, evidence of J.S. Bowden.

the war politicians were discussing Adam Smith's ideas with a sense of realism born of American independence and a vigour born of industrial success. A Parliamentary Select Committee appointed to consider the means of maintaining and improving the foreign trade of the country reported in 1820 (among other things) that "the time when monopolies could be successfully supported, or would be patiently endured, either in respect to subjects against subjects, or particular countries against the rest of the world, seems to have passed away."[5] If this really was the case, it remained to be seen whether a trade founded on bounty and nurtured by protection could survive should the legislature see fit to remove either of its ancient and supposedly essential props.

So far as the bounty was concerned, the expected blow came in 1824 when the government refused to renew it for a further term, as governments had done regularly since 1733. A source of bitter controversy for half a century, it had, nevertheless, survived at the reduced rate of twenty shillings per ton and now suffered as one of those unjustifiable financial advantages given to "subjects against subjects." So slight, however, had been its true value as a stimulus to the trade that its passing was hardly noticed and produced few protests compared with the waves of petitions that greeted proposed changes to the bounty in the 1770s and 1780s. Far more serious in its effect on the number of whalers operating in the 1820s had been the drastic decline in oil prices to £18 or £19 per ton in 1820-1821, when over-expansion in the trade was met for the first time since the 1780s with a slowing down in the growth of the market. The whaling fleet was cut by a quarter between the 1821 and 1822 seasons, while owners endeavoured to use political pressure to maintain their privileged position against both British and foreign competition. If in the long run they failed it was because their chief opponents were no longer Dutch whalermen but British industrialists intent on introducing or maintaining commodity substitution in the two main outlets for whale oil.

The earliest threat to wartime prosperity arose in the woollen industry, where whale oil had gained ground in recent years, firstly because of the vast quantity of army cloth processed entirely with whale oil, and secondly because of the substitution of whale oil for rape oil in the manufacture of medium quality cloths when the shortage of imported seed pushed the price above £50 a tun. As a leading oil merchant told the Parliamentary Committee on the seed trade, in 1816, "The large demand for whale oil was in consequence of the scarcity of Rape oil; there was not a sufficient supply; I was therefore obliged either to let

---

[5]*BPP*, 1820 (300) II, 367-379.

my customers go to other houses or find them a substitute for Rape oil."[6] In 1816 the price of whale oil, which in Hull had averaged £36 over the last dozen years, tumbled to a mere £26 at a time when £32 a tun was thought essential to cover costs. When asked to what he attributed this reduction in the price of whale oil, Samuel Cooper, one of Hull's leading whaler-owners replied, simply, "To the low price of Rape oil." William Mellish, a leading London owner, claimed that his colleagues were withdrawing ships with oil at such a price, "fearing to embark too much on the present appearance of trade."[7] "What the Greenland Ship-owner wants," said Samuel Cooper, "is a market for his produce, free from the competition of foreigners."[8] There was no longer competition from foreign whalers, but the foreign seed was equally ruinous, and must be stopped. The trade as a whole was adamant that something must be done to keep rape oil at over £50 a tun: "I have no doubt whatever," another owner told the committee, "that the Fishery would be continued without any material interruption, if there was a duty upon the importation of foreign Rape seed, and it had to contend only with English Rape seed."[9] Fortunately the whaling interest found an ally in the agricultural interest, which also wanted to build up the supply of native seeds in face of foreign competition. Both factions got their way, and a duty of £10 per last was imposed on foreign seed, enough, it was estimated, to raise the price of rape oil by £12 per turn. As a consequence the price of whale oil rose again in 1817, and owners were sufficiently heartened for 1819 and 1820 to witness the greatest effort of the period; but long-term plans were brought to naught by the emergence of the Free Trade spirit within the Board of Trade. The interests of whaler-owners clearly conflicted not only with the interests of the better end of the cloth trade, but also with the interests of the expanding seed-crushing industry, and with the benefit of hindsight one can hardly fault the Board of Trade for sacrificing the whaler-owners to what, in the circumstances, was both their natural fate and the national interest. The duty on rape seed was reduced from £1 per quarter to fifteen shillings in 1822, six shillings in 1825, three shillings in 1826 and one shilling in 1827, and imports

---

[6]*Ibid.*, "Select Committee...of Seeds," 167, evidence of Thomas Todd.

[7]*Ibid.*, 189.

[8]*Ibid.*, 184.

[9]*Ibid.*, 190, evidence of J.S. Bowden.

rose from 9000 quarters in 1821 to 41,000 on average in 1822-1824 and 58,000 in 1827-1830.[10]

Whale oil was never a preferred oil for fine textiles so far as its attributes were concerned, and the inflow of foreign seeds and availability of cheaper seed oil saw its virtual elimination from the textile trade. When in 1844 a Parliamentary Select Committee investigated the state of British shipping, this withdrawal of protection against seeds was held up as one of the chief causes of the decline of whaling. The American government, it was alleged, had pursued the opposite course and laid duties on imported seeds with the result that that country now had seven or eight hundred whalers operating in the Pacific Ocean.[11] Moreover, having refused British whaling interest the protection against seeds enjoyed by their American rivals, the British government proceeded to compound the damage done by refusing to continue the high level of protection against American-caught whale oil.[12] In 1843 the duty was reduced from £27 18s 7d per tun to £6 6s for whale oil and £15 15s for sperm oil, as part of the general reduction in duties on raw materials in the budgets of 1842-1844. From the point of view of British owners, with higher production costs than their rivals, this reduction in duty was a serious challenge to which they had no adequate answer. However, its importance to the Northern trade should not be exaggerated, since colonial whale oil had always been imported to the detriment of native enterprises, and the British themselves were responsible for only twenty-nine percent of the whale oil imported into the country in the years 1831-1840 (see table 16).

Whatever the justice of their case, whaler-owners were as adamant as they had ever been that their valuable and strategic trade could not exist in a context of unsubsidised open competition, and argued that the government was sacrificing shipowners to its own Free Trade principles. A leading London whaler-owner, G.F. Young, spoke for the whole trade when he addressed the Shipping Committee: "if you will follow out the policy which has for its object solely the benefit of the consumer, as far as that is connected with subjects of maritime commerce, you will destroy British navigation."[13] It is hard to imagine

---

[10]*Ibid.*, 1836 (79), VIII (1), 218, Select Committee on Agricultural Distress, Report, Account of Rapeseed Imports, 1821-1835.

[11]*Ibid.*, 1844 (545), VIII, 221, q. 203, evidence of G.F. Young.

[12]*Ibid.*, q. 516, evidence of J. Somes.

[13]*Ibid.*, q. 204, evidence of G.F. Young.

any other policy finding political favour in the 1840s, and whaling was cast adrift to manage as best it could.

III

The second blow from a substitute commodity – though one which was slower to take effect – came with the spread of coal-gas lighting, which threatened to oust whale oil from the street lamps and sperm oil from the drawing rooms. Coal-gas, manufactured in equipment developed by Boulton and Watt, had been applied to factories since about 1805, and had proved sufficiently attractive for the Gas Light and Coke Company to be formed in 1809 to sell coal-gas in London. The evidence in support of its Bill said a great deal about the qualities and advantages of gas and little about its likely effect on the whaling trade, and it is doubtful if the latter realised the potentialities of gas in the early days. Nevertheless, it was soon discovered that the gas men intended to supply lighting fuel in profitable cases only and to leave the remainder to the oil men. Thus in 1817, when the Gas Company was trying to move into some of the principal London streets, the London whaler-owners petitioned for government support against their competitors.[14] "The Gas Company," said the whalermen, "wish to leave the lighting of the narrow streets etc. to oil lamps which they say give no light, where it appears to be absolutely necessary to have the best lights." In the early stages of the conversion from one fuel to another there was something to be said for the whalermen's case that the best service was secured through a monopoly which gave both profitable and non-profitable customers to the one supplier, but the government refused to interfere with market forces; whaling was no longer protected from competition in the home market.

It was left to the Southern rather than the Greenland owners to raise the matter of national strategy, since sperm oil seemed likely to suffer more than whale oil from the first round of competition with gas:[15]

> they [the whaler owners] deny its being a public benefit to light shops, houses and other buildings internally. They contend it is a private benefit to individuals which ought not to be allowed to interfere with the existence of important national fisheries, and therefore the Shipowners say they hope they will not be allowed to light houses, shops, etc., with gas –

---

[14]British Museum (BM), Add. Ms. 38, 367, folios 107 ff.

[15]*Ibid.*, folios 109-110.

There being no consumption for spermaceti oil except in shops, houses, and public places, it is not used in our manufactories, and for that reason the fishery must be lost if the light from gas is allowed to be used indoors.

Whatever its effects on the whaling trade, the spread of gas lighting was inevitable. Between 1814 and 1823 the number of gasometers in London grew from one to forty-seven, their capacity from 14,000 cubic feet to 917,000 cubic feet.[16] Gas was safe and good, Humphrey Davy told the Select Committee on Gas Light Establishments in 1823, notwithstanding explosions in London, Edinburgh and Manchester, and the period around 1820 saw the building of gas works in many of the major towns that had relied on whale oil lamps if they had lamps at all. The superiority and convenience of gas was, by 1823, beyond dispute, and the only way the whalermen could fight back was to convert their oil into gas!

Fortunately oil gas was a feasible proposition. J.B. Emmett of Hull had succeeded in making it in 1816 by decomposing oil in a heated retort, and John and Philip Taylor invented an apparatus for making purified oil gas which was patented and manufactured by Taylors and Martineau in 1817. According to the government's adviser on gas works, Sir William Congreve, "oil of any inferior description is capable of producing good gas," and oil gas would produce a light three times as good as that obtained from the same volume of coal gas.[17] As a result all the equipment was smaller, cheaper and safer, and he was surprised that only one company – the Oil Gas Co – has been set up in London to manufacture the superior sort of gas. The reason may have been that Taylors and Martineau's equipment could be fitted into a domestic kitchen, and could, in theory, dispense with the need for central gas works and mains, at least so far as the better class private houses were concerned. Certainly the provincial towns took up the oil gas faster than London, and in the early 1820s oil gas works were to be found in such inland towns as Norwich, Cambridge and Taunton, and such ports as Plymouth, Bristol, Liverpool, Dublin and Hull.[18] "In places where coal is not very cheap," said Scoresby, "gas, it seems, can be produced

---

[16]*BPP*, 1823 (529), V, 225, Report from Select Committee on Gas Light Establishments, evidence of Humphrey Davy.

[17]*Ibid.*, 326.

[18]*Ibid.*

from oil, at about the same expense as coal gas; consequently, the numerous advantages of the former, will render it highly preferable."[19]

Oil gas also had disadvantages which the oil lobby were eager to play down. Chief of them was the difficulty of offering a guaranteed supply of oil at contract prices. As a result, the oil gas works were offering gas at between forty and forty-five shillings per 1000 cubic feet in the 1820s compared with around twelve shillings per 1000 cubic feet for coal gas. Since 3000 cubic feet of coal gas was reckoned equal to 1000 cubic feet of oil gas, there was a smaller disparity than appeared at first sight, but there was, nevertheless, a disparity.[20] Even at the higher price the oil gas companies made very little profit, and while the availability of coking coal increased and its price declined, there was no way in which the price of whale oil could be forced down without also diminishing the supply of oil as owners left the trade. For a decade or more, the oil gas plants were a valuable market for the whaling trade, but they could only delay the full impact of the discovery of coal gas. As early as 1829 Hull, for all its involvement with whaling, abandoned oil for coal.

After 1830 there was only one area in which oil gas maintained its position. Both the equipment and the gas itself were portable. David Gordon of Edinburgh discovered that oil gas could be condensed in cylinders, and Sir William Congreve spoke in 1822 of the Portable Oil Gas Company which was about to be formed in London to manufacture bottled gas. It was particularly valuable, eventually, on the railways, and the North Eastern Railway Company, for instance, was still manufacturing oil gas in Hull at the beginning of the twentieth century. It was also important in the development of navigational aids in the nineteenth century, and formed the basis for the Pintsch gas buoys which speeded up the movement of shipping into and out of ports in the 1880s, though by this time the gas was usually made from seed or mineral oil rather than from animal oil, leading to the modern bottled gas industry.

IV

Competition from gas and vegetable oil reduced prices and provided the context for the long decline in Arctic whaling beginning in 1821, but the basic causes of that decline must be sought within the fishery itself. In the short term the remaining owners were saved, to some extent, by the rising level of productivity

---

[19]Scoresby, *Account of the Arctic Regions*, II, 428.

[20]Prices and the change from oil to coal gas can be followed in the *BPP*, 1847 (734), XLIV, 359, Return of Gas Companies since 1820.

as the declining number of ships in competition in the Arctic secured relatively larger catches: the average number of whales caught by each whaler in 1830-1835, despite a disastrous year in 1830, was almost double the figure for 1815-1819, and the average tunnage of oil was still at a relatively high level (table 10).

Table 10
The Northern Whale Fishery, 1815-1834
(5-yearly averages)

		Whalers		Whales		Oil	
Greenland		Davis Straits	Total Ships	Total Number	Avg. per Ship	Total Tuns	Tuns per Ship
1815-1819	97	54	152	1017	7	12,205	81
1820-1824	66	67	133	1282	10	14,241	107
1825-1829	11	84	95	848	9	10,279	108
1830-1834	7	75	83	948	13	8,527	103

Source: J.R. McCulloch, *A Descriptive and Statistical Account of the British Empire* (2 vols., London, 1834), II, 33.

Equally important for owners was the degree of resilience imparted to the trade by the revived interest in whalebone which, in Hull at least, was worth only ten percent of the value of the oil brought home in 1815-1817 and no less than fifty-five percent in 1825-1827. Statistics prepared in that port would seem to indicate that in the late 1820s an owner might reasonably expect a greater return on his capital than had been obtained in the more obviously "prosperous" days before 1821 (table 11).

Table 11
Number of Hull Whalers and Average Value of Their Catches, 1815-1833
(5-yearly averages)

	Whalers	Oil	Bone	Total Catch
1815-1819	58.2	£3139	£309	£3448
1820-1824	45.2	2528	769	3296
1825-1829	30.6	2763	1481	4244
1830-1833	26.5	2641	1030	3671

Source: W. Gawtress, *Report of an Enquiry into the Corporation of Hull* (Hull, 1834), 382.

The years 1830-1833 include one unfortunate season; if this is excluded the figures for the remaining years would be 24.7 whalers with oil worth £3151 and bone worth £1225, making an average total catch value of £4376.

In view of such inducements, the trade would almost certainly have continued, and may even have found new markets as new uses for oil were found, had the supply of oil and bone remained secure. In fact it did not. It is clear from table 10 that as the Greenland fishery collapsed, whaling efforts were concentrated on the Davis Straits, but though initially the returns there were good it was not long before the most accessible areas were suffering from over-fishing. When G.F. Young was questioned about the decline of whaling by the 1844 Shipping Committee he attributed it, as did some other owners, to government tariff policy, but he would have done better, perhaps, to have followed Joseph Somes and attribute it to a shortage of whales, or rather to a shortage of easily caught whales.[21] Compared with Greenland, the Davis Straits fishery was soon unreliable, and while some years produced results as good as anything that had gone before, other years were terrible.

V

The simple truth is that, in their search for further stocks of whales in Baffin Bay, expeditions in the 1820s were approaching the limits of physical endurance; and by the 1830s Arctic whaling had entered a new and fearful stage. As the whalers moved ever northward after their elusive quarry, "rock-nosing" through uncharted waters and ignorant of ice-bearing currents, the Arctic moved southward to meet and overcome them with forces more vicious and successful than economic laws. After a decade of increasing difficulties, the 1830 season was the worst ever experienced in the Arctic. There had been heavy losses of ships in the past, and seasons with very poor results, but never a combination of the two at this concentration. Of the ninety-one whalers sent out, nineteen were lost, twenty-one returned clean, and most of the survivors were heavily damaged. The total catch was 161 whales, the lowest on record. The loss of life was slight because of the custom of fishing in packs, but at one time there were said to be 1000 men out on the ice awaiting rescue after nine ships had been lost and four badly damaged in a single day.[22]

---

[21]*Ibid.*, 1844 (545), VIII, qq. 553-554.

[22]Details of the Arctic fishery after 1820 are best followed in B. Lubbock, *The Arctic Whalers* (Glasgow, 1936), *passim* (in chronological arrangement); and in Hull sources such as J.J. Sheahan, *General and Concise History and Description of the Town*

A single devastating season might still have been acceptable, but there was bad weather again in 1831, when many of the ships could not get into Baffin Bay, and disaster in 1835 when they could not get out. It was this crisis of 1835, and the consequent publicity, that more than anything else marks the turning point in the attitudes to Arctic whaling of owners, crews and the general public. Books about whaling in the late eighteenth century had hardly progressed beyond the romantic and heroic stage, recognising occasional hazards but not dwelling on them in any very realistic way. They still expressed the excitement of the chase, with dangers from whale and weather thrown in merely to spice the story. As late as 1820 Scoresby's comprehensive work did little to elucidate the growing physical problems facing whaling and nothing to foretell the sudden decline in whaling after 1821. By the 1830s the situation was quite different. In its beautiful little history of whaling published in 1833 the *Penny Magazine* drew attention to the shift of interest to Baffin Bay since the publication of Scoresbby's book. "In these high latitudes," it wrote, "whales still exist in large numbers, but from the greater prevalence of ice mountains, or icebergs as they are called, the fishery in Baffin's Bay is probably still more perilous than that which used to be carried on in the animal's more ancient haunt."[23] By 1835 there was no probability about it; books about whaling experiences now "revealed all," and since they were often written by surgeons, the revelations were quite horrific.

The 1835 troubles illustrate the general problems facing ships every year, though not usually with the same degree of severity.[24] With a sudden and unpredictable change in both weather and ice movements, six ships were sunk and nine frozen in, to the despair of the owners and of the families of some 600 men. With nothing but ice as far as the eye could see, the whole fleet was demoralised by October when food began to run low and the intense cold of winter began to bite into the men's undernourished limbs. With frozen condensation a quarter of an inch thick on their bunks, they stamped around below decks or engaged in unnecessary pumping to keep warm as driven snow turned the vessels into glistening icebergs, or the wind howled like banshees

---

and Port of Kingston-upon-Hull (London, 1864), *passim*; T. Sheppard and J. Suddaby, *History of the Hull Whaling Industry* (Hull, 1906); and J. Sibree, *Fifty Years Recollections of Hull* (Hull, 1884), chapter 7.

[23]Anon., *Monthly Suppplement of the Penny Magazine,* No. 74 (1833), 103-104.

[24]See J. Spencer, *The Messmate. A Companion for Sailors* (Hull, 1836) for life on the ice-bound *Jane* of Hull, and Anon., *Sufferings of the Ice-Bound Whalers* (2nd ed., Hull, 1836).

through the spars and rigging. Periodically all hands were out on the ice as it heaved in earthquake-fashion and threatened the ships. "The ice," wrote an officer of the *Viewforth* of Kirkcaldy on one such occasion, "is now warring and crashing in a most awful manner. It would, indeed, be difficult for the imagination to conceive what is now going on around us, and the prospect that lies open to our view."[25] For those already rotting with scurvy, and those with frostbite turning to gangrene, there was no prospect at all save the hope of a speedy end to their suffering.

Those who endured the fury of Baffin Bay – and not just late in the season – were torn between rapture at scenes of "unparalleled loveliness and grandeur" and dismay at their own helplessness. "In these wild regions," it was said, "the elements are on terms alternatively of peace and war...," and the fears of the Greenland coast gave way to the terrors of Baffin Bay: "Another awful day, such as I wish I may never forget, nor again behold. What a helpless creature is man, when the king of terrors lays hold on him!"[26] In 1835 the men were overwhelmed by the forces of nature: "It is really awful – hunger, cold, fatigue, dangers all upon us at once; and it requires a fortitude to bear up under them which few can command." Many turned to the religion that had been spreading through the fleet during the last quarter of a century, and pinned their hope to the Bethel flag, taking comfort from the prayers of the mate of the *Jane* of Hull, "expressing our belief that it is not by the hands of men that the ships are to be relieved, and that we look up to a higher power whom the winds and the seas obey."[27] Nevertheless, the hands of men did play some part, for on 4 December 1835 the whaler-owners of Hull, to which six of the ships belonged, petitioned the Admiralty for a relief expedition, both for humanitarian reasons "and that losses already sustained by your memorialists through the total failure of the fishery may not be aggravated by the destruction of such a number of their fellow creatures and the valuable property entrusted to their charge."[28] An expedition led by Captain James Clark Ross (who had himself been rescued some time previously by a whaler) managed to get the men out when the ice

---

[25]Anon., *Sufferings*, 23.

[26]*Ibid.*, 14 and 21.

[27]*Ibid.*, 10 and 26.

[28]Wilberforce House Museum, Hull, "Ships Beset at Davis's Straits. Copies of Memorials to the Admiralty, 1835."

began to break, but the very next year found another six ships blocked in by huge ice fields. Again there were relief expeditions, and on this occasion only one ship was beset for the winter, though the *Dee* of Aberdeen had only nine men alive when she managed to get free.

The poor seasons that were now becoming too common were as ruinous for the owners as they were terrible for the men, and there was little inducement for the weaker-willed on either side to continue. Certainly there was nothing to encourage the replacement of lost whalers, and the number dropped from seventy-one in 1835 to fifty-two in 1837. Another bad summer in the latter year – though mercifully no ships were lost – drove the number down to thirty-nine, and things were becoming desperate. The 1838 season was an "open" one, that is to say the ice was clear and the fishing quite good, but the weather in general and the ice in particular were bad again in 1839, 1840, 1841 and 1842. The despair in the trade is evident from the small number of ships remaining active:

Table 12
Number and Tonnage of Northern Whalers
1830-1832 and 1841-1843

	No.	Tons	Men		No.	Tons	Men
1830	91	30,484	4120	1841	19	5742	897
1831	86	28,137	4093	1842	18	5118	830
1832	81	26,147	3706	1843	25	6971	1146

Source: Great Britain, Parliament, House of Commons, *Parliamentary Papers* (*BPP*), 1845 (504), XLVII, 515.

Of the English ports, only Hull and Newcastle remained, London having faded out in the 1820s as she concentrated on the Southern Fishery, sending her last vessel northward in 1835. Whitby left the trade at the same time, leaving only the Scottish ports to compete with Hull, which steadily maintained her thirty-five to forty percent of the national whaling fleet until the mid-1830s. But Hull, with her fleet of large and splendid vessels, could not stand the losses of the late 1830s when her importation was literally decimated, and the entire national fishery for half a decade produced barely more than Hull alone had caught in 1833. Peterhead was the only port prospering after 1835, and that was because her whalers were not whaling, but had diverted their attention to the safer and, as it turned out, more lucrative pastime of sealing off the Newfoundland coast. In 1840 Hull's fleet, which had for so long ruled the Arctic waves, was reduced to two ships, and though she recovered to some

Gordon Jackson

extent in the 1840s, the initiative in the trade appeared to be moving northwards to the Scottish ports:

Table 13
Whalers Equipped by Individual Ports, 1834-1845

	1834		1843		1844		1845	
	No	Tons	No	Tons	No	Tons	No	Tons
Hull	27	8906	4	916	10	2609	14	3396
Newcastle	3	1131	2	796	3	1186	1	391
Aberdeen	17	5055	11	2616	15	4072	19	4768
Bo'ness	–	–	1	322	1	322	1	322
Dundee	8	2789	5	1625	5	1624	5	1624
Kirkcaldy	5	1591	2	696	2	696	2	696
Leith	5	1847	0		0		3	389
Others	11	3636	–	–	–	–	–	–
Total	76	24,955	25	6971	36	10,509	45	11,586

Source: 1834: McCulloch, *Descriptive and Statistical Account*, II, 33; 1843-1845: *BPP*, 1846 (183), XLV, 417.

Certainly the emphasis was moving from whaling to sealing, and it is reasonable to conclude that the great Northern Fishery was in decline after 1830.

Chapter 7
Expansion and Failure of the Southern Fishery
c. 1808-1840

I

The southern fishery was in no better shape, though it had promised so much at the turn of the century, when it appeared to offer limitless regions for the exploitation of the more valuable sperm whale. In fact, after the major expansion of the 1790s, the Southern Fishery stagnated in comparison with the Northern Fishery, which expanded both its catches and value with the opening up of the Davis Straits grounds. Between 1804-1805 and 1814-1815 the tonnage of Northern whalers grew by sixty-six percent, whereas that of Southern whales actually declined by twenty percent as the trade was forced to make time because of the troubles created by war. Whalers going south-east were disturbed on the Cape of Good Hope fishery, at least four being captured by the Dutch and taken into Capetown in 1804 alone. Whalers going south-west faced the historic difficulties of navigating and victualling in Spanish wasters. The chief Pacific sperm fisheries were still off the coasts of Chile, Peru and California, and around the Galapagos Islands and most of the victualling places, so vital for the Pacific trade, were in Spanish territory: Concepcion and Valparaiso in Chile, Lima and Payta in Peru, and Guayaquil in Ecuador. Captains were once more reluctant to double the Horn, though equally dangerous was the long haul through the south Atlantic for ships that missed the St. Helena Convoy.

Faced with naval conflicts that were reminiscent of Spitsbergen two centuries earlier, owners armed their ships or withdrew them from danger areas. The sister ship *Caerwent* and *Cambridge*, for instance, were heavily armed and provided with letters of marque before being sent round the Horn to hunt as a pair for both whales and shipping. When eventually they came across a Spanish schooner they plundered it in such a drunken and disorderly manner as to endanger the crews and ships falling into the hands of the enemy, and the captains were forced to draw up a set of regulations for the plundering of enemy vessels.[1] Other ships were less fortunate and fell to Spanish, French and Dutch ships, while the outbreak of war with the United States brought that country's frigates out to the whaling coasts to preserve their own whalers and attack the British ones. As if straightforward warfare was not enough, the Spanish colonies

---

[1]Wilberforce House Museum, Hull, Caerwent Papers.

were already moving towards revolution, as the *Comet* of Hull found to its cost in 1813. She happened to be in Concepcion when revolution broke out, and the insurgents took armaments and whaling boats for their cause. Having recovered her boats and "escaped" some few miles to Talcahuana she was again boarded by the revels and more arms and boats taken, together with most of the crew, who were kept ashore as hostages so that the ship might be ready should the rebels want it. A month later the "Patriots" released the crew, but kept officers as hostages, and it was not until Spanish battleships put down the revolt in June 1814 that the *Comet* was able to get away, without most of her small arms and ammunition. She had been in port for twelve months and twelve days.[2]

II

With such a large proportion of the southern fishing grounds occupied or claimed by aliens and enemies, it was natural that the English should turn increasingly to what was probably the most important development in the early nineteenth century, namely the extension of whaling and sealing around the new Australian colony. To the north-east of Botany Bay lay Norfolk Island, occupied almost at the same time and destined to become a great centre for sperm whaling, though paradoxically Captain Mitchell had successfully pleaded against taking his convicts there in 1791 because he wanted to get on with whaling along the Australian coast, where the fishing was actually more difficult. In 1805 the governor of New South Wales justified the retention of Norfolk Island partly on the grounds that it provided invaluable sustenance to whalers in the Pacific area to the east of Australia. With fresh food and water in plenty the crews remained in perfect health, "instead of being the scorbutic and debilitated men returned when their cruising was confined to the coast of South America."[3] To the south-west Macquarrie and Campbell Islands provided a similar service for their areas, though to a lesser degree. Further afield there was Tahiti, a savage paradise that became for a time the crossroads of the Pacific, for the sake of supplies, repairs, water and women.

While the islands were chiefly favoured as bases for pelagic fishing for the sperm whale, the Australian colony and potential colonies were soon discovered to be admirable places for old-fashioned bay-fishing for the Southern Right whale (*B. Antipodarum*). Within months of the establishment of the new

---

[2]Trinity House, Hull, Log of the *Comet* (copy in Wilberforce House Museum).

[3]Governor King to Lord Camden, 30 April 1805, quoted in W.J. Dakin, *Whalemen Adventurers* (Sydney, 1934; rev. ed., Sydney, 1963), 23.

colony of Tasmania (1803), it became apparent that the river Derwent, on which Hobart had been established, was a major breeding ground for the Right whale. For three months from the end of May the river teemed with whales, and it was dangerous to venture up it in light craft. "Soon," wrote a recent historian of Australia, "it was dangerous for whales to go up the river."[4] By July 1804 the commanding officer at Hobart had drawn up an elaborate plan for capturing Right whales in the winter and spring, and sperm whales in the summer. He sent it to Sir Joseph Banks with the hope that some at least might be "upon Government account" and so help to pay for the transportation of convicts, but as usually happened it was private enterprise, not government initiative, that got things going and reaped the profits.[5] The slaughter was immense, yet still the whales came. The *Ann* of London caught no fewer than thirty within the river during her 1818 expedition.

The same thing happened time and again along the coast of the Australian mainland, with the whalermen taking the lead in coastal exploration. The first settlements in Victoria and Western Australia were whaling settlements, and the first profitable industry in South Australia was whaling. The bays "were a kind of maternity hospital which suddenly became a slaughter house."[6] Immigrant ships were sometimes met by a stench along the coast rivalling that in Lancaster Sound or Pond's Bay in the Arctic, and John Eyre, one of the great Australian explorers, found Fowler's Bay "literally strewed in all directions with the bones and carcasses of whales."[7] In some places the massive ribs were so tightly packed as to give the impression of decaying mango swamps. The carcasses could be counted in their hundreds, and the bays in their tens. In Tasmania there are said to have been thirty-five bay fisheries in 1841, while New Zealand's southern island had between twenty-five and thirty as early as the 1820s,[8] when whalermen were already well-established as the first major intruders and were conducting in a small, but violent way what an early

---

[4]G. Blainey, *The Tyranny of Distance. How Distance Shaped Australia's History* (Melbourne, 1966), 103.

[5]Quoted in Dakin, *Whalemen Adventurers*, 31-32.

[6]Blainey, *Tyranny of Distance*, 112-113.

[7]A. Moorehead, *The Fatal Impact. An Account of the Invasion of the South Pacific, 1767-1840* (London, 1966), 198-199.

[8]Dakin, *Whalemen Adventurers*, 43; K. Sinclair, *A History of New Zealand* (Harmondsworth, 1959), 39.

New Zealand historian called "a war of races."[9] The Enderbys wanted the British government to annex New Zealand for the sake of the whale fisheries, but their interests did not, on this occasion, coincide with those of the government, and so, as Alan Moorehead has put it, "with equal ferocity the sailors killed the whales at sea and the Maoris on land."[10]

The natives in New Zealand and the victualling islands fought back, using the very weapons the whalermen had given them in exchange for food and women. Bay fishing in Australia and Tasmania might have been lonely work, but bay fishing in New Zealand could be terrifying. The crew of the *Boyd* was eaten in 1809, and many ships desperate for supplies or shelter found that the Friendly isles, for instance, were inappropriately named. Yet it was increasingly common for whalers to put men ashore in lonely places to engage in bay fishing or seal skinning, while the ship went off for a few months' sperm fishing. If the men did not engage in bay fishing, the voyage for sperm whales alone might well last for twice as long. Not unnaturally the Southern Fishery declined in popularity as ships went further into the Pacific and voyages increased from two years to three, and finally to four. Crews, who had never been very well paid in the Southern Fishery, were increasingly difficult to come by. According to the owners, they were "the best sailors in the world" in 1801; by 1844 they were "the worst description," and owners were forced to take what they could get.[11] Historians of the Pacific habitually refer to whalermen as a curse that spread across the ocean, bringing "the debauchery natural to a whaling port," and no matter how much they exaggerate, the impression remains that Southern whaling was not an experience widely sought after, at least in England.

III

By the 1820s the owners were also entering a period of demoralisation, in the more usual sense of the word. Despite the immense and undisputed potential of the Southern Fishery, they were already losing heart. At its peak the Southern fleet was no more than seventy-five percent of the Northern, and in terms of the number of ships sailing annually, it was only thirty-eight percent. During the

---

[9]Sinclair, *History of New Zealand*, 35.

[10]Moorehead, *Fatal Impact*, 202.

[11]British Museum (BM), Add. Ms. 38,356, "Information supplied by Mr. Enderby, 1801;" and Great Britain, Parliament, House of Commons, Select Committee on British Shipping, Report, q. 531, evidence of J. Somes.

malaise that set in after 1821 the Northern fleet declined by twenty-one percent, whereas the Southern fleet declined by no less than fifty percent between 1820-1821 and 1824-1825. After levelling off in the middle of the decade, the Southern Fishery contracted violently in the 1830s, and by 1840 was a shadow of its former self.

Table 14
Number and Tonnage of Southern Whalers Clearing,
1820-1843

	No.	Tons		No.	Tons		No.	Tons
1820	n.a.	19,755	1830	32	9682	1841	13	4836
1821	n.a.	14,398	1831	24	8335	1842	6	1835
1822	n.a.	11,432	1832	35	12,066	1843	9	3096
AV.	—	15,195	av.	30	10,028	av.	9	3256

Source: 1820-1822: Great Britain, Parliament, House of Commons, *Parliamentary Papers (BPP)*, 1828 (469), XIX, 464; 1830-1843: *BPP* 1845 (504), XLVII, 515.

Coal gas is often blamed for causing this decline in Southern whaling – as the owners themselves had forecast when it first appeared – but there are good grounds for questioning this easy assumption. Owners were specifically asked by the Select Committee on Shipping (1844) if gas was the cause of their troubles. "By no means," said G.F. Young: "the quantity of spermaceti oil consumed has increased since the period at which the fisheries were very flourishing."[12] Some years earlier, in 1827, merchants trading with Morocco had complained to the Board of Trade that their imports of wax had been affected by the growing use of spermaceti.[13] In fact the total importation of sperm oil in 1831-1832 was nine times as great as it had been in 1801-1802 and, moreover, its price was increasing in the 1830s at least to contract customers.

Nor was the depletion of stocks more than a contributory factor in the Southern Fishery, compared with its devastating effect in the Northern. The basic reason for decline was simply competition, or rather Britain's failure to withstand competition.

---

[12]*Ibid.*, q. 220, evidence of G.F. Young.

[13]Great Britain, Public Record Office (PRO), Board of Trade (BT) 1/248, Morocco merchants to Board of Trade, 25 March and 19 November 1827.

Table 15
Retained Imports of Sperm Oil, and Contract Prices
Paid by Commissioners of Northern Lights and Trinity
House, 1831-1844
(per tun)

	Imports	N.L.	T.H.		Imports	N.L.	T.H.
1831	6774	n.a.	n.a.	1838	6466	£78	£82
1832	7236	n.a.	n.a.	1839	5415	93	95
1833	5637	£64	n.a.	1840	4397	102	105
1834	6307	66	n.a.	1841	5657	94	99
1835	7389	63	63	1842	3395	80	80
1836	7005	68	67	1843	5940	62	67
1837	6142	86	86	1844	5552	67	69

Note: 1833 figure for imports exceeds total imports for 1833, and should almost certainly be 5367.

Source: Imports: *BPP* 1842 (259), XXXIX, 53; and 1845 (126), XLVI, 591. Prices: *BPP*, 1845 (607), IX, 442 and 570, Select Common Lighthouses.

There were two areas for competition: one the fishing grounds and in the British market. So far as the former was concerned, the chief trouble, as noted above, was the vast growth of the American whaling fleet. In many areas, because of the earlier restrictions by the East India Company, British vessels followed in the wake of experienced Americans; in others, the flood of American vessels forced them out, while in the high seas sperm fishery they were overwhelmed. As happened with the Dutch in earlier centuries, the prospects of the British whaling fleet were determined not by the number of British whalers, but by the total number of whalers in any one fishing ground. As early as 1818 there were two hundred American vessels roaming the Pacific and invading the bays; and twenty years later their fleet was of the order of seven hundred vessels serving their vast market of pioneers' oil lamps. They caught more in one day, wrote Herman Melville, than did the British in ten years. The southern seas were free for all, in stark contrast to the virtual monopoly which the British had established for themselves in the north; and for reasons not hard to identify, the Americans retained the leadership they had long enjoyed outside the Northern Fishery.

The British did not have to contend with foreigners alone. There was also a growing competition within the British market from the colonies themselves. It was not entirely unwelcome. They truth is that the Southern Fishery in the Pacific never enjoyed the popularity of the earlier Southern Fishery in the Atlantic, despite the somewhat larger tonnage of vessels involved for a few years after the Napoleonic war. Indeed, a larger tonnage was necessary simply because so much time was taken in moving backwards and forwards between Britain and the fishing grounds. At a fairly early stage, the rising class of merchants in Sydney and Hobart discovered that whereas it cost some £4000 to fit out a Southern whaler (quite apart from the cost of the ship), it cost only £300 to equip a simple bay whaling station. It made economic sense for the oil to be secure cheaply by the colonists, and shipped home in normal merchant vessels which were still searching for bulky return cargoes to balance the convicts and supplies they carried out to Australia. The fact that this latest stage of whaling took place in a hospitable climate within an area of British settlement completely changed the nature of the trade and re-established the sort of conditions that had existed before the American revolution. There had been considerable imports of oil and bone from Sydney for some years when William Wilson of Leith decided to emigrate to Australia to pursue the whale fishery there.[14] By 1827 Walker and Jones of Sydney owned five whalers, and three years later the port as a whole was reckoned to own seventeen that were engaged in deep sea whaling, as well as the various bay stations operating for merchants who may not have been whaler-owners. In Hobart the Derwent Whaling Club was established in 1825, and the local merchants were soon deeply engaged in sperm whaling, again partly with capital and expertise imported from Britain, though the Australians were already developing their own skills in the trade. By 1835 there were more Australian than British whalers operating in the Pacific.[15]

The London trade declined as the Australians' trade developed, and most observers were inclined to see a causal relationship. The statistics would seem to bear them out, as competition moved from the fishing grounds to the home market. Between 1831 and 1833 the Australian share of total British imports of sperm oil rose from nineteen to thirty-six percent, while the share brought home by British whalers declined from seventy-nine to fifty-eight percent. Although the colonies could not maintain this position, their share nevertheless averaged thirty-one percent of total imports for the years 1833-1840. So far as ordinary whale oil was concern, competition was even more severe, with imports from Australia passing the production of both Southern and Northern fisheries in 1836, to stand in the years 1836-1840 in a ratio of 2.4:1.

It is this great advance in the importation of colonial-caught oil that explains, at least in part, why the Southern Fishery did not expand to replace

---

[14]D.S. Macmillan, *Scotland and Australia, 1788-1850* (Oxford, 1967), 101.

[15]Blainey, *Tyranny of Distance*, 107.

supplies from the Northern Fishery during the natural calamities in the 1830s. For good or ill the British whaling fleets no longer determined the quantity and price of oils on the British market. Their diminishing role can best be seen in a comparison of the major sources of oils and bone during the 1830s (table 16).

IV

Though competition came first from Australian whalers, with their many cost advantages over London-based ones, it came finally and devastatingly from the Americans, whose activities determined the world price for oil.[16] By 1844 the few remaining owners were in despair when they appeared before the Shipping Committee. Young, whose firm had operated whalers for twenty-five years, was inclined to give up, having come to the conclusion that the Southern trade "would never again be a remunerative one."[17] First the removal of the seed duty, then the partial removal of the oil duty, persuaded prudent men to withdraw their capital. "Fiscal and other changes," it was said, "have nearly annihilated the northern and southern whale fisheries." "No consideration," said Young, "would induce me voluntarily to embark £1000 in the whale fishery, from a conviction that we never can, by any change or diminution of cost which it is in the power of the Legislature to effect, be enabled to meet the competition to which we are exposed in those trades."[18] When, however, he tried to sell his three ships he found a stagnant shipping market which added still further to the difficulties of the whaling owners, who were not able to liquidate part of their capital to support the remainder. Young sent his *Offley* to sea again "very reluctantly" rather than lose on her; the *Kingsdown* which he valued at £4000 fetched only £1800; and the third ship could not be sold at all. Joseph Somes, who also had three ships in the Southern Fishery, was as anxious to get out as Young: "as soon as they come home," he said, "I shall retire from it." His motivation was simple: "it did not pay."[19]

There was nothing that owners could do to improve their profit margins because they no longer enjoyed protection and could not reduce their costs to a

---

[16]*BPP*, Select Committee on British Shipping, Report, q. 199, evidence of G.F. Young.

[17]*Ibid.*, q. 10.

[18]*Ibid.*, qq. 197 ff..

[19]*Ibid.*, qq. 519 and 544, evidence of J. Somes.

competitive level. Their prime costs had always been greater, and in the 1840s, for instance, English whalers cost £12,000 when American whalers cost only £8000. Even more damaging was the fact that Australian vessels for use in their own waters could be had for as little as £1000.[20] British running costs were also greater, not least because of the greater distances involved. The proportion of profits going to American crews was also thought to be lower, while those crews, bred in the trade and enthusiastic in their pursuit of it, were said to be better whalermen than the British. Certainly in the 1830s and 1840s the Americans and Australians were approaching whaling in the Southern hemisphere with an energy and boldness that was no longer to be found in London, where owners and crews alike were faced with the choice of giving up or moving to a more suitable place.

It is fitting that the English Southern Whale Fishery should have ended as it began with the Enderbys. Samuel and his sons came from Boston, Massachusetts, to London when it was economically sensible to do so. Almost three-quarters of a century later, when there was no longer any justification for London's direct involvement in the Southern Fishery, the family moved again. Charles Enderby founded the Southern Whale Fishery Company and sailed for New Zealand, in the *Samuel Enderby* in 1849. He established a whaling station on Auckland Island, and did not return. So far as the British were concerned, the Southern Fishery was finished.

---

[20]*Ibid.*, q. 519; and Blainey, *Tyranny of Distance*, 109.

Gordon Jackson

Table 16

Oils and Bone From Major Sources as a Percentage of Total Imports, 1831-1840

	1831		1832		1833		1834		1835		1836		1837		1838		1839		1840	
Sperm Oil	Tuns	%	Tuns	%	Tuns	%	Tuns	%	Tuns	%	Tuns	%	Tuns	%	Tuns	%	Tuns	%	Tuns	%
Australia	1297	19	1616	21	1985	36	1984	32	2159	28	2364	34	2232	35	2370	37	1170	20	1407	27
Brit. No.	48		0		10		102	2	8		327	5	309	5	164	3	129	2	146	3
USA	0		1		0		0		1		0		588	9	84	1	168	3	1408	27
Whale Fisheries	5373	79	5618	75	3158	58	4130	66	5320	70	4244	60	3065	49	3782	58	4054	70	2141	40
TOTAL	6186		7540		3484		6276		7645		7028		6312		6483		5815		5289	
Other Train Oil	Tuns	%	Tuns	%	Tuns	%	Tuns	%	Tuns	%	Tuns	%	Tuns	%	Tuns	%	Tuns	%	Tuns	%
Australia	1329	7	1469	6	2087	8	2098	11	2780	17	3128	25	4077	26	7333	34	5875	36	6509	32
Brit. No	10,971	61	9199	40	10,596	39	8211	43	9920	60	7954	64	9085	59	9301	43	8330	51	11,939	59
Whale Fisheries	5059	28	12,141	52	14,252	52	8235	43	3416	21	1318	11	2047	13	4782	22	1893	12	1291	6
TOTAL	17,853		23,234		27,391		19,057		16,552		12,460		15,491		21,798		16,384		20,292	
Whalebone	cwt	%	cwt	%	cwt	%	cwt	%	cwt	%	cwt	%	cwt	%	cwt	%	cwt	%	cwt	%
Australia	1282	18	1907	11	1714	9	2388	19	3282	45	4068	69	4322	61	7899	57	6216	67	6711	86
Brit. No.	52	1	242	1	223	1	0		462	6	295	5	370	5	629	5	513	6	205	3
USA	143	2	0		0		0		0		0		529	7	385	3	363	4	392	5
Whale Fisheries	5230	73	14,216	85	16,742	89	9422	76	3400	46	1120	19	1708	24	4867	35	2177	23	458	6
TOTAL	7191		16,766		18,873		12,465		7337		5929		7087		13,852		9324		7805	

Source: British Trade Returns, 1831-1840; and *BPP* 1842 (375), XXXIX, 53, 78 and 101.

Chapter 8
The End of the Northern Fishery in the
Late Nineteenth Century

I

With the run-down of both Northern and Southern fisheries, the second half of the nineteenth century experienced the same sort of marking-time as had occurred in the late seventeenth century. As a consequence the period is relatively unimportant compared with the great exertions before 1840 and the vast expansion after 1900, and it is only necessary here to outline the main lines of development. None of them led on to the modern industry, and important though British whaling may have been to individual persons and places, it had already departed from the mainstream of whaling and was sailing up a backwater as dangerous and ruinous as any in Baffin Bay. No amount of incentive, capital investment, technical advance or human bravery could save the Arctic trade, but it fought its painful death-struggle for three-quarters of a century, periodically encouraged by remissions that eased the pressure and sometimes brought a measure of prosperity.

Although whaling never actually ceased, except when frustrated by appalling conditions, there was no improvement on the position obtaining in the mid-1840s. Changes favouring the trade were slow to appear, and for a long time most developments worked against rather than for the whaling men. The final triumph of gas lighting in towns was self-evident; the eventual triumph of mineral oil in domestic lamps and industrial usage was inevitable. There were few industrial processes for which whale oil was uniquely suitable, and the forerunners of applied chemistry were already turning their attention to substitutes even for these. Against this sort of background entrepreneurs in the middle of the century withdrew their capital and their ships, following the lead of men such as the Gees of Hull, who made their mark and some of their money in whaling before going into general shipowning and steamship-owning in particular. In the years following the American Revolution shipowners had seen whaling as a valuable employment for ships. Now, with huge changes taking place in the shipping world, it seemed a sensible time to move in the opposite direction, and one after another of the Hull owners withdrew from the trade and came to terms with their port's position as the centre of the seed-crushing industry. Though there was a final flirtation with whaling in the 1850s, when more new whalers were fitted out than in either of the two preceding decades, by 1861 there were only six vessels active in the port, and as these were lost or withdrew they were not replaced. There was plenty of adventure and heroism in the last years, but business is about profits, not heroism, and from this unromantic point of view the trade was bankrupt.

By contrast the Scottish ports remained in the trade, showing perhaps a greater degree of initiative in developing the seal fishery as a subsidiary of whaling and in employing steam whalers, their enterprise encouraged particularly by the growth of the jute industry.[1]

Seals had always been a possible make-weight on unsuccessful whaling expeditions, but it was left to the northern ports to make a flourishing trade out of sealing and to employ ships successfully in both branches of the Arctic trade. Peterhead in particular sent vessels adventuring along the Greenland coast, though by far the largest concentrations of seals were to be found off the coast of Labrador, which had long been a source of fur, but which was only recently of interest to the British whalermen as the Greenland seals were diminishing and as they made their wide-ranging explorations of the western side of Davis Straits in their search for new whale and seal stocks. Almost a million seal skins were taken by British vessels in the years 1848-1857 (table 17), but equally important was the seal oil represented by these skins, at roughly 100 seals to the tun.

The period around the middle of the century was that of Peterhead's dominance in the Arctic trade. After reaching a peak in the early 1820s her effort and achievement had diminished, in company with that of other ports, from an average of sixteen ships and 104 tuns of oil in 1820-1824 to twelve ships and eighty-one tuns in 1830-1834. Interest and optimism nevertheless remained: "there are still ten vessels employed in that trade," it was said in 1845, "and it is not improbable that it may again become more successful, as the late failures have been occasioned more by bad seasons and an altered state of the ice at the fishing grounds, than by a decrease in the number of whales."[2] Any hope of a revived whaling trade was undoubtedly misplaced, but the sealing trade was increasingly attractive to Peterhead, which took three-quarters of all

---

[1]The relationship between jute and whale oil may best be followed in the annual Dundee trade figures published in *Dundee Year Book* (Dundee, 1881-). Official notice of the whaling trade was slight after 1840, the best general source being B. Lubbock, *The Arctic Whalers* (Glasgow, 1936), *passim*. For Dundee, see S.G.E. Lythe, "The Dundee Whale Fishery," *Scottish Journal of Political Economy*, XI (1965), 158-169; and *Dundee Year Book* (1881), 82; (1890), 109; and (1894), 208.

[2]*New Statistical Account of Scotland* (15 vols., Edinburgh, 1845), XII, Aberdeen, 365.

the sealskins brought home in the years 1848-1857, compared with Hull's fourteen percent.

Table 17
Relative Performance of Whaling Ports, 1848-1857
(Average Annual Catches)

	Seals	Whales	Tuns of Oil	Cwts of Bone
Peterhead	72,631	24	1216	321
Fraserburgh	7970	1	110	4
Aberdeen	1074	20	192	223
Dundee	169	27	271	373
Kirkcaldy	901	16	151	188
Bo'ness	—	3	47	57
Hull	13,182	20	371	280

Source: *Dundee Year Book* (1894), 210.

In 1853 she sent out twenty-seven vessels, of which two-thirds were sealers, compared with Hull's thirteen, and in 1859 she equipped over thirty vessels. For a quarter of a century Peterhead was the most deeply committed port in the country, relieved from the embarrassment of undue competition and blessed with a fund of experience that remained in the north long after it had been allowed to die in the south. The Grays – Peterhead's leading family in the trade – and their local friends and rivals recognised an opportunity for enterprise and initiative which those in the traditional whaling centres were either unable or unwilling to exploit. Further down the coast, for instance, the old whaling town of Dundee showed almost no interest in sealing, though on the strength of the growing demand from the jute industry she was already the country's leading whaling port.

Table 18
Average Number of Whalers Fitted Out, 1861-1879

	Dundee	Peterhead	Kirkcaldy	Hull	Fraser-burgh	Aberdeen
1861-1864	8	17.5	2	4	2.5	4.3
1865-1869	10.5	12.2	0.2	1.2	1.6	0.8
1870-1874	11.0	10.0	—	—	—	—
1875-1879	13.4	7.0	—	—	—	—

Source: B. Lubbock, *The Arctic Whalers* (Glasgow, 1936), 460.

The Peterhead era came to an end in the 1870s as Dundee began to consolidate her whaling and sealing interests by investing in a newer type of larger vessel which her northern rival had difficulty admitting to her harbours. As a result Dundee forged ahead of Peterhead, while all the other ports withdrew from the trade.

Although faced with heavy competition in the sealing grounds from other countries, chiefly from Norway, Dundee sealers enjoyed a considerable long-term success. The *Aurora* caught an average of 13,647 seals over eighteen years, the *Esquimaux* 12,152 over seventeen years, and the *Terra Nova* 17,613 over ten years.[3] The value of such regular cargoes, with prices between 3s 6d and five shillings per skin, is obvious, and to the value of skins must be added the seal oil, worth only a little less than whale oil. In 1881, for instance, six Dundee vessels returned from the Newfoundland sealing with 139,985 skins worth on average five shillings, and 1797 tuns of oil worth £29, making a total of £87,109 or £14,518 per vessel. By comparison, all but one of these vessels also engaged in whaling, and earned an average of £3253 from that side of the trade, a clear indication of its relative importance, at least in 1881. After 1877 the volume of seal oil almost always exceeded the volume of whale oil brought home to Dundee.[4] It was beyond doubt that during the more prosperous years sealing was "carrying" the whaling trade.

Within Peterhead and Dundee the processing of sealskins became an important industry. At first they were handed over to merchants for disposal, but eventually Stephens of Dundee, one of the chief firms remaining in the trade, established their own factory. Here the skins were graded, the finest young skins to be cured and dyed as furs and made up into expensive muffs, boas and capes on the premises, and the rest to be tanned as leather, graded from old sealskins suitable for japanned coach-leather to the young skins suitable for female accoutrements. The prize of the lot was the beautiful white fur of the pup less than ten or twelve days old, and seals, for all their prodigious abundance, began to disappear from the Greenland coast, and became more difficult to find in Labrador. Although there was no great diminution in value, the number of ships engaged in sealing declined abruptly in the 1890s and, except in 1900 and 1906, the numbers caught were very small.

The greatest boost to both sides of the trade (apart from changes in fashion) came with the application of steam power to whaling. In 1857 Brown and Atkinson and Bailey and Leetham, two of Hull's leading shipowners, had

---

[3]*Dundee Year Book* (1894), 216.

[4]*Ibid.* (1881), 29 and 39; and (1889), 31.

experimented with auxiliary engines while a third, Thomas Ward, sent out steam tenders to assist his sailing vessels. The advantages of steam were immediately apparent so far as manoeuvrability was concerned and demoralised sailing crews told of their disappointment as they watched the rival steamers pass them by or force their way through hitherto impenetrable pack ice. "With powerful steamship the work is play now to what it was then," Captain William Barron wrote as he looked back on his days in sailing whalers.[5] Vessels were no longer so entirely at the mercy of unpredictable gales, and men, at least in theory, were no longer required to take to the ice to warp their ship along. The steamer's greater capital and operational cost was, from the point of view of the owners, more than compensated for by the versatility and speed with which it operated, especially in the northern ice beyond the reach of sailing vessels, and in the fjords where currents and winds would have wrecked them. "I have gone through Melville Bay with steam," wrote Captain Barron, "in twenty four hours without losing a moment's rest, whereas I have been six weeks going through with a sailing ship, and no better prospect in view. So things are more easily done than formerly."[6] Steam provided speed in the passage between home port and the fishery, as well as within the fishery, with the result that vessels were able to make two voyages a year, one to the traditional whaling grounds and one, at the start of the year, to the sealing grounds.

The combination of steam, whales and seals appeared to offer yet another period of prosperity, and a number of companies were formed to exploit the new situation, often with the aid of the limited liability laws which, in Hull if not in Scotland, enabled smaller investors to return to a trade which for a generation or more had been in the hands of major shipowners. For those seeking new employments for steamers the prospect was exciting. In 1860 Brown and Atkinson had reformed their interests and offered shares to the public as Hull Whale and Seal Fishery Company Limited, formed, said their prospectus, "for the purpose of extending the whale and seal fisheries...which have dwindled away in importance for want of some such opportunity as is now presented by the operation of the limited liability act."[7] By that time Hull had at least six iron screw steamers including, for a brief spell, Bailey and Leetham's

---

[5]W. Barron, *An Apprentice's Reminiscences of Whaling in Davis's Straits. Narrative of the Voyages of the Hull Barque Truelove, from 1848 to 1854* (Hull, 1890), 33.

[6]*Ibid.*, 62.

[7]Wilberforce House Museum, Prospectus.

Corkscrew, the first screw steamer in Britain.[8] Dundee experimented with steam in 1858 and had three steamers – *Tay, Dundee* and *Narwhal* in 1859, the year in which Peterhead's first steamer, the *Empress of India* was commissioned. Both the Scottish ports had their Seal and Whale Fishing Companies founded in the late 1850s, and Aberdeen followed suit in the 1860s, but the enthusiasm for monolithic companies soon died away, and whaling passed back into the hands of individual shipowners or groups of shipowners.[9]

The final burst of enthusiasm for whaling in Hull had been associated with yet another of the periodic improvements in the price of whale oil, which had risen from less than £30 to more than £50 a tun between the 1840s and 1860s, but while the incentive might for a short time be there, the technical ability was somewhat diminished. In short, Hull's experiment with steam whaling was probably the most unfortunate part of her long involvement with the Arctic. Steam alone could not guarantee success, and those who had expected it to conquer adverse conditions and expand the fishery were disappointed. Whether through bad luck or bad seamanship, her steamers did not return with catches of either whales or seals that were sufficient to encourage prolonged effort, particularly when the price of oil declined once more. Above all, perhaps, Hull made the wrong choice of steamers. Her great iron vessels were, because of fuel problems, almost all underpowered, as the men of the *Diana* discovered in 1866-1867 when she was trapped for the winter in ice through which Dundee vessels (one of which had refused to help her) were able to make their escape.[10] Indeed, unless some system could be found for getting fuel to the Arctic there was a very real limit to the usefulness of steamers in far distant waters. Moreover, compared with the old wooden sailers, the new iron ships were cold and damp and extremely uncomfortable for their crews, who lived in a nightmare of frozen condensation. And they were, in Arctic conditions, relatively unseaworthy. It was not unknown for wooden whalers to return with their hull and superstructure completely misshapen after nips in the ice, but iron vessels had no such resilience under pressure. Most of the Hull steamers experienced varied degrees of damage which discounted any chance of useful profits and encouraged steamship owners to find more satisfactory and

---

[8]Hull Custom House, Hull Shipping Registers, *passim*.

[9]*Dundee Year Books, passim.*

[10]C.E. Smith, *From the Deep of the Sea* (London, 1922), is the edited diary of the *Diana's* surgeon, and is the best account of the terrible conditions faced by unfortunate crews in Baffin Bay, though it must be emphasised that the *Diana's* situation was unusual.

secure outlets for their investments. They could point, for instance, to the case of the 600-ton *River Tay* of Dundee, built by John Key of Kirkcaldy. Supposedly with double the strength of a normal iron vessel, reinforced both internally and externally, and divided into forty-two water-tight compartments, she nevertheless sank in a mill-pond sea after being struck by ice. "Like other ships of her class," it was reported in the *Dundee Year Book*, "the iron whaler came to an untimely end...This was the last experiment of its kind."[11]

Despite Hull's unhappy experience with steam whaling, her withdrawal from the trade coincided with its general adoption by Scottish owners. Only thirteen percent of the whaling and sealing fleet were steamers in 1861, but seventy-one percent in 1871 and ninety-five percent in 1881, when there was still twenty vessels engaged in the trade. Dundee owners had learned their lesson quickly: steamers must be wooden, and equipped with adequate sails for use whenever possible, especially – by agreement between captains, who distrusted the noise – in the fishing grounds. With no more competition from Hull, the local firm of Alexander Stephens turned out a whole succession of first-rate steam whalers between their *Narwhal* of 1859 and *Terra Nova* of 1884. They also started whaling on their own account, and operated the two largest steamers out of the port, the 828-ton *Arctic* from 1875 to 1885 and the 740-ton *Terra Nova* from 1884 to 1894, when they withdrew from the trade.

The final factor encouraging Dundee whaling (and, so far as the oil was concerned, her sealing) and confirming her superiority in the trade, was the growth there of the jute industry, which soon became almost a Dundee monopoly. The rapidly expanding use in the 1850s and 1860s of Indian jute for sacking and associated things such as carpet backing and linoleum opened up an exciting market, since no other oil was so suitable for the batching of jute, the process whereby freshly opened bales were soaked in emulsion to soften the fibres before spinning. Despite attempts to replace it by mineral oil, most notably by James – "Paraffin" – Young of Glasgow in 1858, whale oil was not finally superseded for general purposes until the 1920s and 1930s, and even then it continued in use for the finest counts of yarn until quite recently. Some indication of potential demand can be seen in the growth of direct imports of jute at Dundee, which rose from around 30,000 tons in the mid-1850s to almost 100,000 tons in the early 1870s and over 200,000 tons in the late 1880s and 1890s.[12] At least until the 1950s most yarns spun from this vast amount of jute had an added oil content of at least five percent.

---

[11]*Dundee Year Book* (1894), 211.

[12]*Ibid.*, *passim*.

Given a local market, good ships, able crews and a fair degree of luck, Dundee whaling enjoyed a couple of decades as good as any in the recent history of the trade. The peak of her activity so far as the number of ships was concerned came in the late 1870s, and so far as catches were concerned in the early 1880s (table 19).

Thereafter, Dundee's interest in sealing declined gradually, as did the availability of seals and the value of their skins, but her whaling activities continued, despite a substantial fall in oil prices in the early 1880s, from over £30 to less than £20 per tun. As late as 1881 the proceeds of sealing amounted to £96,119 compared with £34,782 from whaling, an average per vessel of £6408 and £3162 respectively. By 1885, with tumbling oil and skins prices, the trades stood at £37,769 and £22,898, with averages of £3434 and £1431. Ten years later sealing brought in about £15,000 compared with £42,130 from whaling. The one or two ships still going to Newfoundland now stocked up with skins and ignored the oil, while whaling received its last great boost from the world of fashion. The decline in the supplies of whalebone had not deterred those who moulded and padded rich females in the final extravagance of wasp-waist and bustle after c. 1870, when the corset became "a veritable cuirass;"[13] and under such pressure the price of bone advanced steadily from around £500 a ton in the 1870s to £1500 in 1885 and £2300 in 1895. After a temporary decline in the 1890s it very nearly reached £3000 in 1902, and at least since 1896 whalebone had been by far the most substantial source of income.[14] In 1905, when the peak of corset construction was reached with the exaggerated "S" curve, the whalebone brought into Dundee was worth almost eight times as much as the oil. Yet within two years the brassière began to replace the bodice, and what was left of the corset was increasingly elastic; the whalebone trade went out of fashion with the contrived "figures" which had held sway in polite society, with only the briefest respites, ever since the Basque whalermen had discovered the economic advantages derived from vanity.

Dundee's activity in the Arctic reached its peak in 1881 before she began to follow Peterhead and Hull into a slow but inexorable decline. Dundee Seal and Whale Fishery Company had bought no new vessels since the 680-ton *Resolute* in 1875 and did not replace vessels withdrawn or lost; in 1894 they were in liquidation, their last vessel sold to David Bruce and Company, who also bought the last vessel of Stephens, the ship builders and whaler operators who had also allowed their fleet to decline since 1884. The Tay Whale Fishery

---

[13]N. Waugh, *Corsets and Crinolines* (London, 1954), 79.

[14]*Dundee Year Books, passim.*

Company ceased operations in 1884, and the Dundee Polar Company sold out in 1892. These firms had been the backbone of the industry which, together with Robert Kinnes and Co., they had more or less created. Though individuals continued, led by Kinnes and Captain Adams, one of the most successful of Dundee whalermen, none of their vessels was more modern than the *Terra Nova*, built in 1884, and the only vessels brought into the trade – by Adams and Kinnes – were old and cheap and, by recent standards, small. A handful of vessels continued to operate in the early twentieth century, but their cargoes were poor and their returns slight. The nine ships engaged in 1907 made an aggregate loss of £50,000, and thereafter the trade faded away. The last two vessels sailed on the eve of the First World War, and returned clean. British whaling in the Arctic was finished.

It must be emphasised that the run down and final demise of British whaling was caused not so much by a failure of the market as by a failure on the supply side. Despite substitution in the early years of the nineteenth century whale oil continued to find users, and not just in the jute industry. In the last quarter of the century imported whale oil was running between 15,000 and 20,000 tuns per annum, and Hull, for instance, was still importing between 2000 and 3000 tuns in the 1890s, over ten times as much as Dundee was bringing home in her own ships. The crucial fact is that whale oil now came from areas and was secured by means that were beyond the competence of English and Scottish whaling entrepreneurs. The final stage of the trade should not be viewed as a minor success because a handful of vessels from Dundee made a modest income in the absence of competition, and the occasional captain could make his five hundred a year. It should be seen rather as a failure on the part of entrepreneurs to cut themselves off from a dying trade before bankruptcy overtook it, and an unwillingness or inability on their part to exhibit that enterprise and initiative that would have directed them towards modern whaling. Even the much-publicised Dundee Antarctic expedition of 1892-1893 was equipped only with the small Henry "Express" gun which was mounted in the boats, and made almost no attempt to catch "modern" whales. The whole object of the expedition, according to W.G. Burn-Murdoch, one of its biologists, was to find the whalebone whale, "for making umbrellas and destroying women's waists – particularly for the latter purpose."[15] The main hope for Dundee's future, so far as Captain Robertson of the *Active* was concerned, lay in his continuing faith "that a whale similar to the Greenland whale exists somewhere

---

[15]W.G. Burn-Murdoch, "Life at the Antarctic," *Dundee Year Book* (1893), 150 ff.

in the Antarctic."[16] In thus turning their hopes to the Antarctic so early they were in advance of their rivals, but their motive was out of data. Dundee men were not afraid to make investment decisions. The tragedy for British whaling is that they made the wrong ones, and having made them were overcome by the sort of icy paralysis that killed men in Arctic waters. They could not save themselves because they could not grasp the lifebelt; it was left to more open-minded capitalists from outside the industry to exploit the abundant whale fishery on Scotland's own doorstep. The British phase of whaling, which had begun around 1780, lasted for little more than a century; long before the First World War whaling had entered its Norwegian phase.

---

[16]*Ibid.*, 146.

Table 19
Dundee Sealing and Whaling, 1875-1904
(5-yearly averages)

| | Sealing | | | | | Whaling | | | | |
| | Total | | | Average Per Ship | | Total | | | Average | |
	ships	seals	oil tuns	seals	oil tuns	ships	oil tuns	bone cwt.	oil tuns	bone cwt.
1875-1879	12.8	70,638	889	5519	69	12.6	677	n.a.	54	n.a.
1880-1884	12.6	97,303	1270	7732	101	10.4	790	n.a.	76	n.a.
1885-1889	8.2	67,295	832	8207	102	10.0	359	39.6	36	4.0
1890-1894	3.2	45,424	n.a.	14,195	n.a.	7.4	342	11.1	46	1.5
1895-1899	1.6	12,060	n.a.	4537	n.a.	6.4	257	8.1	40	1.3
1900-1904	—	—	—	—	—	5.8	188	8.4	32	1.4

Source: Dundee Year Books, passim.

Chapter 9

New Whaling Techniques

I

In the middle of the nineteenth century the British whaling trade had been overtaken by an entrepreneurial and technical paralysis that was barely hidden by the continuing activity in Scotland. Faced with difficulties on both the demand and supply side, the industry prepared itself for its supposedly inevitably doom. Here, as elsewhere, modern scholars might detect not so much a realistic acceptance of fate as a diminution of the enterprise and initiative that had created the trade in the first place. Capitalists were leaving the trade; young whalermen were no longer entering it. A huge fund of bravery and skill was resting on its laurels, its only answer to changing conditions being to push both bravery and skill beyond the limits of physical endurance. This very doggedness of the last whalermen has earned them a fine reputation; but as businessmen they were ultimately a failure. They lacked the resilience and ability to change that was essential for survival. They did not seek out and exploit new opportunities. Above all, in their determination to press traditional whaling to its limits, they consistently ignored the most significant developments that were to lead to modern whaling. The sad irony is that despite the sacrifice in fortunes and fingers, there were more whales off the coast of Scotland than there were off the coast of Greenland. But the Scotsmen could not catch them, and, apart from unsuccessful experiments by Peterhead men in the 1840s, made no serious attempt to do so.

Thus, by default, the initiative in whaling passed to those who could approach it afresh, adopting new methods to answer new circumstances. The crucial decision was how to use steam power. There were two possibilities, one obvious, and the other less so. The obvious one, chosen by the British, was to use steam to drive the traditional pelagic whaler; basically, that is, to get it to and from the whaling grounds, and assist its mobility while there. The less obvious one was to apply steam to the boats which actually did the fishing, thus increasing their speed and manoeuvrability, and enabling them to go more than a rowing boat's distance from base. The British were undoubtedly correct in surmising that such vessels would not earn their keep in the declining Arctic fishery. What they did not recognize was their immense potential if used along the coastline of Europe.

It had always been something of a paradox that the Arctic whalers had had to cross the migration routes of a huge stock of whales in order to reach the straggling specimens in the Arctic. The problem, as noted above, had always been that the more abundant rorqual whales defied capture by traditional methods. Unlike the placid Greenland whale, they moved too fast for a rowing boat to approach them, and sounded too energetically for a rowing boat to hold them. Even had a kill been possible, there was little that a rowing boat could do with a hundred tons of sinking whale on the end of its line except follow it to the bottom, as the people of Peterhead found. A small steamer might stand a better chance of reaching a fin or blue whale, and of resisting its immense power; but it took a great deal of experimentation before theory became reality.

Svend Foyn, a seal-catcher of Tønsberg, was apparently the first man to appreciate that modern technology was opening the way for a revival of the earliest type of whaling from European shore bases; or at least he was the first man to match vision with inventiveness and entrepreneurial skill.[1] He realised that the smaller vessels employed in sealing might, with suitable modifications, be more satisfactory for catching the types of whales found in European waters than the traditional whalers employed by the British, and he set about proving it in 1863 with his *Spes et Fides*, the first modern whale-catcher from which all others descended. There was no comparison between *Spes et Fides* and anything that Scoresby would have recognised. With a length of only ninety-four feet and a gross tonnage of eighty-six, she was "all engine." Everything – including crew space – was sacrificed to strength and speed so that she could stalk whales at seven knots and then tow them back to the shore base where the making off operations took place.

Foyn's claim to fame does not rest on the application of steam power alone. There was a series of inter-related problems to which he also found answers without which the steamer would have been useless. In the first place, no rope on earth could hold a rorqual when it sounded, and even a dead whale produced an intolerable strain if heavy seas produced much movement in the catcher. Foyn's solution was ingenious yet simple: the strain on the rope was taken up by a series of pulleys and springs – initially on the mast and eventually in the hold – which was commonly called the accumulator. Its effect was the same as the bending of the rod in fishing. With the accumulator, and a carefully operated steam winch – which was another Foyn development – it was possible

---

[1]The best work on Foyn has not been translated from the Norwegian, but useful accounts may be found in L.H. Matthews, *et al.*, *The Whale* (London, 1968); F.V. Morley and J.S. Hodgson, *Whaling North and South* (London, 1927); and most of the modern texts, such as F.D. Ommanney, *Lost Leviathan* (London, 1971).

to avoid breaking the rope so long as the strain did not go on for too long. In the second place, the old method of "playing" the whale until it died from loss of blood or shock was clearly impossible, as was the old method of delivering the *coup de grace* with lances. No one who got that near to a stricken rorqual survived to tell the tale; even the steam-catchers invariably went astern in order to avoid them after a strike. Again the answer was simple, though it took years of experimentation before a perfect solution was arrived at: a swift death must be brought about by a lethal, as opposed to a "hook," harpoon, and this must necessarily be projected by a gun.

The idea of using a harpoon gun in whaling was no novelty. Elias Bird, an ex-South Sea Company captain who had continued whaling on his own account, experimented with one in the 1730s, and various gunsmiths – in Hull, for instance – had developed simply instruments for projecting harpoons, as illustrated in Scoresby's *Account of the Arctic Regions*. They were generally rejected because in Arctic whaling they had little advantage over the hand-harpoon, which most harpooners preferred. "The harpoon gun," wrote Scoresby,[2]

> has been highly improved, and rendered capable of throwing a harpoon nearly forty yards with effect; yet, on account of the difficulty and address requisite in the management of it, and the loss of fish, which, in unskilful hands, it has been the means of occasioning, together with some accidents which have resulted from its use, – it has not been so generally adopted as might have been expected.

The chief drawback to the old guns – apart from the conservatism of harpooners – lay in the fact that because traditional whaling shallops were unsuitable for carrying anything but the smallest of them, they were capable of projecting only small harpoons which were generally thought unsuitable for fin and blue whales: they drew too easily and did not cause a sufficiently extensive wound. For example, a Dundee steam whaler that once got six normal harpoons into a fin whale was towed for fourteen hours without any apparent flagging on the part of the whale, and when eventually the engines were used as a brake the

---

[2]W. Scoresby, *An Account of the Arctic Regions, with a History and Description of the Northern Whale Fishery* (2 vols., Edinburgh, 1820), II, 228.

only result was six broken ropes.[3] Sticking four-foot harpoons into the largest and most powerful animals that have ever lived was more suited to Gulliver's travels than modern commerce. There was therefore a tremendous advantage to be gained from Foyn's design for a gun to project a six-foot hundredweight of Swedish steel, with vicious barbs that opened when they began to take the strain, and produced a massive wound and an effective hook. The final devastating version contained an explosive charge, thus combining the functions of harpoon and lance. As the barbs opened, umbrella-fashion, their base crushed a glass phial of sulphuric acid which set off a fuse and exploded the gunpowder in a cast-iron shell, weighing some eleven pounds, which was screwed into the tip of the harpoon and formed its "point." The "balance" of the harpoon was again a matter for lengthy experimentation. If the head was too light the harpoon might glance off; if it was too heavy it might go straight through the whale's blubber and out the other side. In the end it was discovered that a long heavy shaft was an advantage, since the momentum after the point had struck was sufficient to bring the harpoon to a vertical path and so downwards into the animal's body. It thus became possible to shoot at whales swimming directly ahead of the boat in a fashion which would have been almost impossible in the old days when they were generally struck in their side.

Who first thought of using explosives in whaling is not clear; certainly it was not Foyn, as is often supposed. A Frenchman named Devisme probably had the best claim to being its "inventor," and French "carbine whale-boats" were operating in the Pacific in the 1840s, as described in an account of voyages made by Dr. Felix Maynard, "ghosted" by Alexandre Dumas:[4]

> After a year spent in almost daily experiments, both upon the living animal and the dead body, it is no longer possible to entertain any doubt as to the great penetrability and force of these terrible projectiles, or that his carbine of special calibre is suited for hunting these great cetaceans...One is justified in stating without fear of error, that henceforth the pursuit of whales will resemble that of hunting ducks on a pond. Devisme's invention will not only result in radical modifications of the equipment of vessels commissioned for the great fishing, but will also influence the future of this

---

[3]Account of the Dundee Antarctic expedition of 1892/1893 in *Dundee Year Book* (1893), 145.

[4]F. Maynard and A. Dumas, *The Whalers* (London, 1937), 293-294.

industry, recently so flourishing, but today languishing and full if disappointment.

Nevertheless, even if modern whalermen would have described their calling as a duck shoot, they would never have regarded it as a French duck shoot, for that nation was no more able than the British to realise the significance of Devisme's work. It was left to Foyn and his compatriots to seize their chance by introducing the necessary radical modifications to whaling as anticipated by Maynard. One the one hand they had the technology available for the successful marriage of the steam-catcher and the explosive harpoon. One the other hand they had many factors working in their favour and pushing them towards whaling: factors such as the happy proximity of migration routes to the Norwegian coastline, the existing experience in the sealing and fishing industries, and, not least perhaps, the absence of alternative outlets for investment and labour.

The importance of the Norwegians' early start in modern whaling can hardly be exaggerated. By trial and error they mastered the techniques of their new art: how to stalk the new sorts of whales in their steam-catchers, how to operate the new gun to maximum advantage, how to manipulate the winches. Long before other people became interested, the Norwegians had developed a co-ordination of activities on board their catchers, a series of new skills which they passed on to their sons – and to no one else. Modern whaling began as a Norwegian industry and expanded as a Norwegian industry. When the time came for it to spread abroad it still depended upon Norwegian personnel; and Norwegian was the universal language of whaling until the Japanese intervened in the 1930s.

Svend Foyn began experimenting in 1863, and caught his first whale, in Varangerfjord, in 1867. He caught thirty or forty a year, and eventually increased his catch sufficiently to encourage another company in 1877.[5] By 1880 there were eight companies operating twelve steam-catchers and for two decades an ever increasing number of catchers ravaged the whale migrations off the coast of Norway. But this was only the beginning. In the 1890s, faced with the decline of stocks on their own coastline, and the hostility of inshore fishermen, the Norwegians moved further afield, fishing off the Faroes, off Iceland, and finally off Shetland and the Hebrides. Here the annual migrations brought a host of victims. The whales caught in European waters were no longer the white whales and bottlenose whales of small commercial value, but giant specimens of blue, sei and fin whales that had previously gone unmolested. Among them was

---

[5]Morley and Hodgson, *Whaling North and South*, 67-68.

discovered the Nordcapper – *Balaena biscayensis* – which is now thought to be the original whale fished by the Basques, and was so long considered extinct that Scoresby had denied its very existence.

So great was the success of modern shore-based whaling that by the end of the 1890s the total annual catch – around 2000 whales – exceeded the yield during the height of the great Dutch fishery of the seventeenth and the British fishery of the eighteenth centuries. This success obviously opened up possibilities for other similar areas, though for the time being the Norwegian catches were already reaching the point where supply exceeded demand, to the detriment of price. At the same time the value of oil was further reduced with the beginning of the importation of vegetable oils and nuts, principally from West Africa. Faced with declining prices on the one hand, and with longer voyages in search of whales on the other, many firms gambled on a secure future by installing equipment for the more efficient utilisation of the same number of whales rather than by increasing their catches. Whaling had always been an extremely wasteful exercise by modern standards. Only the blubber and baleen had been taken, and the rest of the carcass left to rot, thought the value of whale refuse as manure had been recognised since the eighteenth century. It was known that both bones and meat contained oil, but its extraction was beyond the capabilities of primitive ship-board try-works. Now that whales were once more processed ashore every part of the carcass could be worked up, with a consequent saving in whale-catchers' expenses and with some slight alleviation of the fairly rapid depletion of local whale stocks.

The move towards better and more powerful long-distance catchers, and the growing expenses of more sophisticated land stations, had a most important effect on whaling. Such large scale investment was beyond the scope of the peasant-type bottlenose catchers, and ultimately of some of those who followed Svend Foyn into the industry with their steam-catchers. They might co-operate to build a processing plant in one or other of the Norwegian whaling ports – Tønsberg, Larvik and Sandefjord – but more usually there was an integration of the trade and production functions as the major purchasers of whale oil provided the capital for what was rapidly becoming "big business." Thus Britain was drawn inexorably into the new whaling trade, not because of her expertise – which was irrelevant – but because she was one of the chief markets for whale oil and the chief source of money. For the third time the British set about whaling as a foreign art, employing foreign harpooners; and once more it was not long before the British dominated the commercial side of whaling. This final stage of British whaling was to be the grandest stage of all.

II

The first British firm to become involved in modern whaling – and the greatest in the history of the industry – was Salvesen of Leith, though a purist might argue that, at least initially, the firm was Norwegian. It represents, in fact, a merging of British and Norwegian interests that was not uncommon after 1900. Christian Salvesen had come to Leith from Norway in 1851 to establish a shipping agency for the Scottish-Norwegian trade.[6] In the 1860s he also opened an agency for Norwegian whale oil which is reputed to have pioneered the sale of Svend Foyn's oil, and by the 1880s he was a considerable importer of whale oil, not only for the Dundee jute mills, but also – and perhaps chiefly – for the west coast of Scotland, where a Glasgow branch office was set up in 1884. For the next twenty years Salvesen imported something of the order of 7000 barrels of whale oil per annum,[7] a total that was greater than the volume caught by Dundee whalers in the Arctic. The steadiness of the trade is, perhaps, a commentary on the activities – or non-activities of that port, but it also reflects the relative stagnation of the market, where whale oil was failing to find new uses, and also, to some extent, the beginnings of difficulties on the supply side. For some time in the 1880s Salvesen had been growing impatient with his Norwegian suppliers, but had been reluctant to commence whaling himself for fear of upsetting those suppliers. When in the 1890s the firm did become involved in a very small way it was by financing whaling companies run by their Norwegian relations. When, for reasons of finance and efficiency, the third of these proved unsuccessful, Christian Salvesen was finally persuaded by his son, Theodore, to take over the company and use the elements of its fleet in the Olna Whaling Company, set up in May 1904 under the control of Theodore Salvesen who, more than any other individual, was responsible for the growth and prosperity of modern British whaling. Here, at Olna, Salvesen enjoyed the same measure of success as the un-named station in Shetland which D'Arcy Thompson of the Scottish Fisheries Board visited in July 1904:[8]

> I have just seen enough whales to last me my lifetime. We
> visited a station last night where they had just caught fourteen

---

[6]Wray Vamplew, *Salvesen of Leith* (Edinburgh, 1975), 153-154.

[7]*Ibid.*, table 16, 274.

[8]*Ibid.*, 138-143; and R. D'A. Thompson, *D'Arcy Wentworth Thompson, the Scholar-Naturalist, 1860-1948* (London, 1958), 145.

and the great beasts were all lying piled up in a heap, sixty feet long or more every one of them. And this morning just after we had sailed, we met a steamer coming in with two more in tow.

The activities of the Olna Whaling Company clearly illustrate the changes that had taken place in northern whaling. The westward movement of Norwegian interests had brought them within British waters. The Norrona and Shetland Companies set up land stations in Ronas Voe in 1903, and the Alexandra Company at Colla Firth, the Bunaveneader company at Bunaveneader on the Isle of Harris, the Bernera Company near Stornaway, and the Olna Company in Olna Firth in 1904. From these places they caught straggling specimens of bottlenose, humpback, nordcapper, sperm and blue whales, and large quantities of sei and fin whales, chiefly to the north of the Shetlands, but also off the Hebrides. Between the years 1908 (when the Scottish Fishery Department began to keep statistics) and 1914, inclusive, no fewer than 2418 fin and 1283 sei whales were caught within the Scottish fishery districts,[9] a number which compares most favourably with the whales caught by Scottish vessels in the Arctic: Dundee and Peterhead each took a century to catch 4000 whales! Salvesen thus acquired a share in a promising fishery, and immediately set about building the most efficient fleet and station their very considerable financial resources could buy. By 1908 the Olna-based whale-catchers were making over 200 fishing trips in a season lasting about four months, and the factory was using every part of the carcass.[10]

Olna, vividly described by F.V. Morley in the 1920s[11] was a typical modern shore base. As the whales were brought in by their catchers they were winched up a ramp onto a large area known as the plan, where a combination of expert flensers and steam winches stripped off the blubber as the skin is peeled from a banana. While the carcass was then dragged along to make way for another whale in the flensing area, the blubber was fed through rotary cutters and, by conveyor belt, into cookers where it was reduced to No. 1 oil. The

---

[9]D'Arcy W. Thompson, *On Whales Landed at the Scottish Whaling Stations during the Years 1908-14 and 1920-27* (Glasgow, 1928), 4-5. This work contains a valuable survey of the development and working of the modern Scottish trade.

[10]*Ibid.*, 39.

[11]Morley and Hodgson, *Whaling North and South*, 11-12; and Vamplew, *Salvesen*, 143-146.

carcass was now set upon by the lemmers, or butchers, who stripped off the meat which was boiled under pressure to produce No. 3 oil. Salvesen had originally tried to market the meat fresh both in Britain and on the continent, and the failure to do so was one of the tragedies of modern whaling. Not only did it deny to whaling an additional income which would have been of the greatest importance to the trade in its later history; it also denied Europe an immense source of badly needed protein.

Perhaps the chief reason for the rejection of whale meat was simple prejudice on the part of consumers. Although meat produced by shore stations was eaten in the Faroes, Japan and, to a lesser extent, in Norway, it had no part in British culture. Generations of British whalermen had rejected the stinking, decaying carcass as a nuisance to be got rid of as rapidly as possible, and no-one who ever smelt Olna was likely to look forward with enthusiasm to whale steaks. Now that whale meat could be produced as fresh as any meat from a slaughterhouse – which is no fairly palace! – its own characteristics unfortunately did little to counterbalance the prejudice. The high level of myoglobin required to carry oxygen for the long dives made the flesh very dark in colour, with a naturally high blood content and a slight "iron" taste. Moreover, while the taste was not unlike that of beef or venison, whale meat did have a unique component – trimethylamine – derived from its krill diet, which was not found in any "normal" meats and which may have been responsible for a distinctive flavour which many people found unpalatable.[12] There was also a tendency to toughness that required careful cooking and an equally careful selection of the part of the whale from which the meat was taken in order to avoid "oily" and "bone" taste. However, it must be admitted that there were also serious problems on the production side. Because of the insulating properties of the blubber, autolysis and bacterial action ruined the meat within twelve hours of death unless the body wall was cut; and bacterial action was frequently accelerated by the internal havoc wrought by exploding harpoons. Nor was it easy to market the meat in its raw state. Whaling stations were not adjacent to markets, and the quality of the meat was quickly affected by the degeneration of the oil contained in it, varying from around five percent in a lean male to thirty percent in a heavily pregnant female. The alternative to fresh marketing, the setting up of costly canning plant, did not seem to be financially justified.

Had the market proved suitable, no doubt some of the problems would have been overcome – as they were in Japan – and enthusiasm for meat production and processing would have been engendered. But for Salvesen there

---

[12]R.A. Lawrie, *Meat Science* (2nd ed., Oxford, 1974), 334-339.

was no point in it and the marketing of meat ceased. Instead, the boiled meat, from which the oil had been extracted, was ground into a meat meal of which Theodore Salvesen was justly proud. It was, he told the Royal Society of Arts, made "exclusively from absolutely from fresh whale flesh, the best parts only being used; this is a most nutritious and wholesome foodstuff, containing about 79 per cent protein."[13] It went chiefly into animal feedstuffs, and this was probably the best solution in view of contemporary technology. Experiments at the Reading Dairy Research Institute in 1925 showed, for instance, that it took 4.8 lbs. of "dry feed" to produce one lb. of pig meat, but only 2.3 lbs. if 7½ percent of whale meat meal was added, and only 1.9 lbs. if 7½ percent of whale liver "flakes" was added.[14] Even so there was very little profit to be made out of the whale-based Gromax marketed by Lever Brothers in the late 1920s.

The removal of the blubber and best meat was by no means the end of the operations. The viscera were usually thrown away, but the remainder of the carcass was reduced to manageable pieces by steam saw, the refuse being boiled down to make No. 4 oil, and then ground, with a certain amount of bone, to make whale guano containing roughly 8.5 percent ammonia and twenty-one percent phosphate. The bones, which are porous and contain a large quantity of oil, were boiled under steam pressure to give No. 3 oil at Olna, though other companies later treated it as No. 2 oil because of its superior quality.[15] (Some of the finest of all whale oil comes form specific bones – usually the jaw – of certain of the smaller whales.) The residue of the bones after boiling was then ground and dehydrated to form a bonemeal containing four percent ammonia and fifty percent phosphate. In fact the only part of the carcass that was wasted was the whalebone. In the Greenland Right whale it was worth over £2500 a ton when Olna opened, whereas that from a blue or fin whale was worth a mere £50 and was not worth the effort involved in preparing it.

Theodore Salvesen was enthusiastic about his whaling venture – though it was only a minor part of the parent company's large commercial empire[16] – and the success of Olna was the signal for expansion. Another station was soon

---

[13]T.E. Salvesen, "The Whaling Industry of Today," *Journal of the Royal Society of Arts*, LX (1912), 521.

[14]Unilever Archive, Blackfriar's House, London, File 8104/TT3793, H.R. Greenhalgh to Lord Leverhulme, 19 January 1925.

[15]Morley and Hodgson, *Whaling North and South*, 146.

[16]Vamplew, *Salvesen*, part I, is a full account of Salvesen's other activities.

opened at Thorsvig in Faroes, and in 1906 a third was opened at Hellisfjord in Iceland. By then the firm was a major whaling company with ten catchers, able to hold its own against its more experienced Norwegian rivals and catching almost eighty percent of the oil which Salvesen sold on the British market.[17] Between 1904 and 1906 the output of oil from Olna was doubled, while in the years 1905-1910 that station caught an average of 280 whales yielding 1087 tons of oil, the Thorsvig station caught ninety-seven yielding 313 tons, and the Hellisfjord station (in four years) caught ninety-six yielding 590 tons.[18] The overall position was not, however, particularly promising. Total receipts had risen until 1907 and then slipped, averaging £60,600 for 1905-1909 and £46,898 for 1909-1914, and reflecting a substantial fall in the number of whales caught after 1909.[19] The Norwegian steam-catchers had offered prosperity through the exploitation of new species of whales in very confined waters, but those new species were no less vulnerable than the old, and it could only be a matter of time before the awful toll produced a drastic reduction in the number of whales visiting European waters where, in any case, the existence of stations was always a little precarious because of the implacable hostility exhibited by local fishermen, for whose commercial shortcomings they were the current popular excuse.[20]

---

[17]*Ibid.*, 149.

[18]The modern whaling trade broke with tradition by measuring its oil in tons of 2240 lbs. (with six barrels to the ton). The old tun measure varied with the temperature. At the standard allowance of 7.5 lbs. to the gallon, a tun weighed 1890 lbs., though at 60°F, it actually weighted 1934 lbs. The modern ton was therefore considerably more than the old tun, and this should be borne in mind when making comparisons over time. The issue appears sometimes to be confused because the old tun was often spelled ton. In practise there is no confusion: in the old industry the tun/ton was *always* a volume measure; in the modern industry it is always a modern ton, though for the sake of convenience the oil might be counted in barrels, as it was by the Norwegians who drew up the *International Whaling Statistics*.

[19]Information from Wray Vamplew; and Vamplew, *Salvesen*, table 30, 285.

[20]See, for example, the many complaints by fishermen in Great Britain, Parliament, House of Commons, *Parliamentary Papers (BPP)* (2138), XLII, 449, Minutes of Evidence of the Departmental Committee on Whaling and Whale Curing in the North of Scotland. Since the evidence was somewhat emotional and largely irrelevant the Committee reported in favour of allowing whaling to continue on condition that all the carcass was disposed of.

Chapter 10
New Whaling Areas

I

By 1909 it was evident that no significant increase was to be expected in the output of the European whaling stations, which were already past their prime; and in their search for more oil the Norwegians spread outwards beyond the Hebrides towards the bay stations of the old Southern Fishery, along the coast of South Africa and Australia. The steam whale-catchers that chased rorquals in European waters could chase them equally well in other areas where they had remained unmolested during the vast slaughter of Right and sperm whales. Above all, they could move with relative ease in the colder waters of the Antarctic where the greatest concentrations of rorquals were to be found. For all their daring, the Southern whalers had made no impression whatever on the whale stocks in this area, chiefly because the climate was poor and land bases were too isolated for old-fashioned pelagic whaling.

Although a new phase of southern whaling was technically possible in the areas of habitation, there were formidable obstacles that deterred most companies from considering fishing in Antarctic waters, and left them watching each other to see who would make the first move and the first losses. The greatest problem was distance. Whale-catchers had no room for try-works and could not possibly carry either blubber or oil. They could not even carry enough coal to get themselves down to the Antarctic, let alone for a round trip and a fishing expedition. The whole point of the catchers was that they were tied to a land base, but there was no inhabited territory – and some people thought no inhabitable territory – where the whales congregated in the cold waters in which the greatest concentration of krill was to be found. Since there was neither food nor fuel there, whaling expeditions in the Antarctic called for a huge transport operation involving both supplies and oil. Above all, there must be a very substantial base capable of working up the whales, catering for the men, and servicing the catchers.

In simple human terms there was the formidable task of attracting labour to the cold and dreary isolation of the deep south. This was quite a different proposition from persuading Norwegians to visit the Shetlands for three or four months in the year, and a firm that was not prepared to pay its men relatively good wages might expect constant labour troubles. Here, as in everything else, the costs involved in southern whaling were likely to be very much higher than in the recent phase of successful northern whaling, and businessmen were faced with new orders of magnitude when making their investment decisions.

The question exercising entrepreneurs' minds at least until 1906 was whether the necessarily large expenditure anticipated in southern whaling could ever be repaid out of profits on oil which was not fetching a high price and which, given a relatively stagnant and inelastic market, would only decline further in price if enough was caught to cover costs in the south. It was a theoretical problem shared at some time or other by most primary produce trades: at what stage in a faltering source of supply should a more expensive source be cultivated? Given competition in a free market, most men prefer to wait for a pronounced advance in demand sufficient to raise prices in general to an economic level. Expeditions in the 1890s which revealed the potential of Antarctic whaling had therefore produced no immediate results, and members of the Dundee expedition of 1892/1893 received a far from enthusiastic reception at a meeting of "interested parties" in Leith. An expedition from Hamburg led by C.A. Larsen, which actually met the Dundee expedition of 1892/1893 received a far from enthusiastic reception at a meeting of "interested parties" in Leith. An expedition from Hamburg led by C.A. Larsen, which actually met the Dundee expedition in the Antarctic and confirmed its report, was no more successful in finding support among Norwegian whaling interests. The attractions of long distance whaling were still very weak, and serious commercial interest in the Antarctic only really began when Larsen, shipwrecked on a scientific expedition in 1903, persuaded his Argentinian rescuers and hosts to back him by forming the Compañía Argentina de Pesca, of which he became whaling manager. He returned to Norway and from there arrived in South Georgia in November 1904 with two sailing ships and a steam-catcher, and built the first Antarctic Station, for Argentina, in a pre-selected bay which he called Grytviken.

Grytviken bay was aswarm with humpback whales, and a prodigal slaughter began. Only the best blubber was boiled in an attempt to make the most money, but the financial returns were far short of those forecast by Larsen. As the sceptics had warned, even a slight increase in the supply of oil (from Salvesen in the north as well as Larsen in the south) was sufficient to reduce its price to the lowest point for decades and probably, in real terms, to the lowest it had ever been (see appendix 10). Although it is by no means certain whether Larsen should be praised for his foresight or blamed for his obstinacy in continuing a losing game, his gamble paid off in the end because the oil crisis of 1906 pushed the price up to a point where his company made very ample profits. Once the future of the market was assured, Larsen's enterprise indicated the most promising line of development for the industry, and the Antarctic whale fishery was born.

Most of the nineteen firms that established themselves in the Antarctic before 1914 were Norwegian, with no fewer than eight of them based on Sandefjord, but very few of the five dozen Norwegian whaling firms could find the sort of capital required for southern whaling. Forward investment was essential, and inventory costs were immense. The Norwegians knew that skill alone would not bring success, and the British knew that skill could be bought. The practical compromise was, as we have seen, the marriage of British resources and Norwegian labour, and this was to be the nature of "British" whaling for the rest of its life. With its secure markets and ample resource "British" whaling moved ahead, eventually accounting for over half the world total of whales, and reviving memories of the great days of the past.

II

The new phase of whaling began, for Britain, in 1908 with the formation of Salvesen's New Whaling Company. Salvesen had intended setting up a base in South Georgia, but were prevented from doing so by the Colonial Office. The area opened up by Larsen could, in fact, only be fished from shore bases on British territory, and from the beginning the Colonial Office endeavoured to control the slaughter by limiting the number of licences for shore bases and by fixing certain restrictions on those to whom they were granted. Since the Colonial Office felt no obligation to further British interests, it took the first of a whole series of "anti-British" decisions (some of which were very serious indeed) when it refused to allow Salvesen to fish from South Georgia, where the Norwegians were already well established. As a result Salvesen were forced to begin building a station in the West Falklands, a much inferior position. Here, in January 1909, was brought ashore the first whale caught in the southern hemisphere by a British company in modern times.[1]

The incongruity of a British territory admitting foreigners and excluding Britons, whatever abstract principles were involved, was unlikely to gain general sympathy in the immediate prewar years, and in fact Salvesen were allowed to establish themselves in South Georgia in 1909. There, on the north of the island, sheltered from the worst of the "Roaring Forties," they built a modern Smeerenberg, beginning in November 1909 and periodically extending and improving until it was finally abandoned to the elements in the 1960s. The base was called Leith Harbour, a permanent reminder of the port of ownership, though it never became a "home from home" for Leith men: Norwegian was the "official" language.

---

[1] W. Vamplew, *Salvesen of Leith* (Edinburgh, 1975), 152.

Leith Harbour was opened in 1910 and was immediately successful, its four catchers working chiefly among the humpback whales which were more economical to work up than the smaller sei whales predominating around the Falklands. In the following year work began on a second British base at Prince Olaf's Harbour, this time for a new firm, Southern Whaling and Sealing Company of North Shields. Southern Whaling, incorporated in August 1911 with a capital of £60,000, was more or less a side-line of the very important trawler-owning and -broking firm of Irvin and Johnson, which operated in Aberdeen, Peterhead, North Shields and Great Yarmouth, and which also had interests, in company with Sir David Graaf, in fishing and whaling in South Africa. In 1913 the capital was increased to £100,000, of which £90,000 was paid up, but this was only a notional sum, since £125,000 was spent on equipping Prince Olaf's Harbour with sixty digesters and boilers, fifteen clearing and storage tanks, an engineering shop, an electricity plant, and accommodation for 250 to 300 men.[2]

How long these land stations would remain productive was a matter for conjecture in the years before the Great War. When in 1912 Theodore Salvesen delivered to the royal Society of Arts the lecture which was later said to have been the first indication to the general public of the changes taking place in whaling, he was told by a member of the audience, an old northern whaling man, "that they had better make hay while the sun shone, as if seven whalers were getting 7000 whales in one spot, it would not be very long before the southern whale fishery would follow the northern whale fishery, and the whales would practically disappear from the sea."[3] It was an unnecessary warning to Salvesen, who was always anxious to avoid exploitation leading to exhaustion, but not all firms – particularly the Norwegian ones – shared his concern, and he was prepared to admit that economics did not always favour efficiency at this stage of the game:[4]

The distance from the markets, with the consequent expense
of bringing to the factory the stores necessary for reducing the

---

[2]Unilever Archive, Blackfriar's House, London, SEC/1304, papers relating to Southern Whaling Company, 1919-1926; and Memorandum of Association of Southern Whaling Co. (copy in Palm Line office, United Africa Company).

[3]T.E. Salvesen, "The Whaling Industry of Today," *Journal of the Royal Society of Arts*, LX (1912), 523.

[4]*Ibid.*, 519.

carcass and the extra freightage incurred in conveying the finished products to the markets, make it questionable whether it is a profitable business to reduce more than the blubber in such places as the South Atlantic; indeed, the work can only be conducted under any circumstances when the products are saleable at high prices.

III

Although the Colonial Office restricted the number of "expeditions" in South Georgia, and the number of catchers which each might employ, a heavy toll was taken of the most easily available whales in the bays, and catchers were forced to go further in search of them until they reached a limit beyond which it was impossible to go. While there was no question of South Georgia waters being fished out, the taking of whales gradually became less easy and consequently more expensive. New companies were therefore wise to go elsewhere, and six of the seven set up in 1910-1911 chose to operate from the South Shetlands. In doing so they emphasized a new departure in whaling. The waters around the Shetlands were equally good for fishing, but the islands themselves were markedly inferior to South Georgia. They were, according to an official photographer with a later expedition, "little more than jagged rocks, ice and snow covered, rising out of the sea, and offering small hospitality in the way of harbourage. No vegetation of any kind can be seen, only turbulent sea and ice-covered rock."[5] They were not suitable for land bases, so the bases took to the sea.

So great was the expense and difficulty associated with land bases that the Norwegians had already turned to a cheaper and more flexible alternative: the old merchantman of two or three thousand tons, equipped with rudimentary try-works and anchored in the fjords of South Georgia. Actually the first floating factories were too small and their try-works too primitive for the adequate working up of carcasses, so that these vessels represented a retrograde step in the fight against waste which the Colonial Office was waging in the Antarctic. Nonetheless, expansion into the South Shetland area would have been impossible without them, while the rapid changes in the Antarctic gave these small and poorly converted vessels a life of only a few seasons.

The first Norwegian factory ships went south in 1905; the first British vessels in 1911 for the Antarctic summer season of 1911/1912. One of them, with two attendant catchers, was equipped by Southern Whaling in advance of

---

[5]F.V. Morley and J.S. Hodgson, *Whaling North and South* (London, 1927), 137.

the completion of their Prince Olaf's Harbour station. The other two, with three catchers, were equipped by Salvesen to work together in an attempt to extract the maximum return from the carcasses, with *Neko* boiling the blubber and *Horatio* pressure-cooking the remainder of the carcass.[6] Already Theodore Salvesen was directing the firm towards a sophistication at sea to match their sophistication on shore, and so ensuring a prime place in the trade. However, sophistication alone was not enough to ensure economic viability, and again the old situation reappeared: the more efficient firms could end up making lower profits than their less scrupulous rivals, and in any case an increase in efficiency would over-tax the market.

This last point became increasingly apparent as Salvesen's profits in 1910/1911 became losses in 1911/1912 and 1912/1913,[7] though their production had increased by eighteen percent, largely as a result of the employment of the factory ships around the South Shetlands. One the one hand the world supply of whale oil was increasing rapidly with the new catching techniques and new whaling areas. On the other, the major buyers of whale oil began to form a "pool," which become effective in 1913, when oil prices were already very low. The producers were therefore in a situation where increased output for individual firms was essential for survival and yet in the long run ruinous, unless some new outlet for whale oil could be found.

There appeared to be two possible solutions to the problem. The first was the bankruptcy of the smaller and supposedly inefficient Norwegian firms, an eventuality eagerly awaited by Salvesen, who regarded such firms as a drag on the trade. A second solution was a producers' pool to counter the consumes' pool. In 1914 the larger producers were moving towards such a pool, though its implementation was difficult because there were many small firms struggling for survival. In the event, all that happened was that the larger companies attempted to starve the market, and this was the position when war began, and natural scarcity drove prices to a more acceptable level.

The early years of the First World War were as difficult for whaling as for most other trades, and the same kind of contradictions appeared in official policy. Whale oil was of crucial importance, not only as a potential food, but also as the principal source of glycerol, a vital constituent of explosives which was obtained in the residue from soap-making when the fatty acids were turned into soap. As existing stocks of oil were used up (at first they were plentiful, having been diverted from foreign markets in 1914), the government relaxed the

---

[6]W. Vamplew, *Salvesen of Leith* (Edinburgh, 1975), 156 ff.

[7]*Ibid.*, table 20, 276.

regulations which had previously hampered British operations in the Antarctic, and encouraged the two British companies to increase their catches. Despite almost continuous difficulties over supplies, fuel, transport and men, the war presented the opportunity for the British companies to consolidate their position in the absence of effective Norwegian competition. Salvesen were able to increase their catchers to sixteen by 1917/1918, and their catch from 11,333 tons in 1913/1914 to 14,000 in 1917/1918, while Southern Whaling operated six catchers during the war and brought home 4600 tons of oil in 1917/1918.[8] Above all, the firms continued during and immediately after the war to equip themselves with the latest and best catchers and equipment that stood them in good stead when competition revived.

---

[8]*Ibid.*, table 31, 287; and Unilever, SEC/1304, Unilever Archive, S.W. Co. Balance Sheet, 30 November 1918.

Chapter 11
Advances in Oil Technology

The rapid expansion of whaling in the decade before the First World War occurred because, after a century in which whale oil had been gradually ousted from its traditional uses, modern science gave it a new lease of life. Whale oil creased to be an elementary product, fit only for burning and other lowly uses, and became, under the influence of chemical technology, a multi-purpose raw material for modern industry. As a consequence whaling was faced with quite unprecedented demands for oil (output, for instance, rose from 47,387 tons in 1909/1910 to 134,000 in 1913/1914)[1] and, like its product, was transformed out of all recognition. In fact modern whaling owed its origin less to Svend Foyn, who invented the techniques, than to the 1906 crisis in the world supply of fat, which provided the incentive for their wide-spread adoption.

The crisis of 1906 occurred chiefly because the production of animal fats failed to keep pace with the growth of the modern soap industry. Moreover, margarine, which was derived from the same basic ingredient, had been rapidly gaining in popularity since its introduction in the 1870s, and had become a staple item in working class diets in Britain, Germany and Scandinavia. Since it was the more valuable product, its manufacturers were able to overbid the soap-makers for the best quality raw materials, and oil chemists, especially in Germany, set to work to find acceptable substitutes for animal fat.[2] For the first time for centuries the soapmakers thought in terms of using whale oil as a raw material, although in its natural form it was suitable only for certain industrial soft soaps.

The new methods of whaling outlined above had already brought about a spectacular improvement in the quality of the oil itself. That whale oil had unpleasant characteristics was common knowledge, and Greenland yards and

---

[1]*International Whaling Statistics (IWS)* (Oslo, 1914), 22.

[2]"The Soap maker has no chance against the Butterine maker. The Soapmaker gets £24 a ton for soap containing 63 per cent of fatty acids and the margarine maker gets £60 a ton for 85 per cent fatty acids...there is practically no good oil or fat but what the margarine maker can make into excellent food." Sir William Lever, 1910, quoted in C. Wilson, *The History of Unilever. A Study in Economic Growth and Social Change* (2 vols., London, 1954), I, 117. For a general survey of margarine raw materials, see J.H. Van Stuyvenberg (ed.), *Margarine: An Economic, Social and Scientific History, 1869-1969* (Liverpool, 1969), chapter 2.

whaling ships had been notoriously offensive. What was not commonly realised was that pure, fresh whale oil (produced from mammal fat, not from fishes!) was no more offensive than port or beef dripping. Scoresby had pointed this out in 1820, when he attributed the objectionable qualities of whale oil to the fact that "when putrefaction commences, a small portion of the blood contained in the blubber is probably combined in the oil, and the animal fibre, in considerable quantity, is dissolved in it."[3] With the beginning of modern whaling, the animals were in general rendered within hours of death and before the degeneration of the oil had reached an undesirable level. There was therefore no reason, beyond prejudice against "fish" oil, why whale oil should not be used as a substitute for any good quality edible oil with similar characteristics, though prejudice took a long time to overcome.

No matter what is quality, the use of whale *oil* was not likely to grow substantially when the chief demand of the soap and margarine makers was for *fat*. The crucial stimulus to modern whaling was therefore the discovery of the process of hydrogenation. It had been known for some considerable time that oils and fats - whether of animal or vegetable origin - are basically similar in composition. They are essentially glycerides, that is esters - or compounds - of various fatty acids and the trihydric alcohol glycerol (glycerine) together with a number of other alcohols - including vitamins A and D - and with a tiny proportion of free fatty acids which are not combined with alcohol.[4] The acids consist of an "acidic" element on the end of a chain of carbon atoms (varying in number with the type of acid) each of which has two arms to which hydrogen atoms are, or can be, linked. Acids which have most of the linkages filled with hydrogen are "saturated" and solid; acids with hydrogen atoms wanting are "unsaturated" and liquid. A mixture with a preponderance of unsaturated acids will therefore be an oil, and one with saturated acids predominating will be fat. The theoretical answer to the fat shortage was simple: oil could be turned into fat by saturating its unsaturated acids with hydrogen, with the degree of hardness being determined by the extent to which saturation was allowed to progress. Unfortunately the practical business of how to do it was not so easily arrived at, and it was not until 1902/1903 that Wilhelm Normann's process of hydrogenation with a nickel catalyst was patented, though not immediately exploited because of technical difficulties. In the following years various

---

[3]W. Scoresby, *An Account of the Arctic Regions, with a History and Description of the Northern Whale Fishery* (2 vols., Edinburgh, 1820), II, 411.

[4]T.P. Hilditch, *The Industrial Chemistry of the Fats and Waxes* (London, 1927; 2nd ed., London, 1941), 144 and 174-175.

experiments in both Europe and the USA produced 183 patents – fifty-one of them in Britain – perfecting the process, and the principal fat consumers began the construction of what were normally called "hardening" plants. On the eve of the First World War there were about a dozen such plants in Europe and Britain, and the first text-book on hydrogenation had appeared.

Almost any oil can be hardened, but it will carry over into the fatty stage the characteristics inherent in its acid mix. There were therefore problems of oil chemistry as well as technology in the early days of hydrogenation, and endless experiments were necessary before the process was entirely reliable or fully understood. Whale oil consists largely of acids with eighteen carbon atoms, and these happen to be suitable for soap-making. On the other hand there were difficulties over odour and fastness of colour. While in theory the odour was removed in the hydrogenation and refining processes, in fact hardened whale oil had a tendency to "revert" with the passage of time. Hydrogenation was in practise aimed at the bulk of the acids and was rarely continued until every particle of every acid was saturated, with the result that the remaining unsaturated acids could absorb oxygen and turn rancid. Even without reversion, soap made from whale oil was said to have a musty smell, while a more fundamental objection was raised against its poor lathering qualities and against its general hardness. As late as 1912 scientists were arguing that hardened whale oil had no future, or only a limited future, in soapmaking;[5] and practical men such as Sir William Lever, while using it in "Lifebuoy," where any possible odour would be hidden by carbolic, would not permit its use in quality soaps: he "would not play with goodwill articles such as Sunlight, Hudson's and Lux, or we might find ourselves before we realised it robbed of the fruits of years of advertising and of the large amounts expended for goodwill."[6] Thus for technical reasons the amount of hardened whale oil did not generally exceed a quarter of the total acid base of soaps, even when processing was improved in the 1920s, though it did become a favourite base for soap powders.

It has always been something of a paradox to laymen, as it was to Lever Brothers' directors before 1914, that hardened whale oil that was not good enough for soap was almost perfect for margarine. Although again there were difficulties over its perishable nature, its mix of acids provided a hard fat

---

[5]C. Ellis, *The Hydrogenation of Oils* (London, 1914), 172-175.

[6]Quoted in Wilson, *History of Unilever*, II, 130.

that was of roughly the same plasticity and digestibility as butter.[7] Whale oil thus became the salvation of margarine as a cheap food, but it was not adopted easily. European agricultural and dairying interests, which had eagerly welcomed the rising tallow prices that threatened both margarine and soap, raised every possible objection to cheap whale oil. They launched a great publicity campaign in which a string of scientists talked of "cadaver fats," "half-rotten whales," "chemically-changed fish oil" and the need for "pure food" regulations. Indeed, so bad did the situation become that, in order to divert attacks on the industry, the Duesseldorfer Margarine Zeitschrift suggested a legal prohibition on the use of whale oil for edible purposes in Germany; and because of the German press campaign Van den Bergh and Jurgens announced in 1913 their intention not to use whale oil in margarine.[8]

Although for technical, commercial and emotional reasons oil was not openly adopted for soap or margarine on any very large scale before the Great War, manufacturers gradually equipped themselves to use it. One of the largest British soap-makers, Crosfield of Warrington, bought the Normann patent and by 1909 were capable of producing a hundred tons of hardened fat weekly. Other manufacturers were less enthusiastic until 1911, when Crosfield were bought by Brunner-Mond, the major alkali producers, who were eager to secure their outlet in the soap trade by vertical integration. Faced with a potential monopoly situation in two raw materials, Lever was stung into action, buying the rival Testrup hardening patent in 1912, defeating the Normann patent in the law courts. and preparing his own hardening plant. On a more immediately practical level, Lever Brothers also bought a half share in a Norwegian firm – De Nordiske Fabriker (De-No-Fa) – which had been set up to harden whale oil in that country and was already the leading European producer. Not to be outdone Brunner-Mond, having failed to reach agreement with Lever Brothers over soap and alkali production, set up Hydrogenators Limited at the end of 1913 to supply hardened oil to consumers outside the Lever "family."

The processing of whale oil had thus become big business. Hydrogenation was expensive and complicated, involving both the treatment of the oil and the production of the hydrogen. When Ellis produced his textbook on hydrogenation in 1914 he subtitled it "The Generation of Hydrogen," and

---

[7]A.J.C. Anderson and P.N. Williams, *Margarine* (2nd ed., Oxford, 1965), 8-9 and 48-49.

[8]Ellis, *Hydrogenation*, 150-152; and Unilever Archive, Blackfriar's House, London, MDMJ, 14 October 1913.

almost half the book was devoted to this topic after an introduction entitled "The hydrogen problem in oil hardening." It took about 2800 cubic feet of hydrogen to harden a ton of oil, and almost inevitably the new industry settled down in a small number of large hydrogen-making and hydrogenation plants associated with specific consumers of hardened oil. The result of the whaling trade was severe. Instead of facing a multitude of small purchasers, as they had done for centuries, the whaler owners were now faced with a handful of immensely wealthy and powerful firms which were almost all willing to work together for the greater good of the group. Already in 1912 Anton Jurgens had taken the initiative in suggesting the whale oil consumers' pool (Jurgens and Van den Bergh in Western Europe, Schicht in Central Europe, and Crosfield, Watson and Lever Brothers in Britain), with the largest share going to the giant Lever concern for soapmaking. Moreover, large consumers used to mass production and constant runs wanted security of supplies, and this led the whaling trade fairly rapidly towards a market situation involving forward purchasing, contractual obligations and quality control. Whaling became, in effect, an adjunct of the margarine and soap industries by 1914, and it remained to be seen how long it would survive in independent hands. As early as 1911 Anton Jurgens had begun buying minority holdings in Norwegian whaling companies gand by 1913 was known by the wits of Rotterdam as the "Prince of Whales."[9]

In view of subsequent developments, the war period was more notable for the shifting attitudes of consumers than for the advantages accruing to the producers. As unprecedented austerity spread across Europe, "fishiness" diminished with necessity and necessity overcame prejudice. Whale oil was accepted – at least by the manufacturers – as a raw material in its own right rather than as a substitute for better things, and the earlier competition and intrigue associated with the supply of fats now turned to the supply of oil, with the three major British soap firms hotly disputing the division of whale oil stocks which the government now controlled. Sir William Lever was particularly annoyed at what he regarded as the unfair – and politically influenced – share (forty percent) which was allocated to his firm,[10] and as supplies eased in 1916/1917 he began buying as much oil as possible. He had also found that Lever Brothers could not harden oil fast enough, having previously relied heavily on De-No-Fa, and so extended their own hardening

---

[9]Quoted in Wilson, *History of Unilever*, II, 120. The widespread hostility to margarine among politically influential agricultural interests, and the consequent adverse legislation, is described in detail in Van Stuyvenberg (ed.), *Margarine*, chapter 7.

[10]Unilever LC/6104, W.H. Lever to C.C. Knowles, 16 September 1916.

plant.[11] This in turn encouraged still further investment in oil stocks as a safeguard against competitors and also as a hedge against price rises expected after the war, when oil stocks might be diverted to central Europe where prices were now much higher and where, in the prewar years, almost half of Europe's margarine had been made.[12]

By the end of the war, therefore, Lever Brothers were heavily committed to the use of whale oil, and the vast stocks which they had accumulated pushed them further in this direction. Efforts were made to maximise whale oil consumption throughout the Lever enterprises to such an extent that in 1920 the technical people were complaining that the toilet soaps were being harmed, and even in the cheaper grades they wished to use more palm oil and less whale oil.[13] Nevertheless, Lever ordered that the stocks must be used up: "Unless we deal energetically with the Whale Oil position we shall never get our stocks down, and, apart from which, by using the Whale Oil we help our finances; by buying Acid Oils outside we do not help them."[14] Although such intensive usage did not continue, the Lever Brothers Board was told in 1922 that "we cannot make both ends meet without whale oil,"[15] and in order to safeguard its position the firm continued to hold heavy stocks of whale oil throughout the interwar period, to the growing annoyance of the margarine makers, who in 1929 formally requested that Lever Brothers should stop using whale oil in soap, since almost any vegetable oil would do for soap, whereas whale oil was better for margarine.[16]

The growing market for margarine was to be of decisive importance to whaling in the postwar years. The manufacture of margarine in England and Scotland – but not in Ireland – exceeded the manufacture of butter long before the war, while imports almost doubled between 1914 and 1916, from 1.5 million

---

[11]Unilever LC/7332, Lever to J.L. Buchanan, 26 March 1916.

[12]Unilever LC/7608, Lever to E. Cooper, 3 October 1916.

[13]Unilever Policy Committee Minutes, 22 November 1920.

[14]Unilever LC/162, W.H. Lever to S. Cooper, 11 March 1921.

[15]Unilever MDMJ, 12 November 1922.

[16]Unilever Managing Director's Conference (MDC), 17 October 1929.

to 2.8 million cwt.[17] Imported margarine from Jurgens and Van den Bergh which was sold in most of the multiple grocers was, however, vulnerable to enemy action, and since only the Maypole Dairy Company made significant amounts in Britain, the government asked Lever, who had been toying with the idea, to go into the margarine business. As a result Lever Brothers set up Planter's Margarine Company in 1914 with their soap rivals Watsons of Leeds, and though at first it was fearsome stuff which Lever's own servants refused to eat, the business expanded as butter supplies diminished and the quality of margarine in general improved. In 1915 Planter's were turning out 13,372 tons; by 1917, partly through buying a Maypole factory, they were producing 27,235 tons and were building a new factory at Bromborough which was ready just before the Armistice in 1918.[18] Other firms had also entered what appeared to be a promising industry.

It is not clear how far these wartime margarines used whale oil, not least because their manufacturers were sufficiently frightened of consumer prejudice to hide the fact that they were using it. Even the textbooks on oil technology are suitably vague. In 1919, for instance, G. Martin, the head of the research department of the CWS, produced his practical handbook *Oils, Fats and Waxes*, in which he referred to the increasing use of hardened whale oil in margarine in his chapter on hydrogenation; but in his chapter on margarine he made no reference whatever to whale oil. On a commercial level, as late as December 1926 Lever Brother's chairman could veto an innocuous reference to the firm's involvement in whaling (for a cigarette card!) with the question: "is it not counter to Lever Brothers' policy to approve any wide dissemination of the suggestion that whale oil and Lever soaps and food products have an association?" He suggested a reference to the use of whale products "in the manufacture of cattle foods and allied products," but even that was through a little risky.[19] In the following year Professor Hilditch, the country's leading expert on oils, condemned the prejudice which still operated in Britain, though it had long since disappeared on the Continent:[20]

---

[17]G. Martin, *Animal and Vegetable Oils, Fats and Waxes* (London, 1920), 176-178.

[18]Wilson, *History of Unilever*, I, 227-233.

[19]Unilever SEC/1304, I. Cooper to F.V. Fildes, 9 December 1926.

[20]Hilditch, *Industrial Chemistry*, 298.

Since raw No. 1 grade whale oil, produced in modern factory ships, is one of the cleanest crude fatty oils available technically, and is superior in colour and free acidity to many of the corresponding raw vegetable fatty oils destined for use in margarine, there can be no valid objection to its use on hygienic grounds.

The growing popularity of margarine probably owed less to the decline of prejudice than it did to the rise of unemployment and to the improvement in margarine itself. Improvements in the hardening process in 1924 encouraged the use of whale oil and brought down costs, while by 1927 advances in oil technology were such that oils of various sorts were broadly interchangeable. Finally, in 1929 the scientists of Unilever, the new combine of Lever Brothers and the Margarine Union, came up with a process which gave a hardened whale oil that was sufficiently soft. (i.e., it had a melting point which was only 28-32°C) for a margarine to be made almost entirely of it.[21] In that year the total European production of margarine was around 1,050,000 tons, compared with 520,000 in 1913,[22] and the advance in the demand for oils and fats on this scale had a favourable effect on the whaling trade, whether or not whale oil was directly involved in the manufacture of margarine in Britain.

One brief but important note should be added. This chapter has dealt exclusively with *whale oil*, which was chemically suitable for hardening for edible or soapmaking purposes. *Sperm oil*, with its quite different composition (see 48-49), was completely unsuitable for these purposes, and though a certain measure of demand remained among consumers interested in its waxy qualities, it did not attract the attention of large-scale whaling until further developments in oil chemistry and technology took place in the 1950s. As a result the sperm whale was largely ignored, and the major effort of European whaling was directed towards the baleen whales in the Antarctic regions.

---

[21]Wilson, *History of Unilever*, II, 317.

[22]Anderson and Williams, *Margarine*, 18.

Chapter 12
Expanding Fleets and the New Fishing Grounds, 1919-1920

I

British whaling in the interwar period cannot be understood, or adequately described, in terms solely of national production or national consumption. The continuation of Anglo-Norwegian rivalry ensured the international nature of the industry, in which the desire to maximise profits under a system of very free competition led to most complicated investment decisions based on factors that were very largely beyond the control of the British firms, or indeed, of any firm. There had always been international competition in whaling, but never before had individual firms produced so much, or had so much capital at stake. The balancing of supply and demand in the producers' favour was by no means easy, and, as with other primary producers, whaler-owners were already moving dangerously close to over-production. At the same time the acceleration of technical change during the war ensured an international market for oil among soap and margarine producers, with the result that purely national needs had little effect on prices. Although British firms served their domestic market more than any other, the returns on their effort might be determined by marginal production in Norway or government purchasing policy in Germany. On the production side it will be necessary from time to time to set British whaling in the context of total whaling activity as recorded in the *International Whaling Statistics* compiled at the instigation of the Norwegian government. On the consumption side the historian is fortunate that the international market was increasingly dominated by one massive consumer – Lever Brothers/Unilever – whose needs and purchasing motivations are a good guide through the complexities of market forces between the wars.

It is worth pausing to consider aspects of the whale oil market between the wars which help to explain, if not justify, some of the difficulties eventually faced by whaling companies. Because of the precise seasonal nature of the trade, whale oil was unique in being possibly the only raw material – and certainly the only oil – of which the annual production come to market at one time. For the major consumers this had the advantage of enabling them to buy a year's supply within a brief period if they wished, so that any firm that could afford the very considerable inventory cost involved could secure its raw material against its rivals. In fact whale oil was the only oil of which huge quantities could be purchased at one time without upsetting the market, and this endeared it to consumers long after its technical advantages had declined relative to other oils. On the other hand, because sales were so concentrated, producers found that pricing was always something of a problem. There was no "long-term" price, as in tin or rubber, and since the "crop" varied from year to year, each set of negotiations was unique, with previous years' prices as little more than a general guide. It was therefore essential for both consumers and producers to know in advance roughly how much oil would result from a season's operations, so that they could play the old commercial game of holding back till the price was "right." Owners could only do this if they knew that the market would not shortly be flooded by rivals, and if they had some vague idea of expected world demand. It was for this reason, basically, that the Norwegian producers notified catches at regular intervals during the fishing to their Association, and why, in 1918/1919, a Norwegian delegation led by Rasmussen came to Britain looking for an agent to sell their oil in something approaching an orderly fashion. In Glasgow, which – because of a long tradition of refining – was still the major British market for whale oil, they reached an understanding with David Geddes and Son, established in 1868 as brokers in grain and mineral oil, who before the war had been the Scottish distributors of Anglo-American (later Esso) petroleum, and who from around 1900 had been major competitors of Salvesen in the sale of whale oil. From about 1919 David Geddes and Son were the lading brokers in the trade, moving to London in 1923/1924 and eventually handling between two-thirds and three-quarters of the world supply of whale oil, acting for almost all the independent producers, including Salvesen. However, while the sale of oil through Geddes simplified negotiations (especially since Geddes were fed with regular and frequent information of catches in progress, kept accurate records of stocks of unsold oil, and were acquainted with the anticipated requirements of all the major consumers), the entrepreneurial decisions remained with the producers. Geddes were selling agents who could put purchasers in touch with sellers, not representatives of the sellers, who still had to decide when to go to market and when to accept an offer or hold out for a better price. In practice whalermen who were expert at sea were rather poor in the market. Restrictive sales agreements generally failed because of the intense individualism of owners (which was not diminished by the close friendships maintained within a relatively small trade), and many firms were damaged by going too soon to market, or by holding out too long for a better price.

Quite apart from excessive individualism, any concerted effort to maintain prices was impossible because of a universal desire to maximise production, and the need for forward selling. As noted below, the Norwegian companies lived on borrowed money, and commonly sold their oil in advance to cover running costs, relying on cost of production and early intelligence from the fishery to arrive at a price. While forward selling made for certainty in an uncertain world, and could be fortunate if an unexpectedly large crop forced prices down, it did not, in general, produce very large profits, and denied owners the very substantial gains to be made in seasons when the crop fell short of demand and consumers bid against each other in the unhappy knowledge that – in the 1920s, but not in the 1930s – it would be another year before they could buy large parcels of whale oil.

Whatever the state of the market, it was always advantageous for bargains to be struck before the oil arrived in Europe, since transports could deliver it direct to the nearest port for the customer and so save considerable transhipment costs and the risk of spoiling the oil by contamination. Transport and storage problems also had a very important consequence for the oil-using trade as a whole. By and large it was not possible for potential customers to purchase small quantities of oil once bulk transport had replaced the barrel: to remove small quantities from a tank led to over-heating and to a degeneration of the remaining oil because of contact with air. Owners preferred to sell by the tank-full, if not by the ship-load, and small parcels were always more expensive if they could be obtained at all. In other words, for purely technical reasons, as well as for financial reasons, it suited the whalermen that their customers were large firms, even though these firms were able to exercise greater power in the market place than the producers.

II

The lack of organization in the production and sale of oil would ultimately have a devastating effect on the whaling companies, but for the time being they were safe in a market apparently eager for oil, and, given the obvious market opportunities at the end of the war, the whaling firms were anxious to return speedily to the opening up of the Antarctic fishery. In particular the British companies hoped to establish themselves by a normal process of competition with the Norwegians who, by virtue of their early start and unwitting protection by the British government, had hitherto dominated the trade. Once again, however, the British companies were more embarrassed by domestic restrictions than by foreign competition. The government retained control over raw materials for some time after the war, with the result that the whaling companies were prevented from selling their oil abroad, while the government gave them a fixed price (£62 10s) for the 1919/1920 oil, which was £10 lower than that obtained by their Norwegian rivals on the open market. Moreover, Salvesen's transports were still requisitioned, and much to their annoyance they had to hire government transports at a rate higher than they were themselves being paid.[1] Since profitability could well determine the direction of investment in whaling, this might be regarded as yet another incentive to the Norwegians.

Such relatively minor things would have caused little resentment had the government allowed the companies to expand their operations at the same time; but it would not. In its desire for a "Return to Normalcy," it believed that Britain's best interests could only be served by returning to the conditions obtaining before the war, and that, in whaling terms, meant a return to the regulations militating against British interests in favour of Norwegians who, Salvesen were quick to point out, had sold whale oil to the Germans.[2] Both Salvesen and Southern Whaling had extended their operations at the express wish of the government; now they were to be prevented from using their resources fully, in one of the rare instances in which the government, having allowed or encouraged excess capacity to develop during the war, actually tried to stop that capacity from being exploited after it.

Faced with the run-down of their operations, both companies petitioned the Colonial Office. Southern Whaling referred to the fears that "the intensive fishing during the war may have seriously affected the future prosperity of the business," and continued:[3]

> If we assume that this is a fact then it follows that additional whalers will be necessary to make the business pay, and if so surely this concession will be made to the British Companies who have launched out so much new capital during the war, even if it should mean the dropping out of some of the Norwegian Companies who have already made so much out of the business.

All that was wanted was an assurance from the Colonial Office that concessions and facilities would be granted "which will enable the British Companies to be run at a profit." It was refused because of "apprehensions which have been expressed as regards the diminution of the stocks," though

---

[1]W. Vamplew, *Salvesen of Leith* (Edinburgh, 1975), 172.

[2]*Ibid.*

[3]Unilever Archive, Blackfriar's House, London, SEC/1304, J.H. Irvin to Under-Secretary, Colonial Office, 29 April 1919.

rather incongruously the British undertakings were offered licences provided they entered into profit-sharing agreements with Norwegian firms.[4] In the end some slight easing of the restrictions operated for a couple of seasons after the war, but it must be emphasised that any significant growth in British whaling at this time was held back by the government against the wishes of the companies. In 1917/1918 the British were within a few thousand tons of Norwegian Antarctic output, and though the British did not have the Norwegian spare capacity, they were eager to expand. In fact the Norwegian postwar expansion began in the 1918/1919 season, while British output declined in 1918/1919 to the lowest level since before the war. The lowest level of wartime output was not exceeded by the British until 1921/1922, when the Norwegian figures were more than double their lowest wartime effort (appendix 15). It would be wrong, however, to give the impression that the divergence was the result of restrictions alone. The Norwegians had the reserve capacity; the expertise and the initiative; and their entrepreneurs deserve the credit for forging ahead while their rivals were indisposed, their chief advantage, perhaps, being the credit system under which they operated. Norwegian whaling companies were all grossly under-capitalised (commonly with around £50,000 paid up for an expedition costing around £300,000), but were able to borrow huge sums from banks both in Norway and London, where several of the better known merchant banks had Scandinavian connexions. As a result, companies could "mushroom" in a way that could not have happened in Britain, and they could, with equal rapidity, disappear. This volatility facilitated the expansion demanded by a fat-hungry Europe, but also created a confusion within the Norwegian trade, with frequent groupings and regroupings of entrepreneurs – or gamblers – and rapid transfers of ships between "owners," which are difficult to follow. In such circumstances many men went bankrupt, but the ships they had commissioned remained to be taken on by anyone else who could raise credit, while there were several families who made substantial fortunes and formed the backbone of the trade: the Rasmussen, Jahres, Christensens, Bugges and Melsoms, for instance.

Although considerable sums were undoubtedly invested by individual Britons and by British banks in Norwegian whaling companies, it was not until the postwar boom was over that any significant new investment took place within British whaling. During the boom itself money went largely into share transactions rather than fixed capital formation, and not surprisingly it came from Lever Brothers. "Gold mining or dice throwing," Sir William Lever said in 1914, "are unexciting occupations compared with whale fishing: this

---

[4]*Ibid.*, Under-Secretary, Colonial Office, to Irvin and Sons, 6 February and 20 April 1919.

profession should be left to people with life-long experience."[5] But things had changed since 1914. In June 1919 the Levers Board learned without apparent surprise – as if it was the most natural thing in the world – that the firm had acquired "the whole crop of whale oil, both British and Norwegian, and it is impossible to obtain further supplies."[6] In such circumstances vertical integration seemed natural, and two months later, while discussing a minor dispute with a director of Southern Whaling, the Levers representatives suggested "out of blue" that the best course was for Levers to buy Southern Whaling.[7] Although it did not have Salvesen's sound financial banking, the newcomer had performed quite creditably during the war and actually made more profit out of whaling than Salvesen in the postwar seasons. There was, however, a hint of strained relations among the directors, some of whom wanted to transfer all their activities to South Africa, while the senior active partner, on his own admission, took no interest in the whaling side of the firm. They were, in fact, glad to be rid of Southern whaling, and Levers, having ascertained that the firm was worth around £405,000, secured it for their own offer of £360,000.[8]

The assets of Southern Whaling Company acquired by Levers in September 1919 included a fleet which was by no means extensive and which might serve as an indication of the relative importance of fleet and land station at that time. In aggregate the vessels amounted to little more than 4000 tons. The *Woodville*, a tanker of 2800 tons capacity, and the *Sound of Jura*, of 1400 tons capacity, were valued at £80,000 and £35,000 respectively, while the four catchers were worth £75,000. The bulk of the assets, for Southern Whaling as for Salvesen, were still to be found in the South Georgia base – Prince Olaf's Harbour – which was now worth well over a quarter of a million pounds, and which at least in 1922/1923 and 1923/1924 produced more oil than any other expedition in the world.[9] (In whaling parlance each land station and floating factory was an independent "expedition.") (appendix 13). The operation was

---

[5]Quoted in C. Wilson, *The History of Unilever. A Study in Economic Growth and Social Change* (2 vols., London, 1954), II, 120.

[6]Unilever Policy Committee Minutes, 23 June 1919.

[7]*Ibid.*, SEC/1304, stated in paper endorsed "Mr. Knowles Notes for Mr. Inglis."

[8]*Ibid.*, Lever Brothers to Sir J. Irwin, 7 August 1919.

[9]*Ibid.*, Mr. Knowles' Notes, and Unilever Archive, Blackfriar's House, London, S.W. Co. Balance Sheet, 30 November 1918.

still basically one of bay whaling, and though Southern Whaling bought another tanker – *Southern Isles* – almost immediately, that was the extent of their investment in new capital stock for the time being.

In view of future developments it was perhaps unfortunate that the British companies concentrated their efforts on land stations, but the justification at the time for so doing is clear from an analysis of the relationship between land stations and floating factories in the early 1920s, which shows the five stations still accounting for around half of the entire Antarctic crop of oil (see table 20). The compulsory cut-back in British whaling from the South Georgian bases in 1920, from twelve catchers to eight, had been less serious than originally feared for the simple reason that the companies compensated by increasing the size and power of their catchers. They were able to go further afield – eighty miles was about the limit in 1923 – and were able to go faster, and a huge increase in oil yield followed their concentration on blue whales instead of on fin whales as hitherto. The British stations in South Georgia produced 12,136 tons of oil in 1920/1921 and 24,535 in 1922/1923 without any theoretical increase in productive capacity, and with only a relatively small capital outlay on the part of the owners. (appendix 13)

Table 20
Oil Production of Land Stations and Floating Factories
in the Antarctic, 1922/1923, 1923/1924 and 1924/1925 (Tons)

	1922/3	1923/4	1924/5
Southern Whaling Factory	4783	5000	5744
Salvesen Factories	6625(2)	4590(2)	3383(1)
All Factories*	42,368(11)	35,952(12)	47,385(11)
Southern Whaling Station	12,392	8743	12,333
Salvesen Station	12,000	7167	16,667
All Stations	51,697(5)	34,833(5)	58,683
Factories and Stations Mixed	8533(2)	6273(2)	9664(2)
Stations as % of total oil	50.4	45.2	50.7

Note: *Except those of A/S Hektor and Tønsberg Hvalfangeri, which did not distinguish between their factory and station oil, here listed as "mixed."

Source: David Geddes and Company, Basingstoke, Geddes Ms., Statistical Tables

III

Leith Harbour and Prince Olaf's Harbour continued to play an important part in British whaling in the late 1920s, though the 1926/1927 season saw the beginning of the end of the South Georgia fishery. Blue whales began to grow scarce around the island, and though the catchers turned their attention once more to fin whales this only meant greater efforts – and higher costs – for a smaller reward. Any meaningful expansion could only occur outside South Georgian waters, and this, in effect, meant the writing down of the value of the old bases and the creation of large sums of new capital for the floating factories that would have to take their place in the waters around South Shetland. Salvesen's *Neko* had been operating as a floating factory there since 1911/1912, but she was a small vessel (3576 tons gross) and her yield was unimpressive, being less than the average per catcher in the late 1920s.[10] In 1922/1923 she was joined by the *Sevilla*, which was twice as big (7022 tons gross) and nine years younger, and after *Neko* was sunk in 1924 another relatively new vessel was purchased and became the *Saragossa*, operating for the first time in the 1925/1926 season. Also during 1924 Salvesen took delivery of six new, powerful whale-catchers, the first new ones they had bought since 1916.[11] They were the first of forty catchers which Salvesen had specially built for them by Smith's Dock, Middlesbrough, in the interwar period in an attempt to employ only the very best catchers and equipment which changing technology could produce. In 1925, for instance, they bought another three catchers, their first to exceed 300 tons and 1000 horsepower. By then they had a modern fleet equal to anything the Norwegians had to offer, and with a profit-earning capacity of a quarter of a million pounds with oil prices in the £30-35 range of the mid-1920s.

Salvesen's eagerness to prepare adequate ships for the more exacting conditions of South Orkney and South Shetland was matched by that of Southern Whaling. Their fleet was remodelled in 1922-1923 and only the best vessels remained. They were joined by a 5648-ton ship of 1902 vintage that was converted into *Southern Queen*, the company's first factory ship, and by three new and powerful catchers, *Southern Pride, Southern Flower* and *Southern Floe*.[12] Southern Whaling never owned as many catchers as Salvesen, not least because they hired them on occasions from other companies, but they always

---

[10]Salvesen catch statistics in Vamplew, *Salvesen of Leith*, 287 ff.

[11]Salvesen whale catchers; *ibid.*, 278 ff.

[12]Southern Whaling Company's official papers are missing for the 1920s, having been destroyed as "salvage" during the 1939-1945 war, but details of ships have been gained from David Geddes and Company, Basingstoke, Geddes Papers, from *Lloyd's Register of Shipping, passim*, and from papers of H. Tyrer and Sons of Liverpool. who acted as agents for the company. I am grateful to H. Tyrer and Sons, Ltd., for allowing me access to these papers, consisting of two notebooks and some letters, and to Professor P.N. Davies for drawing them to my attention.

had enough; the number of catchers that could operate was fixed by law, and there was no great merit in accumulating unusable catchers, although both companies held catchers in reserve or used them for towing purposes. At least two Southern Whaling catchers had no guns and were officially classed as bumboats, their chief duty running between fleet and islands and standing by to be fitted with guns should any of the licensed boats be disabled. The loss of a catcher was a very serious thing when the season was only three months long and factories had to work at full cook to make ends meet and show a profit.

The Southern Whaling expeditions (including the land station), serviced by nine catchers and two transports, were capable of producing around 18,000 to 19,000 tons of oil and producing profit in the same order of magnitude as Salvesen. But the amount of money involved in this sort of operation was immense compared with prewar whaling. For insurance purposes the floating factory, *Southern Queen*, was valued at £108,000, and the tankers *Southern King* and *Southern Isles* at £64,000 and £36,000 respectively. Of the catchers, eight were worth around £13,000 each and the latest – *Southern Flower* – £24,000. In aggregate the basic fleet – i.e., hulls and machinery alone – was valued at more than £325,000 (including the Prince Olaf's Harbour catchers),[13] and in order to finance it Southern Whaling's nominal capital was advanced from £100,000 to £1,000,000, of which £650,000 shares were issued to Lever Brothers to cover expenditure on Southern Whaling's behalf of £662,521.[14]

The importance of the new factories is obvious from the increased catches in the South Shetland area, which swelled the profits coming in from the newer catchers operating from South Georgia (see appendix 12). Salvesen returned an average of £304,976 in 1924/1925-1925/1926 compared with £166,071 in 1922/1923-1923/1924, and though Southern Whaling's profits are not available, an advance estimate of their 1924/1925 profit was no less than £400,000.[15] With prices fairly steady between 1922 and 1926 (see appendix 16), these were prosperous years for whaling, though both companies used their

---

[13]Tyrer Note Books, I, 147 ff.

[14]Unilever SEC/1304, Notice of Extraordinary Meeting of S.W. Co, 31 October 1924, and inter-office memoranda, 29 October 1924 and 3 November 1924 and 11 May 1925. The Policy Committee ceased in 1921 and the Managing Director's Conference was not established until 1925, so that the usual sources for southern Whaling are not available for the early 1920s. See Wilson, *History of Unilever*, I, 269-270. Presumably the £662,521 expended by Lever Brothers included the £360,000 paid for the firm in 1919.

[15]Unilever 8104/TT3793, H.R. Greenhalgh to Lord Leverhulme, 20 January 1925.

earnings for building up huge reserve funds which were now regarded – at least by Theodore Salvesen and the Lever Brothers' Board – as a necessary part of whaling. Neither was fully convinced that market intelligence supported a massive investment in factory fishing, and Salvesen in particular had doubts whether the expensive new equipment required for wide-ranging fishing could pay for itself before the stocks of whales ran out. Modern whaling was reaching that stage of technical – and therefore expensive – sophistication that was likely to be self-defeating for a firm hoping to pay dividends, and the balance between efficiency and anticipated exhaustion of stocks had to be taken whenever new investment was considered. Large reserve funds would help to smooth out difficulties caused by seasonal fluctuations in catches or in markets, and they were, moreover, essential to finance forward investment in a time of dear money when, as Dr. Vamplew had pointed out, the Norwegians were having to pay up to fourteen percent to finance their fleets for a seasons' fishing.[16] Since it cost over £300,000 to put each of the British companies' expeditions to sea, self-financing was in fact good business.

IV

The new fleets of Salvesen and Southern Whaling had hardly put to sea before doubts were raised about their long-term efficacy as the way opened for another massive expansion of Antarctic whaling. The waters around South Georgia and South Shetland were soon seriously depleted, and once again the trade was set for migration. There were more and better whales over the horizon, and just as Smeerenberg in the north and Hobart in the south had given way to ships combing the high seas, so the shore bases and fjord-bound factories, though they kept going, surrendered pride of place to pelagic factories that steamed with their catchers and opened up the entire Antarctic ocean to the most intensive exploitation the trade had ever seen. Again it was the Norwegians who drew first blood, when in 1923/1924 the veteran Captain Larsen took the Ross Sea Whaling Company's *Sir James Clark Ross* along the edge of the ice and found a passage through into the ice-free region known as the Ross Sea. An abundance of whales was found there by the ship's five new 100-ton catchers, but the factory itself (and therefore the whole expedition) proved unsatisfactory. Although it had a set of the latest Hartmann cookers (costing £70,000) to cope with a swift succession of whales, the factory experienced the greatest difficulty in getting the blubber on board. She had been fitted out for working at anchor in sheltered bays, and though her gear could deal with humpbacks, she could not

---

[16]Vamplew, *Salvesen of Leith*, 178.

lift fin and blue whales on board. When flensing was tired alongside that too was a failure because the equipment could not take the strain as the ship rolled and the whale fell in the trough.[17] In the end she had to retreat to anchorage in an ice bay called Discovery Inlet, and the expedition was less successful than it would have been had she cruised with her catchers, which now spent too much time towing whales for great distances.

Larsen had proved what everyone wanted to know: whales were abundant throughout the Antarctic Ocean and particularly in the vicinity of the ice. The Norwegians, Lever Brothers' Board was told in 1925, had made large profits in the previous season in Ross Sea, and the Colonial Office had promised the next licence for that area to the Southern Whaling, whose manager had committed himself to the rash opinion "that the number of whales was more and more on the increase and that Ross Sea was the best area of all."[18] Larsen's troubles, however, were only the first of many to be countered, often by trial and error, before ice fishing could become general. For instance, the first Southern Whaling factory – *Southern Queen* – to venture from her bay made no adequate provision for the fact that in order to steam at full cook she required something of the order of the three hundred tons of water a day, and her race for base was a ignominious as that of *Sir James Clark Ross*. But worse was to come. After a generation of relatively safe fishing, the old whaling hazards struck again, and *Southern Queen* went down, a victim of the ice. Navigational aids were poor, fog hampered communications, and "pack hunting" was impossible before the introduction of radio. In short, for a few years the entrepreneurs were pressing ahead of available technology. None of the early factories could cope adequately with the capacity of its catchers, and all of them relied on the speedy and wasteful exploitation of abundant whale stocks.

Faced with the many problems accompanying true pelagic fishing, the trade underwent a major overhaul in the late 1920s which lifted it still further into the "big business" league. Existing factory ships of four to six thousand tons, which allowed little deck space for even the essential cooking, were

---

[17]This had not been such a problem in Arctic whaling because the ship and whale, being little different in size, tended to move together, whereas the much larger factory ships did not respond to the action of the seas as readily as the whales. While modern whaling might still be unpleasant and certainly cold, it had lost much of the old hardship and danger, leaving flensing as the most hazardous part of the whole operation. It was a dreadful job which greatly impressed A.J. Villiers who went with the Ross Sea expedition and described it in *Whaling in the Frozen South. Being the Story of the 1923-24 Norwegian Whaling Expedition to the Antarctic* (London, 1925), 130-135.

[18]Unilever MDC, 2 December 1925.

replaced by vessels twice that size equipped with advanced cookers and equipment for working up the whole carcass; and in 1925/1926 the Norwegian factory *Lancing* confirmed the final independence of the pelagic factory with her stern slipway permitting ship-board flensing at virtually any state of the sea.

For both the British companies the move to the ice could only be accomplished successfully by rebuilding their entire fleets. Southern Whaling were first off the mark, scrapping or sending elsewhere most of the smaller catchers and replacing them with modern vessels of great power, equipped with radio to facilitate more co-ordinated "pack-fishing." The loss of the *Southern Queen*, without casualty, had been, in the words of Lever Brothers' chairman, "not inopportune, as we should have had to spend £50,000 on converting her to meet the changing conditions of the whaling industry."[19] She was replaced in 1928 by the 12,398-ton *Southern Empress*, an ex-Eagle Oil petroleum tanker which was converted, at a cost of at least £72,000, into the first "modern" floating factory to operate in the Antarctic ice and the first one, according to Harold Salvesen, to have adequate plant in relation to the number of catchers employed.[20] She could handle four or five whales at a time, and with tanks capable of storing 16,000 tons of oil she was expected to save £15,000 a year by avoiding the necessity for sending a separate tanker out to bring back the oil.[21] Valued at more than £175,000, her anticipated profit was put at £100,000 per annum from an estimated catch of 10,000 tons,[22] a figure which exceeded the catch of the entire Hull fleet of sixty vessels in its heyday in the Arctic. Indeed, in 1928 it was confidently announced that Southern Whaling's fleet was "second to none in the world," and in the 1928/9 season it brought home no less than 22,600 tons of oil which, at £10 per ton profit, produced £230,187.[23] It was, however, oil caught in traditional waters: Lever Brothers' Board would not allow the ship to operate in the Ross Sea. Not until March 1929, when another

---

[19]*Ibid.*, 1 March 1928.

[20]S.W. Company Minutes, 17 October 1929 (Palm Line, United Africa Company); and H.K. Salvesen, "Modern Whaling in the Antarctic," *Journal of the Royal Society of Arts*, LXXXII (1933), 423.

[21]Univlever MDC, 9 August 1928.

[22]Tyrer Note Books, I, 114.

[23]Unilever MDC, 19 July 1928; and S.W. Co. Minutes, 17 October 1929.

Eagle Oil tanker came onto the market, did they accede to their manager's plea for more extensive and adventurous operations. She was bought for £96,500, extensively converted for something over £125,000, and – as *Southern Princess* – was ready for sail with five new 250-ton catchers – built like Salvesen's catchers by Smiths of Middlesbrough – for the 1929/1930 season. *Southern King* went to South Shetland while the old *Southern Empress* went, as usual, to pick up the oil from whatever whales remained around Prince Olaf's Harbour.

Some indication of the size of the new enterprise can be gained from the insured value of hull and machinery alone, which was £244,600 for the *Southern Empress* fleet, £280,000 for the *Southern Princess* fleet, and £187,200 for the *Southern King* fleet. The total capital outlay was just short of a million pounds, and a further £324,000 was put into a depreciation reserve.[24] Such a sum was daunting even to a huge enterprise like Lever Brothers, and since expenditure of this order was likely to hamper soap factory development an approach was made to the Margarine Union to see if it would join forces in whaling. When it refused, Lever Brothers decided to persevere alone, consoled by the thought that factory-produced oil was costing them £15 a ton and selling for £27.[25]

Salvesen also approached the question of new fleets for pelagic fishing with a caution which was well founded when one considers that a popular estimation of success was such that in 1929 Southern Whaling cold insure their anticipated profits from South Georgia at ten shillings percent but had to pay 38s 9d percent on profits from Ross Sea.[26] Harold Salvesen, a university economist who had recently joined his father and brother in the firm, was sent on a full-scale examination of Antarctic possibilities in 1928. He reported that there was still a future for whaling along the ice for the most efficient firms, and this most efficient of firms responded by selling off the *Sevilla* and smaller catchers considered unsuitable for ice fishing, and buying two liners for conversion to floating factories, *Salvestria* and *Sourabaya*, two transports, and thirteen new catchers, at a total cost of around £700,000.[27]

---

[24]Tyrer Note Books, II, 156-145 (numbering in reverse order).

[25]Unilever, MDC, 21 March 1929.

[26]Tyrer Note Books, II, 156 and 148.

[27]Vamplew, *Salvesen of Leith*, 179-180.

British whaling was further strengthened by the formation in 1928 of a third company, Hector Whaling, with a nominal capital of £250,000. Although its principal directors were drawn from merchant banks with Scandinavian connexions – Sir Karl Knudsen of Hambros and K.W. Hickman of Edward de Stein and Company – the drive behind the company for the whole of its existence was provided by Rupert Trouton, whose career was remarkably similar to Harold Salvesen's. One of Keynes' bright young men, Trouton served as his personal assistant at Versailles, and later joined the City broking firm in which Keynes made his fortune. There he specialised to some extent in the shares of the many whaling firms springing up in the 1920s and, after his marriage into the Bugge family, who owned A/S Hektoria, it was natural that a British branch would emerge. Although at first the company was small, and more Norwegian than British, the three floating factories – of which *Hektoria* was the newest and best – and the small land station were transferred to Hector Whaling after the financial crisis in 1930. Although only *Hektoria* was operated as a floating factory after 1930/1931 she had, in fact, a greater theoretical capacity than any of the Salvesen or Southern Whaling vessels and made a valuable contribution to the total group of British-caught oil.

The new factories were very different from the old.[28] They were all over 10,000 tons, which at last provided room for the adequate working and storage space on which modern efficiency depended. Stern slips, up which the whales were drawn by a clew which gripped their trails, permitted ship-board flensing and so removed one of the chief hazards of operating in difficult waters and one of the chief causes of wasteful processing. For ease of loading, the mouths of a larger number of modern digesters were flush with the decks. *Southern Princess* for instance, had forty-eight of them, fifteen-feet deep and varying in kind from the ordinary cookers that were best for blubber to the more cumbersome high-pressure cookers and the rotary Hartmann cookers that were best for flesh and bone. Harold Salvesen, in his Royal Society lecture, calculated the number of cookers in terms of equivalents of ordinary old fashioned digesters, and assessed *Southern Empress* at eighty-eight, *Southern*

---

[28]There are many excellent accounts of the working of the more modern floating factories, of which the best are probably A.G. Bennett, *Whaling in the Antarctic* (Edinburgh, 1931), and H. Ferguson, *Harpoon* (London, 1932). The latter is a lively account of work on board the *Southern Princess*, from the point of view of one who did it.

Princess at seventy-six, *Salvestria* at 109 and *Sourabaya* at eighty-nine.[29] Once the space was available on board the factories, experiments were possible to arrive at the combination of different kinds of cookers required to give the desired results (which varied from firm to firm), while the speeding up in the charging of cookers and the introduction of a shift system, enabled the factories to handle the larger number of whales brought in by their improved catchers, and to produce oil of a uniformly good quality. At the same time the introduction of large-scale water-purification plants rendered the factories independent of land bases, while the supply of fuel and provisions and the removal of oil by transport vessels extended both the range and the season of ice fishing. Finally, accommodation and recreation was improved for the crews – c. 1500 men on the five factories – that had to be enticed to sail in British rather than Norwegian vessels.

---

[29]Salvesen, "Modern Whaling," 422.

Chapter 13
Crisis and Contraction, 1929-1932

I

"We should get as large a share as possible for ourselves and this country by greatly extending our operations now without licences," Harold Salvesen wrote in his report on the viability of pelagic fishing in 1928, and so the firm rebuilt their fleet. The immediate result – an increase in their Antarctic oil production of seventy-four percent between 1928/1929 and 1929/1930 – certainly appeared to justify investment, and Southern Whaling and Hector Whaling were no less pleased with the performance of their new expeditions (appendix 13). Nevertheless, though total British Antarctic catches of oil rose from 44,879 tons in 1927/1928 to 61,781 in 1929/1930 and 120,533 in 1930/1931, her share of the world trade in oil actually declined slightly in these years of maximum effort on the part of the Norwegians. Total catches from the Antarctic rocketed from 145,394 tons in 1926/1927 to 601,391 in 1930/1931 as the number of factories operating there grew from seventeen to forty-one and the number of catchers, perhaps a more meaningful figure, from eighty to 232 (including those attached to land bases; see appendix 15).

Expansion could hardly have come at a worse time. After a generation of uncontrolled investment in raw materials of every kind the world had more than it needed – or more than it could afford – of most things; and as the boom of the late 1920s gave way to the greatest slump in history the whaling trade suffered with the rest. It was the Norwegians – according to the British – who caused the trouble by over-expansion in the late 1920s. Despite an easing of prices, profits remained high, and with their three leading companies paying out forty-five percent, 23½ percent and 57½ percent in dividends in the four years prior to 1928, and with most shared highly valued, it was easy enough to raise money to go after the £12.5 million which the 1929/30 catch was worth.[1] Over £2.5 million was poured into 140,000 tons of new construction, and companies also took advantage of the general run-down of international trade by buying up 250,000 tons of laid-up British steamers for conversion into factories and transports. But it was simply a case of transferring excess capacity from one

---

[1]J.T. Jenkins, *Whales and Modern Whaling* (London, 1932), 128-129. Norwegian profits must, however, be viewed with caution. They represent here the return on paid-up capital, which was generally small, and not the return on working capital, most of which was borrowed.

trade to another, and natural retribution followed. The Norwegians suffered heavily during the nadir of the slump, with many of their new ships laid up in 1930/1931, and all of them in 1931/1932. Only the British firms, with their formidable financial backing, were able to continue, Southern Whaling because they supplied Unilever, and Salvesen and Hector Whaling because they were prepared to stockpile, although on two occasions Hector had difficulty financing their stocks and had to sell at a low price to please their bankers.

The crisis in whaling could have been foreseen. Already in 1926 and 1927 Lever Brothers had been discussing the "problem" of declining oil prices as they affected Southern Whaling, and had decided firstly that Southern Whaling, with its superior fleet, was better able than most companies to withstand a reduction (with some of it passed on in lower wages), and secondly that "the low price for whale oil was an advantage to the consuming companies" and therefore suited the Port Sunlight Management Board. "We came to the conclusion," said Lever Brothers' chairman, "that on the balance it paid us when whale oil was cheap; we are bigger buyers than sellers."[2] Lever Brothers were not using Southern Whaling to force down the price of oil; they were concerned that the low price of oil might reduce profits to a level where Southern Whaling would be making losses and the independent suppliers would be forced out of the trade. The situation in the late 1920s was saved largely because the new pelagic fleets pushed down the costs from £25 a ton in 1927 to £15 a ton in 1929.[3] But any significant increase in production would immediately produce the same problems, and it might not be possible to force down costs again. Nobody appears to have appreciated this fact, or to have checked on what other companies were proposing in their dash to be first in the Ross Sea. Thus, at the end of the 1929/1930 season the total oil produced was forty-eight percent more than at the end of 1928/1929, and Unilever, who had contracts with many expeditions, found themselves with unexpectedly large quantities on hand. One more orders went out to Unilever subsidiaries to maximise the use of whale oil, especially on the Continent, and once again the soap men protested that twenty percent was the maximum whale oil content if the quality of soap was to be maintained.[4] It was left to the margarine men, who less than a year earlier had wanted to stop whale oil being used for soap, to take

[2]Unilever Archive, Blackfriar's House, London, MDC, 28 April 1927.

[3]*Ibid.*, 29 April 1927 and 21 March 1929.

[4]*Ibid.*, 14 August and 18 September 1930.

up some of the increased production; but even so a great deal of money had to be sunk into additional storage capacity and inventory costs.[5]

The fury of the slump finally overtook the whaling trade in the 1930/1931 season. Never before had so much effort promised such a huge yield, and Unilever took fright before the season was over. Already one of the subsidiaries were complaining that home-melt tallow was cheaper than hardened whale oil, and if oil prices in general continued to fall Unilever stood to lose an immense sum on its large raw material stocks, which ought to be cleared before further excessive stocks were built up. Early 1931, therefore, Unilever contacted the twenty-nine expeditions with which they were under contract and told them that they could not possibly take all the oil likely to be offered. The Southern Whaling vessels were recalled, and most of the Norwegian companies followed suit in a desire to maintain friendly relations with Unilever. As a result Unilever were relieved from having to take 55,000 tons of oil, but even so their stocks amounted to eighty-eight weeks supply, which was considerably greater than their normal holding. Most of the whaling companies began making arrangements to store oil which fetched only £12 on average in the market, and when Unilever informed the trade that they were unlikely to purchase any 1931/1932 oil a general depression set in.[6] There was little point in going to sea in such circumstances, and in the end none of the Norwegian companies did so.

The 1931/1932 season was therefore unique in being a British season alone. Southern Whaling vessels were sent out for a number of sound commercial and technical reasons. In the first place, Unilever decided that prices were sufficiently low to justify extending their stocks to two years' holding, but they were reluctant to buy up any of the 100-150,000 tons still on the market because to do so might encourage the Norwegians to put to sea and thus add to the surplus oil; they would moreover obtain fresh oil. In the second place, the margarine men were apparently unhappy with some of the 1930/1931 oil. Dr. Vamplew has suggested that this was because Unilever were trying to break contract, but in fact they also objected to Southern Whaling oil.[7] Some of the oil may indeed have had fuel oil in it (the same tanks – cleaned – were used for both sorts), and this, by affecting its edible qualities, would greatly reduce its value; but the chief objection appears to have resulted from changing

[5]*Ibid.*, 24 July 1930.

[6]*Ibid.*, 19 Mar. 1931.

[7]*Ibid.*, 26 March 1931; and W. Vamplew, *Salvesen of Leith* (Edinburgh, 1975), 176.

attitudes to specifications. Southern Whaling had actually lowered the quality of their oil by mixture and still maintained the official specification. They were asked in future to produce the best quality oil possible – that is with the lowest possible level of free fatty acids which could lead to degeneration – and leave any mixing to the margarine scientists.

There was another very important technical reason why Southern Whaling had to send out at least one expedition. They were still the only firm to pay much attention to the recovery of by-products such as vitamins from whale liver, and these were essential additives to margarine because the vitamins present in the oil were destroyed during processing. Again for reasons that are not now clear, some of the 1930/1931 crop of liver flakes was also below standard.

Table 21
Profit and Loss Account, South Georgia Company and
Southern Whaling Company, 1928/1929-1932/1933

	1928/29	1929/30	1930/1	1931/2	1932/3
Southern Georgia Co.	£238,278	56,554	122,182	-16,132	53,309
Southern Whaling Co.	£230,187	79,641	210,386	89,465	154,127

Sources: W. Vamplew, *Salvesen of Leith* (Edinburgh, 1975), 276; and S.W. Co. Minutes, *passim*.

The knowledge that Southern Whaling intended sailing for the 1931/1932 season confirmed Salvesen's intention to do the same. They were never convinced that the best way to tackle the depression was to run away from it,[8] and their estimate of Unilever's likely needs was probably better than Unilever's own. So rapidly were the whale oil stocks used up by the margarine men that orders went out to reduce whale oil consumption for soap in Holland and Germany and to use more copra instead.[9] Later in the year Unilever made an offer for the whale Norwegian whale oil pool, and by January 1932 they were considering substituting sardine oil, for whale oil in soap production, partly because it was cheap, but also because whale oil stocks were running low.

---

[8]Vamplew, *Salvesen of Leith*, 197.

[9]Unilever, MDC, 10 September 1931.

Between March and June 1932, for instance, Unilever consumed 100,000 tons of whale oil,[10] and Salvesen had no problems disposing of their catch.

Thus by 1931/1932 the stage was set for a revival of whaling, but the industry would not easily regain its old prosperity. The British firms performed reasonably well, as indicated by their profits (scc table 21).[11] It was far from clear, however, whether the Norwegian firms could recover their position in view of the very low prices that were now common for all sorts of oil. Certainly their ability to do would be determined more than ever by their relationship to Unilever.

II

In one notable respect the slump accelerated the ending of "old-fashioned" whaling, and helped to establish pelagic fishing as the only possibility for the foreseeable future. Salvesen had been operating from the Olna station since 1904, and though this was where they gained their experience, output was, within a decade, only a tenth of the output of their Antarctic operations. Although the northern station was re-opened again after the war, only once – in 1924 – did output exceed that of 1907.[12] How long it might have continued in decline is a matter for conjecture, but the middle of a slump in prices, coinciding with a massive increase in Antarctic fishing, was no time to play at whaling in the north, and Olna was closed in 1929.

Unilever were also involved in northern whaling. With the example of Olna before him it was natural that the "Lord of the Isles" – as William Lever was sometimes called – should want to do something in the whaling line to help his beloved Scottish islands, and in 1922 he bought out the old Norwegian-owned Bunaveneader Company at West Tarbert on the isle of Harris. Three whale-catchers operated from this station, making a hundred trips per annum in the 1920s, but it was obvious from the start that the Scottish fishery was no longer economic. In 1924 some £35,000 of Harris Whaling and Fishing Company's debts was transferred to Southern Whaling, and similar provisions had to be made from time to time, their justification being that Bunaveneader acted as a research station for Southern Whaling and for Lever Brothers. Here

---

[10]*Ibid.*, 24 March and 16 June 1932.

[11]Southern Whaling Company's income was calculated on the price paid by Lever Brothers/Unilever for oil in the open market.

[12]Vamplew, *Salvesen of Leith*, 285.

William Lever, as appalled by the annual waste of 6000 tons of "good food" as Theodore Salvesen had been at Olna, cajoled the staff into producing tinned meat and whale sausages, but the results were such that he thought them unmarketable even in West Africa, which did not have the British prejudice against whale meat.[13] He wanted the firm to produce something like the corned beef he remembered from his grocer days and assumed was still available, but it was not until 1925 that a form of dried and canned whale meat was "perfected." The *Daily Record* (26 May 1926) carried a headline "Whale Flesh for Food," but it turned out to be a special consignment for natives employed by Levers in West Africa, and though the *Daily Mail* (1 June 1926) had a feature on "Whales I have eaten," Lever whale meat was no more sought after than Lever fish sausages. Although experiments with meat meal and whale liver extracts were more successful, they did not produce adequate revenue for the station. In 1927, in a last attempt to make the Scottish venture pay its own way, the "Harris boats" were replaced by better vessels withdrawn from the Antarctic fleet, but they made no difference. It was reported in the following year that "there were practically no whales in the waters near the station,"[14] and with losses running at £15-25,000 a year the Harris Whaling and Fishing Company went into liquidation – its debts again covered by Southern Whaling – in 1929. Scottish whaling was over, but for those who loved the Scottish islands there was at least the consolation that whaling had always been hated by the inshore fishermen.

The slump also brought to an end the direct British involvement in South African whaling. Ever since the days of the old Southern Whale Fishery, in the early nineteenth century, there had been bay-fisheries along the South African coast exploiting the breeding grounds. Steam whalers gave South African fishing the same sort of fillip they gave to Norwegian Atlantic fishing, and for some years, in the early decades of this century, it was extensively pursued by British-South African firms. In 1910 there was one station operating three catchers. Two years later there were five stations and eighteen catchers responsible for almost a third of all British-caught whale oil. Irvin and Johnson, founders of Southern Whaling Co, had a South African subsidiary which they offered to Southern Whaling/Levers in 1920. It was rejected because Levers already had a South African whaling firm, Premier Whaling Company, acquired by a subsidiary in 1911. Salvesen arrived in South Africa somewhat later, when they compensated for the wartime closure of Olna by buying a station in

---

[13]Unilever, 1246, W.H. Lever to Sir H.E. Morgan, 4 August 1922 and 19 September 1923.

[14]Unilever, MDC, 9 August 1928.

Saldanha Bay in 1917. There was also, as might be expected, a representative of Norwegian interests in Union Whaling Company, which was managed by A.E. Larsen.

There was a great deal to be said for a South African station in the 1920s. In the years when bay whaling still predominated, the African stations regularly caught more whales than the British South Georgia stations, and though they were smaller whales, the total yield oil continued to be a most valuable component of the British total. South African was, moreover, the only source of sperm oil which, though inedible, was much in demand for toiletries.

There was, however, a great deal more to be said *against* South African whaling. The increasing catches in the middle of the decade came under heavy fire from zoologists working on whale migration, culminating in the Report of the Discovery Committee of the Colonial Office in 1929. It was pointed out that the whales chased off the African coast were the same whales as those chased in the Antarctic, and that through African whaling was on a comparatively small scale it was doing the maximum damage to whale stocks by attacking the breeding grounds rather than the feeding grounds.[15] Perhaps more telling argument was profitability. By 1925 Southern Whaling were tired of their Premier Whaling cousins and trying to sell out their African interests to put the money into the Antarctic where higher profits were obtained,[16] and though in the end Premier Whaling was retained as a possible bargaining counter in whaling diplomacy, its best catchers were transferred to the Antarctic in return for the worst Southern Whaling catchers and the last of the Harris Boats. The average produce per catchers in African waters was only about a third of that in the Antarctic even when the same vessels were involved (since the African season was later than the Antarctic season), and the concentration of activity in the south was the only possible course of action during the slump. Salvesen closed their Saldanha station in 1930, and Unilever sold Premier Whaling to Union Whaling in 1931, the price to be taken in the whale oil.

Bay whaling continued in Natal and Cape Colony during the 1930s, aided to some extent by the removal of the Salvesen and Unilever interests, but it never recovered its former position (see appendix 14). More interesting and important was the movement outwards of South African firms to swell the British catch elsewhere. Irvin and Johnson had founded the Kerguelan Sealing and Whaling Company early in the 1920s to establish a base on that island, and

---

[15]N.A. Mackintosh and J.F.G. Wheeler, *Southern Blue and Fin Whales* (Cambridge, 1929), 469.

[16]Unilever, MDC, 2 December 1925 and 17 February 1926.

as they judged correctly the direction of modern whaling they commissioned, in 1930, the 13,640-ton *Tafelberg*, the largest and newest of the British factory ships.[17] Their example was followed some years later by Union Whaling who, with the run-down of Norwegian operations and the growth of fishing in the Indian ocean, acquired the old Larsen factory *Sir James Clark Ross*, and sent her out as *Uniwaleco* with a fleet of brand new catchers.

---

[17]Details of fleets not owned by Salvesen or Southern Whaling Co. are taken from *Lloyd's Register of Shipping*, *passim* and Geddes papers.

Chapter 14
Regulated Recklessness, 1932-1939

I

The great slump of 1929-1931 may have aggravated the difficulties in the whaling trade, but it did not cause them. They sprang, rather, from a reckless investment in relatively cheap shipping which produced too much oil and killed too many whales. The ships could be laid up and the investment written off, but only slowly did it dawn upon consumers and producers alike that the whales could not be replaced. Whales are not a wasting resource like coal or mineral oil; given sensible exploitation they would reproduce themselves for ever. But exploitation was not sensible and whales were being wasted. They were slaughtered in unprecedented numbers less because the additional oil was needed, than because additional ships went out to take them; and competition that was ruinous for whalermen was equally ruinous for whales!

It was a difficult problem to discuss because nobody knew much about whales. Research initiated in the 1920s by the Discovery Committee of the Colonial Office and by various Norwegian agencies was beginning to reveal unwelcome indications that the perennial problem of over-fishing was entering its final stage as pelagic whalers covered the whole of the Antarctic, and Sir Sidney Harmer, a prominent cetologist, had appealed in 1925 for "a rational system of regulating the industry." Nevertheless, when Lever Brothers' board discussed the possible effects of pelagic whaling in 1928 it was reported that "the view held in all well-informed quarters was there was no likelihood of a shortage of whales generally."

In the following year there was said to be no probability of extinction,[1] but by the early 1930s scientists were no longer so confident. There appeared to be no more unexplored fishing grounds and no more species of whales in reserve as there had always been in the past. (This prognostication was later proved false: there was still a huge stock of sei and sperm whales in warm waters, and these formed the basis for the final phase of whaling). Mackintosh and Wheeler, in their Discovery Report on the Southern blue and fin whales, had investigated migration and feeding patterns because "with a knowledge of these processes it is possible to say in what circumstances hunting is liable to do

---

[1]S.F. Harmer, "Whales and Whaling," a lecture delivered at Woolwich Polytechnic, reported in *The Times*, 9 February 1925; and Unilever Archive, Blackfriar's House, London, MDC, 9 August 1928 and 14 March 1929.

the most damage, and to judge the general ability of the stock of whales to withstand or recuperate from the effects of hunting on a large scale."[2] The authors drew attention to the "economic extravagance" of South African whaling, and other cetologists took up the theme. A.G. Bennett summed up current concern in 1931 with a novel turn of phrase: "The rapid progress made recently in outfit and machinery in the whaling industry is alarming."[3] Nobody in the past had ever regarded "progress" as alarming, but so much capital was being poured into whaling that an increase in catches was imperative simply to cover expenses. It was therefor essential for the major whaling companies to reach agreement limiting catches not only to protect prices, but also for the far more serious purpose of maintaining the industry. Only if this was done, and done quickly, could whaling continue for long. The Norwegians, said one of them, "were now loading so much weight on the whale's back that it must soon sink with its load."[4]

There had been regulations of a sort since the days before the First World War.[5] Norway had restricted whaling off her coast, and the Scottish fishery had been regulated in 1908, though in both cases with more concern for inshore fishermen than for whales. In the Antarctic the British Colonial Office had restricted the activities of individual companies by limiting the number of catchers they could operate, though the probable intention and the certain result was not so much the preservation of whales as the protection of small companies which unfortunately, if understandably, were eager to grow bigger by intensifying the slaughter. While therefore, there was no diminution in whaling, there was a proliferation of companies whose methods were wasteful as they made a swift and rich killing in new whaling areas within reach of the shore bases. As often happened, there was actually a premium on inefficiency so far as carcass utilisation was concerned, and the more reputable firms aiming at the

---

[2]N.A. Mackintosh and J.F.G. Wheeler, *Southern Blue and Fin Whales* (Cambridge, 1929), 260.

[3]A.G. Bennett, *Whaling in the Antarctic* (Edinburgh, 1931), 35.

[4]Quoted in *ibid.*

[5]There are lengthy discussions on regulations in J.T. Ruud, "International Regulation of Whaling," *Norsk Hvalfangsttid*, XLV, No. 7 (1956), 374-387; J.T. Jenkins, *Whales and Modern Whaling* (London, 1932); N.A. Mackintosh, *The Stocks of Whales* (London, 1965); and the introductions to volumes of *International Whaling Statistics*. A useful summary is W. Vamplew, "The Evolution of International Whaling Controls," *Maritime History*, II (1973), 123-139.

creation of a permanent fishery could do nothing as others sought the maximum profit in the minimum time. A far more satisfactory state of affairs may have developed had the Colonial Office limited the total number of catchers, or the total number of whales to be killed, but this they resolutely refused to do because it ran counter to their distorted sense of "fair play," trusteeship and, not least, of free trade.

Despite, therefore, the Colonial Office's attempt to regulate whaling, the commercial life of the South Shetland fishery was no more than twenty years. By about 1927 it was more or less finished, and the South Georgia fishery was also suffering from rapid depletion of those stocks of whales – especially humpbacks – that came within reach of catchers attached to shore bases or anchored floating factories. It was at this stage that the factories put to sea, and even the poor regulations governing the British territories became ineffective. As the two British companies moved out of their territorial waters they were able to expand their operations in a way that was previously impossible, and at the same time the Norwegians flooded in for a quick kill along the ice. Many people forecast disaster as these unsupervised pelagic factories attacked the fin and blue whales hitherto largely protected by their preference for an oceanic habitat, but the only obstacle to excessive and unrestricted killing appeared to lie in regulations adopted in 1929 by the Norwegian government, roughly following the lines of British regulations and, with the agreement of the Norwegian Whaling Association, applying to all their ships in the Antarctic. With the support of the British firms, a concerted policy might have emerged, but it was still too early to breach the ramparts of *laissez faire* and there was no control over the crucial issues: the total number of whales killed, and the number of factories killing them. Attempts were made to stop the slaughter of Right whales and small specimens of fin and blue whales, but for the Right whales and small specimens of fin and blue whales, but for the Right whales preservation came too late, and for the other two it was difficult in practise to enforce. Too much still depended on the honour and good sense of captains making their fortunes, and whatever might have been the level of their honour, the delicate balance between earning a living and over-fishing was difficult to make by those with a pecuniary interest. Always, throughout the history of whaling, there was the argument that those men who only took "size" fish, who never slaughtered calves or pregnant and nursing whales, and who tried to preserve the future of the industry, simply lost ground to those whose scruples were fewer or whose greed was greater.

It was against this background of irresolution and confusion that one of the leading experts on whales, J.T. Jenkins, wrote his *Whales and Modern*

Whaling (1932) to show "the probable influence of man's persistent hunting on the future of the stock." "Few people," he wrote,[6]

> have any conception of the magnitude of modern whaling operations. No one unconnected financially with the business of whaling can possibly approve of the present methods of unrestricted slaughter. It is in the hope that effective action may be taken in time to prevent the larger whales from total extinction that this book has been written. In any remedial measures to be undertaken the primary motive must be the prevention of the extinction of any species of whale, the secondary motive being the preservation of whaling as a reasonably productive industry. If at any time or anywhere the interests of the whales and the whalers clash, the former alone must be considered.

Since official action, in Britain or elsewhere, needed public support, Jenkins hoped his book would assist the public in coming to the right decision, but in the long run it was the opinion and decisions of the whaling firms that counted. No truly effective system of regulation could survive unless they agreed to slow down the slaughter by adopting a maximum annual kill, and this, by the nature of things, required agreements guaranteeing each participating firm's position. "There is general agreement that in the interests of the future the figures should not be much larger," Harold Salvesen told the Royal Society of Arts in 1933, "but companies are becoming increasingly unwilling to impose upon themselves restrictions unless these are accepted by all their competitors – increasingly unwilling to take less than their fair share of the diminishing stock."[7] *"To impose upon themselves"* was really the nub of the issue, though to some extent a measure of agreement had already been forced on firms by the effects of the slump on whale oil prices, which had caused the laying up of the bulk of the Norwegian fleet. The failure of prices to pick up again was a clear warning that a conservation policy was now also an economic necessity if many firms were not to face bankruptcy.

---

[6]Jenkins, *Whales and Modern Whaling*, 5-6.

[7]H.K. Salvesen, "Modern Whaling in the Antarctic," *Journal of the Royal Society of Arts*, LXXXII (1933), 423.

At government level the possibility and desirability of regulations had been taken up by the League of Nations in 1927 and again in 1930, when an International Whaling Convention was called for the following year. Here the whaling companies were called upon to accept and guarantee quotas to be administered by a committee of five, in which Harold Salvesen was to represent the non-Norwegian companies. Although the quotas, due to come into operation in 1932/1933, would have limited total catches to a good deal less than the capacity available in 1931/1932, it was difficult to see how the limit could be kept down, and a more practical approach came with a Norwegian Act restricting the Antarctic season for Norwegian companies to 1 December-31 March. In order to maintain a measure of solidarity, it was also agreed by the signatories that no land station or factory ship should be sold to any party who was not, or would not become, a subscriber to the International Agreement.

Although Harold Salvesen was eager for conservation – he called it a crusade in 1933 – the British firms were somewhat embarrassed by the terms of the International Agreement of 1932. They were too big, with too much capital locked up in modern shipping, to take easily to quotas that threatened their profitability. Salvesen would have preferred the bankruptcy of the inefficient, and was angered by limitations on this firm's operations for the sake of newcomers, though the firm reluctantly signed the Agreement when they were allowed a higher quota giving them ten percent of the world catch. Southern Whaling would have preferred no limitation because they wished to keep prices down, and resolutely refused to have any part in the agreement. A public appeal to them to sign, by Harold Salvesen, brought a reasoned statement of their case by one of their directors. The company were concerned about over-fishing and desired some agreed system of control, but "he made no secret of the fact that Unilever's interest was to have a constant and steady supply of the maximum quantity of whale oil at the lowest economic price."[8] They did not desire an uneconomic price because they did not desire to increase their interest in whaling and therefore needed independent suppliers, but they thought it quite unreasonable that any quota scheme should try to restrict their own vessels catching whales for their own use. Without indicating how they thought such a state of affairs should be arrived at, what Unilever really wanted was the elimination of all waste, a steady supply of oil at a steady price, and a conservation policy to maintain the whale population. The International Agreement came part of the way towards meeting Unilever's wishes. There was a slight reduction of waste through the imposition of quotas in numbers of whales rather than barrels of oil, and through the limitation of the fishing

---

[8]*Ibid.*

season, which now opened on 20 October. But their effectiveness was strictly limited.

II

There is, in fact, little point in going through the details of the annual restrictive agreements for the simple reason that they did no good. Regulations which many men had welcomed as an earnest of good intent were in practice accepted when necessary and broken when possible. Al the grand words about preserving whales were irrelevant, since in the early 1930s world demand was generally lower than the amount allowed by the quotas. Indeed, it could be argued that the quota system encouraged over-production by implying that all was well so long as quotas were not exceeded; in any case, once demand rose above the quota it was ignored.

If, therefore, there was a chance of continued contraction in whaling it lay rather in the economic circumstances than in the regulations of 1932. De-No-Fa, the chief Norwegian hardening company, lost £792,000 on whale oil stocks in 1931 alone, and Unilever lost £114,000.[9] Hector Whaling was in dire trouble and forced by its bankers to sell oil stocks at a loss. Christensen could see no future as an independent producer and tried to sell out to, and become an employee of, Unilever,[10] whose centralised buying was a formidable problem for producers compared with the competitive buying of constituent companies before the amalgamation in 1929. The Norwegian companies could only pay for their outfit by mortgaging their fleets, and would not even put to sea until they had notice of the price Unilever was likely to pay for the 1932/1933 oil. Even though the Norwegians had agreed to limit their output there were fears in the Unilever boardroom that the company's oil purchases were likely to be too small to encourage whaling firms to continue.[11] In the end only ten Norwegian factories put to sea, and it looked as if all the negotiating over conservation had been rather academic. Before the season had really started, the banks had, after consultation with Unilever, decided not to finance the forthcoming whale oil stocks, and in December Unilever announced their intention of buying only

---

[9]Unilever, MDC, 24 March 1932.

[10]*Ibid.*, 17 November 1932.

[11]*Ibid.*, 9 June and 18 August 1932.

200,000 tons of 1932/1933 oil at £13 a ton; any further oil would be bought for only £8 a ton (i.e., for No. 1 oil).[12]

As a result of the poor returns for 1932/1933, when Salvesen, for instance, made only £53,309 profit (the lowest, save for 1932/1933, since 1920/1921), the Norwegians toyed with the idea of staying at home again in 1933/4, and the ball was placed firmly in Unilever's court. "Should we," asked the chairman, "agree to the Norwegian Companies not going out which would put up the price of stocks, or leave them free to do as they like and go out ourselves which would mean cheap whale oil?"[13] There were two relatively new factors to be considered, which added a great deal of confusion to the whale oil market in the following years.

The first factor was the ability to stockpile. At least until 1932, "old" oil was written off as inferior, and lengthy stockpiling was thought impossible. In that year, however, the scientists reported that there was nothing in their tests to suggest that oil deteriorated through keeping. (Indeed, pure whale oil had better keeping properties than certain vegetable oils, though much depended on the free-acidity – brought on by decomposition – of the original oil.) Once oil could be stored, the closing down of whaling for a season became a possibility, but the problem of over-supply was immediately magnified, as will be seen below, and, to make matters worse, governments could now upset the market by creating their own stockpiles for strategic purposes.

The second factor was one which had always bedevilled whaling: commodity substitution. Since the Great War the whaling trade had produced a vast amount of relatively cheap oil, but at the same time the major consumers had been awaiting the maturity of earlier investment in other sorts of oil. Unilever had vast interests in West Africa, and smaller interests in the Pacific, and they were particularly anxious about the performance of their United Africa Company subsidiary. Although their over-all policy was to encourage cheap oil prices, in fact there had been very serious doubts about encouraging whaling in 1933/1934 in case a glut of whale oil damaged the position of United Africa Company by dragging down the price of vegetable oils.[14] The influence of palm oil became still greater in 1935, when the scientists at last came up with a

---

[12]*Ibid.*, 1 December 1932.

[13]*Ibid.*, 27 April 1933.

[14]*Ibid.*, 9 June 1932.

margarine made almost entirely from it,[15] and the French, particularly, while not favourably disposed towards margarine, did everything in their power to import vegetable oil from their empire rather than whale oil from Britain and Norway.

In the end the Norwegian companies decided to sail south in 1933/1934 chiefly, it would seem, because Proctor and Gamble, the American giant which bought Hedley's of Newcastle in 1930, had entered the market for oil, and because there were rumours of increasing demand in Germany. Moreover, Salvesen and Southern Whaling opposed the general desire to restrict individual output,[16] and though Salvesen gave way, and the total production was slightly less than in the previous year, activity was still at a dangerously high level. In March 1934 Unilever's experts calculated that there were 300,000 tons of surplus oil on the market, and that since the Norwegians were talking of going out again in 1934/1935 there would be at least 400,000 tons of oil, of which Unilever would only want 100,000 tons. What in fact was happening was that the whaling companies had continued producing oil for margarine that was everywhere facing difficulties. For a variety of reasons the world price of butter had been halved since the 1920s, with the result that in Britain, for instance, butter consumption increased by 47.5 percent between 1929 and 1934, while margarine consumption fell by 37.8 percent. Governments eager to protect their dairy farmers or their foreign exchange placed restrictions or taxes on the manufacture of margarine – in Holland in 1932, in Germany, Denmark, Norway, Sweden and Finland in 1933, and in Czechoslovakia and Italy in 1934, when Unilever's European sales were a third lower than in 1929.[17] In these circumstances the prospects for whaling were so bad that when Christensen made yet another approach to Unilever in March 1934, to get them to guarantee his cost of production, he met a cool reception because Unilever expected large quantities of oil to become available at less than cost price. In fact they offered to help Christensen, and all the Norwegian companies, by buying their existing stocks if they for their part would limit catches for 1934/1935.[18] However, any

---

[15]C. Wilson, *The History of Unilever. A Study in Economic Growth and Social Change* (2 vols., London, 1954), II, 326.

[16]Unilever, MDC, 15 June 1933.

[17]Wilson, *History of Unilever*, II, 330-341. A comprehensive survey of margarine legislation is in J.H. Van Stuyvenberg, *Margarine: An Economic, Social and Scientific History, 1869-1969* (Liverpool, 1969), chapter 7.

[18]Unilever, MDC, 14 June 1934.

serious attempt to cut back production was spoiled by the German government which, having already upset the market somewhat by refusing to allow oil to be removed from Germany, now moved into the market with an offer – which came to nothing – for 150,000 tons of oil.

The year 1934 witnessed the lowest level of prices in the decade (appendix 17) and marked the turning point for whaling. As the butter mountain melted, the margarine trade revived, and a general feeling among captains at the end of the 1934/1935 season that whales were growing scarcer acted not as a deterrent but as a spur to greater efforts in the expectation of higher prices in future. Oil exceeded £17 a ton in 1935 and in consequence a larger number of factories were equipped for the 1935/1936 Antarctic season. Other expeditions were sent off in search of new fishing grounds, and catches were made off the coast of Western Australia and – in this case by Salvesen – off the coast of Peru. In the following season Madagascan waters were visited by British factories from South Africa, and whaling probably reached its greatest geographical extent before the 1950s. Some thirty factories were roaming the seas in that season (1936/1937) compared with only nineteen in 1933/34, and they returned with oil worth, on average, over £20 a ton. It looked as if whaling was back to its old level of prosperity.

In fact the appearance of prosperity was somewhat artificial, for though the number of floating factories had increased by fifty-eight percent, the amount of oil had increased by only eleven percent, and individual catches began to decline (appendix 13). In other words, the provocation of higher prices had once again led to over-capacity which put up unit costs and so wiped out most of the expected gains in profits. There was, in any case, too much oil. With immense stocks expected at the end of the 1936/1937 season, Unilever gave their usual order in the middle of the season for the maximum use of whale oil throughout the concern; but for the first time the order was immediately rescinded. Estimates showed that processed whale oil was only ten shillings a ton cheaper than palm oil, and it was not worth interfering with technical processes in the short term for such a small sum. It was a decision that could have serious consequences for the whaler owners, for though they may not have known it, the response of Unilever – and presumably of other manufacturers – to over-production previously had been to increase the whale oil content of soap.

Faced with impending disaster, through over-production or over-killing, the Norwegian owners and government had begun the 1936/1937 season with a valiant effort to restrict fishing, largely – it seemed to the British – in their own favour. Jahre, the Norwegian owners of the *Kosmos* fleet, one of the best in the country, suggested limitations on catches that would have cut back British more than Norwegian catches, and the unions joined in by refusing to man British ships which did not accept the Norwegian demands and which did not impose a ban on non-Norwegian labour. So worried were the Norwegians that the unions struck in August 1936, and the British ships, which normally wintered in Sandefjord, were blockaded there when the season was due to commence. It was too late in history, however for "Norwegian tyranny" – as Unilever called it – and within the month the men gave way. It was an important victory for the British owners, for though they accepted limitations on their catches which were, indeed, more severe than those on the Norwegians, they had effectively broken the union hold on British ships. As a condition of re-employing a percentage of the Norwegian men, Unilever and Salvesen insisted that they should allow the training of British gunners, hitherto forbidden by the union, and the number of British men on board the factories rose rapidly.

III

Any serious attempt to regulate whaling after 1936 was inhibited, if not entirely frustrated, by the nature of the expansion taking place. The new factories appearing in 1935/1936 came not only from the old established participants – Britain, Norway and Argentina – but also from Japan and – no doubt to avoid Norwegian regulations – from Panama. In the following season they were joined by further vessels from Japan (which trebled her catch), by one from Denmark, and by three from Germany (two of them hired from Norway by Henkel, Unilever's chief central European rival). Japan, though obviously she contributed to the over-killing of whales, was too far off seriously to affect the European market for whale oil; but some at least of the trouble in the last few years of the decade resulted from the confused – and confusing – position of Germany.

When the German government first made tentative proposals to buy whale oil the Norwegian producers appear to have assumed that this would increase the over-all demand. They were only partially right. The German government entered the market because of the country's difficult foreign exchange position: it did not wish to use scarce foreign exchange to buy whale oil from Norway or Britain and, moreover, would not allow Unilever to withdraw profits from their German operations. One solution seemed to lie in restricting major purchasing of oil to the German government, which would pay for the oil by barter arrangements with Norway, and then sell the oil to Unilever and other consumers in Germany in return for German "inland" marks. In theory, then, all that was proposed was to transfer the purchasing of oil for Germany from private companies to the state. In practice there was a slight increase in oil consumption because more was used now that it could be obtained by using inland marks. Actually the original proposals came to nothing because the barter agreements fell through, and at this stage the German government turned to the alternative, namely a German fleet catching for the "private" German market. Thus, early in 1935, the German government approached Unilever and offered a small subsidy and "the preference for the supply of whale oil to Germany" if Unilever would build a fleet to operate from Germany. Since this would enable them to use up German marks, and since their southern German factories were short of oil, Unilever agreed. The *Unitas* fleet was built, and this, together with two fleets hired from Norway by Henkel and Rau was used to supply the Central and Eastern European demand from 1937 onwards, with a German government guarantee of £1 per ton profit.

Once the German fleets put to sea, for the more or less exclusive servicing of the largest margarine consuming country in Europe, the Norwegian fleets found themselves scrambling to sell their oil in a constricted market. To some extent there was an adjustment in relative catches, as Norway's share of Antarctic whaling fell and that of Germany, Britain and Japan rose. However, since developments were taking place for political rather than purely economic considerations, it is hardly surprising that the necessary adjustments came too slowly, and that in consequence the 1937/1938 season – which Harold Salvesen described as "phenomenally lucky with weather and supply and condition of whales"[19] – ended with the largest surplus of oil since 1930/1931 and the second largest volume ever recorded. For the Norwegian companies, now obviously under pressure from both Britain and Germany, the future seemed insecure to say the least. When David Geddes, Jr., visited Norway in November 1938 he found Peder Melsom in despair, thinking the end of whaling "will come very abruptly and probably quite soon," and Jahre, having decided to go into the tanker trade, had already got his shareholders to agree to the disposal of the *Kosmos I* and *Kosmos II* fleets should a favourable opportunity occur. Two months later a gloomy Rasmussen arrived in Geddes' office with the news that he intended laying up his ships as soon as they arrived home without bothering to unload their cargoes.[20] Even the Japanese were getting worried, and offering to join a sales ring if Geddes could negotiate suitable terms with the Norwegians.[21]

How far the Norwegians would, in the end, have been forced to cut back, and how far the subsidised Germany intervention would or could have

---

[19]David Geddes and Company, Basingstoke, David Geddes' Notebooks, Notes of conversations in Norway, 19 November 1938.

[20]*Ibid.*, 18 January 1939.

[21]*Ibid.*, 17 August and 25 November 1938.

been controlled in the interest of whaling as a whole – and especially of conservation – is by no means clear. In fact the issue was never put to the test, and the outbreak of war in 1939 (the prospect of which had been an important factor in depressing recent oil prices) has tended to obscure the fact that both Norwegian and British whaling were in a state of relative decline, even if that decline was only of very recent origin. Some indication of the severity of the changes that had taken place can be gained from table 22:

Table 22
Major Countries' Share of Antarctic Oil Production

	1936/1937		1937/1938		1938/1939	
	tons	%	tons	%	tons	%
Norway	170,744	38.5	162,874	29.3	120,722	25.7
Germany	32,699	7.4	89,601	16.1	82,088	17.5
Japan	26,098	5.9	64,780	11.6	80,579	17.1
Britain	162,970	36.8	192,228	34.5	148,632	31.6
World total	443,018		556,722		470,129	

Source: Calculated from tables in *International Whaling Statistics* (Oslo, 1942), 32-33.

IV

By comparison with Norway, and in the general context of over-production and international confusion, the British whaling industry performed remarkably well in the 1930s. The brunt of the depression had been borne by the Norwegians, whose activities were severely curtailed after 1932/1933. The land stations in Scotland and South Africa closed down by the British firms were of little importance compared with the Antarctic expeditions; and the Prince Olaf's Harbour station which Southern Whaling abandoned (because it had been of diminishing value) was in any case taken on by Salvesen, who operated two South Georgian land stations in some years during the 1930s. One of Southern Whaling's factories did not operate after the depression, but this had been part of a planned reorganisation of activities. In other respects the firm continued as before and sent out expeditions every year, still arguing against those who would have restricted their activity that their special position as a firm which did not sell its products absolved it to some degree from the restrictions imposed on other firms. To the annoyance of Unilever, the other firms would never openly admit that the giant had any specific "right" to do its own fishing: the last thing they wanted was vertical integration, which would have threatened the

Norwegian position. Salvesen were no better liked by the Norwegians, for they shared with Southern Whaling/Unilever the large reserves and other interests which enabled them to take the slump in their stride. While the Norwegians were having the gravest difficulties putting to sea, neither of the British firms gave much serious thought to the financial implications of their own continued activity. Indeed, so confident were Salvesen that when *Saragossa* was lost in 1932 she was immediately replaced by another vessel – *New Sevilla* – which, at 13,801 tons, was twice her size and the largest floating factory operated by Salvesen before the Second World War. They obtained her by buying out the Norwegian Sevilla Company, thus eliminating a rival in the process. "With an eye to future years also," they told their Sandefjord agent in April 1932, "we desire as far as possible the elimination of small groups, whose interests might run counter to those of the majority."[22] It was a policy not of greed, but of economic common sense.

The British companies were eager, for the sake of prosperity, to reduce the number of competitors, and, for the sake of posterity, to reduce the level of catches. The first, as we have seen, was more easily accomplished than the second. Southern Whaling had to keep up their efforts for the sake of the whale liver vitamins that other owners would not process for them, and Salvesen were determined to squeeze the maximum oil out of their international quota. In 1936/37 they reached their maximum effort, buying out yet another rival and sending its factory – *Strombus* – to join the three which operated throughout the 1930s: *Salvestria, Sourabaya* and *New Sevilla*. In fact *Strombus* operated only for the one season, but Salvesen remained the leading firm in the country, if not in the world, with a vast number of catchers approaching fifty in 1939.

Some of the British growth in the 1930s was attributable to new firms: Southern Whaling and Salvesen owned all the factories operating in 1926/1927 but only a third of those in 1936/1937.[23] The building of *Tafelberg* by Irvin and Johnson's Kerguelen Sealing and Whaling Company in 1930/1931 and the acquisition of *Hektoria* by Hector Whaling have already been noted. The remaining factories were Norwegian or Anglo-Norwegian vessels transferred to British companies following the financial devastation of the Norwegian companies during and after the slump, so that some at least of the British "rise" and the Norwegian "decline" overlapped. The old *Sir James Clark Ross* was sold to Union Whaling and became *Uniwaleco*. The Rasmussen group sold its South Georgia base and a tanker (*Peder Bogen*) to Salvesen, while their brand-

---

[22]W. Vamplew, *Salvesen of Leith* (Edinburgh, 1975), 211.

[23]Details from Geddes' papers, Annual Reports.

Gordon Jackson

new *Svend Foyn* had had to be sold unused to the A/S Tonsberg Hvalfangeri group, which in turn ran into grave difficulties. Their floating factories *Anglo-Norse, Polar Chief* and *Svend Foyn* were transferred to English companies (Anglo-Norse Ltd., Polar Whaling Company and Star Whaling Company) backed by merchant bankers Dawnay-Day, though the ships continued under Norwegian management. It should, perhaps, be emphasised that with these smaller companies it is almost impossible to define what is meant precisely by "British" or "Norwegian." The two nations were inextricably mixed: the ships might come to the British register, and make use of British finance, but the effort was still basically Norwegian. The same was true, though to a lesser extent, of the most significant development in the 1930s: the formation of Hector Whaling's subsidiary United Whalers, which made the new combine a very effective rival of Southern Whaling and Salvesen. Hector Whaling had sprung from Trouton's marriage into a Norwegian whaling family; United Whalers sprang from the marriage of his brother-in-law into a Swedish bank or, more specifically, into a bank owning blocked German marks. Just as Unilever built *Unitas* to use up marks, so Trouton agreed to build the 20,638 ton *Terje Viken* for the same purpose in the same Bremen yard, using almost identical plans. Since *Unitas* was technically owned by Unitas Deutsche Walfang Gesellschaft m.b.H., and operated from Germany, *Terje Viken* was the largest floating factory ever to operate from Britain, and firmly established a leading role for Trouton among whaling entrepreneurs.

Table 23
British and Norwegian Antarctic Whaling Catches, 1929/1930-1939/1940
(tons and percentages of world catch)

	Britain	%	Norway	%	World
1929/1930	120533	28.4	288019	67.9	424460
1930/1931	182358	30.3	381949	63.5	601391
1931/1932	126641	94	-		134760
1932/1933	186004	45.4	214309	52.3	409410
1933/1934	185283	46.4	203009	50.8	399257
1934/1935	200675	49.1	197316	48.2	409000
1935/1936	165861	40.8	186006	45.8	406056
1936/1937	162970	36.8	170744	38.5	443018
1937/1938	192228	34.5	162874	29.3	556722
1938/1939	148632	31.6	120722	25.7	470129

Source: Calculated from tables in *International Whaling Statistics* (Oslo, 1942), 22.

While admitting the difficulties in distinguishing between British and Norwegian interests within whaling companies, it should nevertheless be stressed that so far as national ownership of expeditions was concerned, catch figures show a very substantial shift of emphasis away from Norway, which by 1937/1938 had a smaller share of the international trade than Britain. On the other hand, the growing difficulties facing whaling in the late 1930s meant that the additions to the British fleet did not bring about a notable increase in its Antarctic catches. (table 23).

The British position was better if other whaling areas are taken into consideration. Whaling could only continue at the existing level if the industry migrated periodically. Thus in the slump period the Ross Sea had been opened up on a grand scale, and in the early 1930s statistics become vaguely "west Antarctic" and then simply "pelagic." In 1935 Unilever's board was told: "our expeditions, in common with other expeditions, were moving on to grounds where there was no experience of whaling."[24] Salvesen were even more adventurous and began using factories outside the Antarctic altogether. The peak of activity was reached in 1936/1937, when there were ten British factories in the Antarctic, one south of Madagascar, three off the coast of Peru and one in Davis Strait – the same factories being used more than once where seasons were different.[25] At the same time, in the middle of the decade, the number of British land stations around the world reached their maximum at nine, though two of them – in New Zealand and Newfoundland – are statistically negligible. From 1937 onwards, international regulations cut back operations outside the Antarctic, partly to remove factories from areas where they were likely to do too much damage to whale stocks, and partly to restrict fishing to the most remunerative areas. As a result the Antarctic became once again the source of almost all the British-caught whale oil.

Table 24
British Antarctic Catches as a Proportion of Total British Catches,
1931/1932-1938/1939

1931/1932	94.4%	1934/1935	93.3%	1937/1938	88.2%
1932/1933	94.4%	1935/1936	80.2%	1938/1939	95.2%
1933/1934	93.2%	1936/1937	75.9%		

Source: *International Whaling Statistics* (Oslo, 1942), table 4; and 1950, table h.

---

[24]Unilever, MDC, 10 January 1935.

[25]*International Whaling Statistics* (Oslo, 1942), table 4, 126-131. See appendix 13.

This hostility to whaling outside the Antarctic was clearly justified insofar as it might prevent the culling of baleen whales in their breeding grounds, but it also served to inhibit a potentially important development. Whaling in the 1930s had expanded not only because new areas of the Antarctic were invaded but also because new species were found or more intensively fished. Thus the blue whale, though fast disappearing from South Georgian catches, provided the greatest boost to whaling after 1928/1929, to be followed somewhat later by the major rise in catches of fin whales, humpbacks and sperm whales. The rapid development of the humpback and sperm trades, however, reflected new departures as South African factories took the former off the coast of Madagascar, and Salvesen took the latter off the coast of Peru. While the stocks of humpbacks might have been inadequate to such an attack, the sperm whales were not. Since they were few in number among catches, and chiefly taken off the African coast, it was assumed in the trade that they were almost extinct, whereas they were probably the most numerous of the larger whales, and Salvesen, rather than taking the last of the sperms, were in fact tapping a huge reservoir which was to become one of the two mainstays of the more recent whaling trade. On the other hand it must be admitted that the great demand in the 1930s was for baleen whales, that is for edible whale oil, not inedible sperm oil, although the latter did have a smaller demand in those soaps and toiletries for which its waxy properties were appropriate.

Table 25
Profits of Southern Whaling and South Georgia
Companies, 1929/1930-1938/1939

	Southern Whaling	Salvesen
1929/1930	£79,641	56554
1930/1931	210386	122182
1931/1932	89465	-16132
1932/1933	154127	53309
1933/1934	73063	93312
1934/1935	nil	323609
1935/1936	107275	425000
1936/1937	31297	200639
1937/1938	597	-79310
1938/1939	11202	–

Source: Southern Whaling Minute Book, *passim*; and W. Vamplew, *Salvesen of Leith* (Edinburgh, 1975), 276.

In terms of catches the British companies certainly performed well in the 1930s, but in financial terms there were many years when profits appeared to provide an inadequate return on capital employed (table 25). While these figures should be taken only as a very rough guide to profitability, since it is by no means clear that they represent the total profit – or loss – on whaling expeditions, they do at least show that whaling was once more something of a gamble, and appear to justify Unilever's growing disenchantment with the Southern Whaling Company and their growing desire to rely on independent producers for their whale oil. Rupert Trouton, having lost £53,000 on *Terje Viken* and £28,000 on *Hektoria* in 1937/1938, was as pessimistic as the Norwegians. Already by January 1939 he was talking of giving up if the British government would not give the British producers a preference in their own market, and had begun negotiations for the sale of *Terje Viken* and *Hektoria* to Germany or Japan.[26]

V

The future of whaling seemed bleak at the end of the 1930s, quite apart from commercial troubles and impending war. Despite the valiant efforts of conservationists, the number of whales killed during the "regulated" 1930s far exceeded that in the 1920s, and though some of the whales are admittedly of "newer," smaller species in the late 1930s, the total volume of oil quite clearly reflects a greater over-all impact on whale stocks.

Table 26
Whales Caught and Oil Produced, 1920-1938
(Averages)

Season	Whales (Number)	Oil (Tons)
1920/1921-1928/1929	20929	171041
1929/1930-1937/1938	38422	463767
1935/1936-1937/1938	50356	540455

Source: Calculated from *International Whaling Statistics* (Oslo, 1942), table f.

A huge increase in the average output of oil per catcher, from 839 tons in 1920/1921-1928/1929 to 1805 tons in 1929/1930-1937/1938, reduced costs very considerably, but costs were already rising again by 1937, partly through union pressure on wages, while the produce of individual factories was declining

---

[26]Geddes' Notebooks, 10 January 1939.

steadily in the late 1930s, as shown in appendix 13. At the same time palm oil was becoming cheaper and more plentiful.

There were also hints that whale oil might eventually lose its place among the soapmakers' raw materials. The rapid growth of the soap-powder market between the wars helped the whaling trade, but the development of synthetic detergents, especially in Germany where the shortage of whale oil was greatest, threatened its future. In 1933 I.G. Farben began selling a soapless base for detergents, while in 1934 Dutch Shell announced the discovery of a non-soapy detergent during experiments with by-products obtained in cracking petroleum. Two years later Henkel, Unilever's main rival in Germany, began using fatty acids obtained from coal. These detergents posed no immediate threat in the 1930s, but they offered an alternative to whale oil soap-powders should the need arise. Thus the interwar period, which began with a rush of scientific enthusiasm, ended on a note of scientific apprehension.

Chapter 15
The Final Fling, 1945-1963

I

The Second World War had a devastating effect on whaling. The European market was soon occupied by Germany; many British whale-catchers were requisitioned for war purposes; and the factories and associated vessels were to be used at the discretion of the Ministry of Food, though the precise relationship between the Ministry and the owners was not yet defined. It took some time, however, for the full effects of war to be felt.

Although war began as the fleets were preparing for sea, they were, after hasty consultations, allowed to proceed normally. The result was that instead of the shortage of oil that might be expected in wartime, there was a greater "surplus" than there had been in the over-production days of peacetime competition. The British government had been stockpiling oil since 1938, and to the 130,000 tons brought home by the British fleets in 1939/1940 was added 90,000 tons which the government bought from Norway and 60,000 tons bought from Japan.[1] There was nowhere to store all the oil on land – it was in any case being dispersed to the West Country – and there was no adequate plant for hardening it in the foreseeable future now that the De-No-Fa factory could not be used. In these circumstances there were doubts if whaling was likely to be a paying proposition for many years to come, and the Ministry of Food, in making a careful appraisal of the country's needs, decided that whaling would be unnecessary in the 1940/1941 season. Nevertheless the government recognised – as prewar owners had recognised – that the trade *had* to continue if the British owners were not to collapse in favour of the Norwegians, who were still active. The question then arose: who should bear the loss; the companies burdened with heavy "war" costs to catch oil they could not sell, or the

---

[1]Unilever Archive, Blackfriar's House, London, MDC, 29 February 1940. Lord Woolton, wartime Minister of Food, later wrote of the very great importance to Britain of an adequate stock of whale oil: "of all the preparations made by Sir Henry French before the outbreak of war, none was of equal importance to the purchase he made on behalf of the Government of the Norwegian supplies of whale oil...It was an exciting transaction, operating right under the Germans' noses, and it gave much satisfaction to Sir Henry French and the negotiators – but not nearly as much satisfaction as it gave me during the difficult period, when it was a constant stand-by." *The Memoirs of the Rt. Hon. The Earl of Woolton* (London, 1959), 237.

government which did not want the oil now but would no doubt want some in the following season?

In March 1940 Salvesen announced that they intended going out in 1940/1941 at their own risk in order to keep their operations ticking over, but neither United Whalers and the other independent producers nor Unilever were prepared to do so because of the increasing likelihood of a glut of oil in Britain should the war last longer than a year. It has been assumed that these companies were frightened by specifically *war* risks, whereas in fact they were far more concerned about the *financial* risks involved in the over-supply of raw materials, even in war-time. With palm oil now £3 to £4 a ton cheaper than whale oil, and more easily available, Unilever expected to make no appreciable loss if their whalers gave way to Salvesen should there be no call for a large fleet, and in fact they sold *Southern Princess* to Salvesen (who had just lost *Salvestria*) for a mere £75,000 because she was no longer useful and was costing £900 a week in laying-up fees.[2] Ironically, when the Ministry decided in August 1940 to cut the proposed fleet from four factories to two (because there was still plenty of oil), they chose to send out the two best, Star Whaling's *Svend Foyn* and Southern Whaling's *Southern Empress*, though for the sake of fairness they were managed by Salvesen. The logical thing, from every point of view, was for Salvesen to buy *Southern Empress*, and this they did, in August 1941, for £495,000, having previously made a joint offer with United Whalers for the ship.[3] Unilever were happy that they had made a capital profit of £440,000 in disposing of Southern Whaling's assets which they now regarded as a liability,[4] and Salvesen were pleased to have acquired a first-class fleet to replace *New Sevilla*, which they had also lost to enemy action.

In view of subsequent developments, Unilever had probably made the better bargain, for the 1940/1941 expeditions were the last to be supported by the Ministry of Food. On the one hand conditions at sea were growing rapidly worse with heavy losses to submarines, while the organisation of whaling was upset by the German occupation of Norway in April 1940. On the other hand whaling appeared increasingly as an unnecessary utilisation of scarce shipping resources. Though Salvesen would have liked to continue alone, no naval protection was available, and within a short time the British vessels and their crews had been diverted to other work in the war effort. Once out of their

---

[2]Unilever, MDC, 14 March, 15 August, and 5 and 12 September 1940.

[3]*Ibid.*, 17 July and 4 August 1941.

[4]Unilever Archive, Southern Whaling Company Minutes, 15 September 1943.

element the factories made rather lumbering tankers, and as such they were extremely vulnerable. By the end of the war none – save the *Anglo Norse* – remained afloat, and the British whaling trade might easily have remained a memory. That it did not do so was due almost entirely, it would seem, to the vision – or opportunism – of Harold Salvesen and Rupert Trouton.

Salvesen and Trouton approached the question of the future of whaling from the opposite end to Unilever. While the latter could see no financial or strategical advantage in reviving Southern Whaling's operations, the independent producers for whom whaling was a far more central pursuit were by no means convinced that whaling was finished. There was, moreover, a growing incentive as the war became longer and the respite from killing allowed the stocks of whales to recover to some small extent, thus whetting the appetite of those who recalled the rich harvest following the partial suspension of whaling in 1914-1918. Early in 1944, for instance, Harold Salvesen was telling his brother that they should get back into whaling as soon as possible after the war since there would be reasonable profits for some years to come, especially since the fleets of their rivals were in ruins and postwar Europe would be desperate for oil.[5] The firm had, moreover, just been allotted first priority by the government which, recognising the need for a revived effort after the war, gave orders for two factories to be constructed ready for peacetime, based, for war-time convenience, on the plans of the last factory – *Svend Foyn* – built by a British yard. The second priority was allotted not to United Whalers, as might have been expected, but to the Norwegian government which, when it began its exile in Britain, had brought a vast amount of Norwegian shipping and a very large number of Norwegian seamen to help in the war effort. To help the Norwegians in this way seemed the least that the British could do in return.

II

The opportunities for whaling after the war were greater than the most optimistic company could have expected in the bleak days of 1939.[6] The European economy was in a sorry state. Industry, agriculture and trade had been disrupted, and everywhere raw materials and foodstuffs were in short supply

---

[5]W. Vamplew, *Salvesen of Leith* (Edinburgh, 1975), 234.

[6]This survey of the postwar period is based largely on *ibid.*, chapters 16-17; on the papers of David Geddes and Son; on the Annual Reports of United Whalers; and on the vast and comprehensive collection of press-cuttings on every aspect of whaling, oil and related trades compiled by David Geddes.

and great demand. This was especially so when a measure of recovery showed just how far raw material production had been disrupted. As late as 1947 the output of oils and fats was about ten percent less than it had been before the war, and the price of whale oil topped £100 a ton several times between 1945 and 1952, when it was providing about a quarter of the British fat ration. Moreover, since rationing and government purchasing were the order of the day, there seemed to be little risk in re-embarking on whaling. The chances of over-supply also seemed remote. The industry had threatened to drown itself in oil before the war, but the decimation of the floating factories appeared to have solved the problem by allowing owners to "realise" some at least of their invested capital and so remove themselves from a trade to which they had been clinging for financial survival. A measure of prosperity might now be expected so long as too many factories were not built, and since they were now so expensive – a new factory would cost around £1,500,000 and a new expedition could hardly cost less than £3,000,000 – it seemed unlikely that excess capacity would arise in the short term.

The British were ready to take advantage of this situation. Salvesen's first new factory, *Southern Venturer*, was ready for the 1945/1946 season, with four new catchers as well as a large number which had survived the war. They caught some 1800 whales which boiled down to 14,480 tons of oil, while the reopened Leith Harbour caught another 2268 tons of oil. In the following season a second factory, *Southern Harvester* went south with more new and powerful catchers, and Salvesen enjoyed three phenomenally good years, with catches (including those from Leith Harbour) averaging 60,444 tons in 1946/1947-1948/1949 compared with an average of 59,529 tons in the "good" prewar years 1936/1937-1938/1939.[7]

United Whalers, while having no new factory of their own for the 1945/46 season, actually managed to secure more oil than Salvesen by chartering two floating factories which the government had seized as enemy property: *Empire Victory* was the old *Unitas*, which Unilever had tried and failed to get out of Germany before the war started, and *Empire Venturer* was the old *Wikengen* (ex-*Vikinger*, the first purpose-built floating factory), which the Rasmussen group had sold to Germany immediately before the war. These, together with nine of the surviving prewar *Terje Viken* catchers and five German catchers chartered from the Ministry of Transport, were a formidable fleet with which to recommence whaling, and in the following season they were replaced by the equally impressive *Balaena*, a new-built vessel which was destined to bring home more oil (315,302 tons) than any other factory, of any nation, in the

---

[7]Vamplew, *Salvesen of Leith*, tables 32-33, 288-291; and Geddes Statistics.

years between the ending of the war and the last effective year of British whaling, 1959/60.

Between them, these three factories secured almost the same proportion of the world's Antarctic whale oil for Britain as the larger number of factories had managed in the late 1930s. Moreover, the "British" proportion is larger still if a fourth factory commissioned by Union Whaling of South Africa is included. She was the *Empire Victory*, for which Union Whaling successfully bid against Salvesen, and although she was older than *Southern Harvester* and *Balaena* she was, at 21,846 tons, almost a third as big again, and as a result South African pelagic production amounted to as much as thirty-six percent of that of the United Kingdom in the boom years 1946/1947-1948/1949, compared with only fifteen percent in the years 1936/1937-1938/1939.

Table 27
Antarctic Pelagic Whaling, 1936-1939 and 1946-1949

Season	World (tons)	Norway Tons	%	U.K. Tons	%	South Africa Tons	%
1935/36	382,192	186006	48.7	133561	34.9	20968	5.5
1936/37	429413	170744	39.8	143532	33.4	13730	3.2
1937/38	541677	162874	30.1	153532	28.3	32279	6
1938/39	451547	120722	26.7	124364	27.5	16824	3.7
1945/46	123296	83588	67.8	39708	32.2	0	
1946/47	299071	156220	52.2	77770	26	34147	11.4
1947/48	323442	165853	51.3	86007	26.6	30176	9.3
1948/49	339076	175,020	51.6	89012	26.3	26788	7.9

Source: Calculated from *International Whaling Statistics,* xxiv (1950), 22.

The key feature of these statistics is not, however, the recovery of Britain's position, but the far more substantial revival in Norwegian whaling, which in the late 1940s was once again accounting for over half the world's whale oil catches. It was the Norwegians who benefited most from the end of German whaling, which was banned by the Allies at the end of the war. Indeed, the Germans themselves had encouraged Norwegian whaling to some extent by reviving it during the war. (Two of the catchers acquired from the Ministry of Transport by United Whalers had been unusual in that they had been built on German orders in Oslo in 1942 and 1943 for the expeditions despatched by Germany from Norway in 1943/1944 and 1944/1945, when the German shortage of edible oil was becoming desperate.) Moreover, as in 1918, the Norwegians were faster off the mark when peace came, sending out forty-four catchers compared with thirty-three from Britain in 1945/1946 and 101 compared with forty in 1948/1949. Any serious chance that the number of catchers and factories would remain small, and the slaughter of whales restrained, was in fact dashed by the urgent demand for oil and by the nature of the postwar whaling regulations.

III

The need for some sort of conservation of whale stocks was almost – but not quite – universally accepted by this time, and the euphoria of postwar brotherly love led all the whaling nations, and others besides, to limit the Antarctic whaling season to the period 8 December-7 April, and to accept a world quota for killing that was set at 16,000 "blue whale units," such units being one blue whale, two fin whales, two-and-a-half humpback whales or six sei whale (this being the approximate relationship between the oil yields of each sort).[8] In terms of oil, this meant an Antarctic production of approximately 325,000 to 350,000 tons per annum, depending on natural conditions. However, since the International Whaling Convention of 1946, which agreed to this quota, was not prepared to assess the "claims" of individual nations, and some nations – particularly the United States, which was not even directly concerned in pelagic whaling – still believed that competition between individual firms on strict capitalist principles was the only way to bring down prices and maintain the "freedom of the seas," no attempt was made to apportion the quota in any way. There was to be a free-for-all, with each factory taking as many whales as it could, reporting its catches weekly to the International Whaling Commission until such time as the international quota was reached, when all factories – which carried inspectors – would be ordered to cease operations. Such a system obviously encouraged firms to engage the maximum number of fast – and expensive – catchers in the hope of securing a full cargo ahead of their rivals, thus increasing the basic costs of whaling while reducing the over-all oil yield, since the larger number of catchers reached the quota earlier in the season, before the last-caught whales had a chance to fatten up during the feeding season. In order to counter-balance this greater effectiveness of catchers, the opening date of the season was gradually put back from 8 December to 15 December in 1948, 22 December in 1949, 2 January in 1951/1952 and 7 January in 1954/1955. Most expeditions obeyed the rules, though some – both communist and capitalist – were ruthless in their disregard for any regulations. The Russian factories were variously accused of failing to report their full

---

[8]Humpback whales were not to be taken south of 40°S, as a measure to protect the few remaining specimens.

catches, or reporting too many in the hope that the quota would be reached and their rivals would withdraw, leaving them to fish on in peace; and at least one factory – Onassis' *Olympic Challenger* – ignored all restrictions until challenged by Norwegian owners in 1956, when Onassis sold out to Japan rather than try to make money under the quota system.

There were, therefore, two major flaws in the postwar whaling regulations. The first was the inadequacy of restrictions aimed at conserving the whale. They went some way towards slowing down the general slaughter, but in the continuing ignorance of true whale stocks they set quotas, based on precedents, that were much too high. Indeed, the postwar slaughter of whales was enormous by any standards. Of the 1,241,970 whales "officially" killed in the Antarctic between 1905 and 1965, no fewer than fifty-three percent were killed in the postwar years; and in terms of oil the total for 1945/1946-1964/1965 (6,672,540 tons) was over fourteen percent greater than the total during the twenty years between the wars. That the quota was too high can be seen in the gradual decline of the blue whale element in catch statistics,[9] and the gradual and excessive reliance on the smaller sorts of whales which required greater efforts for poorer returns.

The second flaw was the absence of any effective means of preserving the trade – as opposed to the whale – by inhibiting the growth in the number of wastefully competing factories. Inevitably there was renewed over-investment in excess-capacity seeking rewards which were, in theory, the richer because there was no limit to the activity of individual factories. With more and better catchers, and with spin-off from warfare such as radar, asdic, aeroplanes and helicopters, old and new owners alike expected to make their fortune. By 1946/1947 there were fifteen factories, and twenty for most of the decade after 1950, when the failure of the African ground-nut scheme – which had been confidently expected to yield 100,000 tons of oil annually – and the prohibition on oil-seed exports by China at the outset of the Korean war, had re-emphasised the continuing need for whale oil, which in any case was still required to maintain the "spreading" characteristics of margarine. A correspondent of *The Financial Times*, excited by the preparations going on around the world – and especially in Japan – for the 1950/1951 season, wrote of the "Improved Outlook for Whaling" (10 October 1950), though he admitted that since the total catch was limited, an increase in the number of expeditions could only mean a reduction in the average catch. His relative optimism was immediately countered

---

[9]As a conservation measure, blue whales were not to be taken before 1 February in 1955/1956 and subsequent years.

by David Geddes, who drew attention to the two main problems on behalf of the
Norwegian Association of Whaling Companies:[10]

> It is a widely held view among active whalers that stocks of
> whales are decreasing. Furthermore, on a mathematical basis,
> the production capacity of the fleet operating this year is about
> one-third greater than the maximum permitted catch, although
> this percentage will vary from expedition to expedition...
> Your headline 'Improved Outlook for Whaling' is too
> optimistic particularly in the long view, although prices today
> are quite satisfactory for the efficient operators.

It was already very clear to the trade, if not to the press, that
companies nurtured in the hot-house of postwar austerity would not survive the
cold blast of post-austerity competition. It was doubtful if either the stock of
whales or the price of oil would remain adequate to maintain them for long at an
economic level of activity. In theory the "best" enterprises would succeed and
the "worst" fail, but in practice all survived with a declining share of the quota
and rising unit costs. For example, with the expanding fleets the time taken to
reach the quota fell progressively from 122 days to take 313,073 tons of oil in
1946/1947 to only fifty-eight days to take 329,371 tons in 1955/1956. Such
short seasons for expensive capital equipment were far from economical and
certainly produced a lower level of efficiency and return on capital than would
have come from fewer expeditions operating for longer periods. In reality the
postwar trade was not the carefully planned search for raw materials that might,
perhaps, have been expected at the end of a war in which governments
organised so much; it was as haphazard as the crazy trade before the war, and
would survive only so long as prices remained "quite satisfactory."

IV

Quite apart from the extraordinarily high oil yields, there was a valuable new
departure in whaling after the war. In a starving world the immense waste of
meat involved in prewar whaling was felt to be unacceptable, and a concentrated
effort was made to do something about it. There had always been guano plants
and meat meal plants in the shore stations, but profits in by-products had been
too low for machinery to be installed to the detriment of valuable oil-processing
machinery on factories. Indeed, it had been argued from time to time that ships

---

[10]*The Financial Times*, 10 November 1950.

made the most profits when they went solely for the oil and threw everything else overboard, which is why prewar regulations had had to have clauses insisting on the recovery of at least the oil from the carcasses of flensed whales. Now the recovery of meat meal was normal, and a further stage in by-product recovery dehydrated some of the juices extracted in the meal-making process to produce meat extract for flavouring foodstuffs, especially soups, meat stews and the like. The processing of whale liver was now fairly general, and attempts were also made to preserve various organs – such as the pancreas and pituitary gland – for the extraction of pharmaceuticals, though these were not a commercial success. The final advance was the logical one of preserving the best meat, and in this the British followed the lead of the Japanese, whose recent success in the industry owed a great deal to their ability to sell the meat as well as the oil. Whale bacon and whale steaks were a delicacy in a land short of domestic animals, though it should perhaps be stressed that oriental methods of cooking and flavouring were more suited to whale meat than were traditional British cooking methods. Nevertheless, for the first time for fifty years or more, whale meat was put on the British market. *Balaena* was from the start equipped with freezing plant, and a refrigerated vessel, *Bransfield*, stood by to receive and transport the meat. Salvesen followed suit with, of all things, an ex-US Army corps ship which they renamed *Southern Raven*.[11] In the end, however, the second attempt to market whale meat was no more successful than the first, though Dr. Edith Summerskill told people how to cook it and Food Minister John Strachey waxed eloquent about the 600,000 tons of wasted meat which he hoped to bring home to Europe.[12] Amid a minor blaze of publicity – most of it favourable – whale meat was "launched," and the Department of Scientific and Industrial Research and the Ministry of Food spent the three postwar seasons researching into the palatability of whale meat. In 1949 Strachey was pleased with the public response, but Rupert Trouton was not. In the press he lashed out at the ignorance of the housewife: "People should not be allowed to express opinions like that," he said after a particularly silly letter had appeared in the *Daily Mail* (26 November 1949). At a more practical level he told his Annual General Meeting in December 1950 that "we have not yet succeeded in overcoming public prejudice – partly created by the poor quality and appearance of much of the early importation, but mainly due to innate conservatism."[13] The

---

[11]Vamplew, *Salvesen of Leith*, 251-252.

[12]Reports in *The Daily Telegraph*, 26 July 1949.

[13]Reports in *The Financial Times*, 29 December 1950.

freezing vessel had been abandoned, and *Balaena's* plant already modified to make more meat meal, though on a note of muted optimism Trouton announced the favourable reception at the British Food Fair in September 1950 of a product which had eluded Lord Leverhulme: canned "corned" whale meat. United Whalers continued to produce about 5000 tons of frozen meat annually, but, though it found an uneasy place in the catering trade, butchers were reluctant to handle it and the government would not allow its use in the easiest outlet, in pies and sausages. Henceforth the British companies concentrated on the old stand-by, meat meal, and on dehydrated meat, both worth about £45 to £55 a ton in 1950, roughly a third of what they might have expected for frozen meat. Most of it was bought by the Animal Feedstuffs Division of the Ministry of Food, and went to fatten livestock rather than human beings. In 1951 the National Farmers' Union Working Party on Protein Supplies reported that "far the best hope of an increase in proteins from whales lies in whale solubles obtained by the evaporation of liquids...,"[14] but there were still major technical problems for which an answer was somewhat inhibited by the high price obtained for oil, which encouraged concentrated effort there rather than on by-products, on which United Whalers lost £57,000 in 1949/1950.[15] Edible whale meat now became almost a Japanese monopoly, with at least five of their factories bringing home 15,000 tons at the height of their involvement, in 1960/1961. It was a pity that British interest died, for the quality of the meat improved considerably with the perfection of the electric harpoon in the early 1950s which, by killing almost instantly, avoided the death struggle which had hitherto seriously affected the quality of the meat. Nevertheless, it can be forcibly argued that both technically and economically it made most sense to concentrate on the meat meal and solubles, of which United Whalers and Salvesen between them brought home around 10,000 tons in the late 1940s and 25,000 tons in the mid-1950s.

V

Despite this second failure to overcome the difficulties in marketing whale meat, the immediate postwar years were among the most prosperous in the history of the trade. Nevertheless, by 1952 the age of austerity was nearing its end, and the phenomenally high price for whale oil obtained in 1950-1952 (with Onassis securing the highest price ever paid – £172 10s – by holding out during the

---

[14]*Public Ledger*, 30 March 1951.

[15]Accounts published in *The Financial Times*, 23 November 1950.

confused situation at the outbreak of the Korean war) could not last. By 1953 the highest price paid had fallen to £80 (appendix 21), even though total output was slightly lower than in the previous season. Once again the consumers were in a position to stockpile and refuse highly priced oil; and in this they were helped, as in the last years before the war, by the enlargement of vegetable oil supplies and by the entry into the European market of the Japanese, who were able to accept a price somewhat below the economic price for European producers. The eventual entry of the Russians into the European market was the final blow to the British owners. They could not compete with the Japanese for whom both oil and meat raised revenue, or with the state-subsidised Russians.

As the number of factories increased and the price of oil declined, the spectre of the 1930s returned to haunt the 1950s. The Norwegians had begun winding down their efforts in 1952/1953 when fewer catchers were employed (though the collapse of the catcher limitation agreement in 1955/1956 brought them back again and plunged the trade into crisis), and the oldest of all the Antarctic companies, the Compañía Argentina de Pesca, was forced into liquidation in 1957. The British companies, which had accounted for a creditable percentage of total Antarctic whale oil well into the 1950s, saw their share rapidly diminishing after 1954 (appendix 18). The "British" South African company, Union Whaling, was forced to sell *Abraham Larsen* (ex-*Empire Victory*) to Japan after the 1956/1957 season, and the United Kingdom companies were thrown back heavily on their still very large reserves. Hector Whaling (as United Whalers was known after 1953), after years of high profits and capital expenditure, and 100 percent dividends, began to feel the pinch by 1953/1954, especially since tanker freights, which earned them a clear pre-tax profit of around half-a-million pounds in out-of-season earnings in 1951, had tumbled from 42s 3d to 22 3d per ton per month in March 1953. Although they still had huge reserves, and liquid assets of a million pounds to finance their expeditions, by 1955 hope for the future of the company was seen not in whale oil but in valuable technical by-products, and three years later no future was seen at all. With £1 preference shares standing at 14s 9d and 5s ordinary shares at 5s 3d (compared with 22s 6d and 28s 9d, respectively, in 1949), the sale of the fleet was discussed. By July 1959 the company could not pay the interim dividend due on preference shares, and by the end of the year announced losses of £490,471. With the collapse, in 1959, of the quota agreements, which made economic whaling impossible, the time had come for the British to get out of the trade, and Hector Whaling were fortunate in being able to sell *Balaena* to Japan in 1960, chiefly because though the over-all quota was only informally recognised, specific quotas related to individual factories had been introduced in 1959, and this gave Hector Whaling something to "sell." (The quota itself could not be sold, but it went with the ship.)

Salvesen were similarly, though not unexpectedly, coming to the end of their long attachment to whaling. In 1947 Harold Salvesen had estimated the useful "economic" life of whaling to be no more than ten years, and consequently the firm had made no further large-scale investment in floating factories. Almost exactly ten years later, in 1957, they were so hard pressed that they attempted to sell *Southern Venturer* to Japan, whose government would not sanction the purchase because they did not wish to give the impression abroad that Japan was trying to corner the whaling market. The origin of Salvesens' disenchantment is clearly seen in the adverse trend of their catch statistics after their best and most lucrative year, 1947/1948.

Table 28
Salvesens' Antarctic Catches,
1946/47-1962/63[16]
(five-yearly averages)

	Tons
1946/1947-1949/1950	57265
1950/1951-1954/1955	48312
1955/1956-1959/1960	38992

Source: Geddes Statistics

Moreover, with the suspension in 1959 of the International Whaling Commission's quota, the rise in the number of whales taken and the continuing decline in the price of whale oil made the future state of whaling more doubtful and the present more depressing. In such circumstances, Salvesen again tried to sell *Southern Venturer*, and finally disposed of her to Japan in 1961, though for only a little over two-thirds of the asking price of 1957. In the same year they ran down the operation at Leith Harbour, Britain's oldest link with the Antarctic, where generations of men had braved the winter repairing catchers and equipment, as well as carrying on, to the end, the original land-based fishery. By now the situation was critical. Prices in 1962 were less than half the figures for a decade earlier, while the increasing difficulty on the high seas is clear from the decline in the total number of blue whale units taken, from 15,242 in 1961/1962 to 11,299 in 1962/1963 and 8425 in 1963/1964. By then Salvesen had withdrawn, transferring *Southern Harvester* to Japan for £450,000, which was more or less the value attached to the quota plus costs; the ship itself

---

[16]There is a slight discrepancy in the figures for 1952-1953, which could give an alternative average of 48,264 tons for 1950/1951 – 1954/1955 (see note to appendix 19).

was to be returned at scrap valuation when the quota agreement ceased, and actually spent the interval laid up in Norway. For Britain the long involvement in whaling – the longest of any nation – finally came to an end, and it would only be a short time before the Antarctic trade as a whole was finished.

The British stopped whaling because there was no longer any money to be made out of their form of the trade. There is little point in comparing labour costs or efficiency with the Japanese or Russians, because these were matters that could make only a season or two's difference. If there is any serious criticism of British whaling it must lie in the failure to extract more value from by-products and to exploit the final phase of whaling to the full.

So far as by-products were concerned, the British had been in the forefront in the early days, and they had been justifiably proud of their meat meal, but, as was seen above, they made but slight inroads into the more lucrative edible meat markets. In the last full year (1959/1960) of British whaling, for instance, the three factories brought home from the Antarctic 13,000 tons of meat and bone meal, 6000 tons of meat and 874 tons of "other products," whereas the six Japanese factories brought home 3000 tons, 86,000 tons and 19,000 tons respectively. Two years later, in 1961/1962, the Japanese secured 136,000 tons of meat and 39,000 tons of other products. Moreover, because they did not cook the meat to extract oil, Japanese oil was always of magnificent quality compared with that of Salvesen, who generally aimed at maximum oil production. Nevertheless, there was no economic advantage for the British in bringing home products for which there was no market, and blame is hardly attributable to the whaling companies for the conservatism of national taste.

Nor were the companies really to blame for taking little part in the final phase of whaling, outside the Antarctic. Their effort had been heavily and sensibly concentrated there in modern times because that region produced around ninety percent of the world's whale oil in the 1940s and early 1950s (appendix 20). There was no incentive to go anywhere else. Only *Anglo-Norse*, the smallest of the British factories, and the only one to survive the war, took baleen whales off Madagascar and sperm whales off Peru rather than return to the Antarctic trade; and she was sold in 1950, leaving only the land stations in South Africa and minor establishments in Australasia to count as regular Commonwealth whaling in non-Antarctic waters. As shore stations proliferated around the world in the 1950s Britain could, for geographical reasons, play no part in their activity. This was especially true insofar as the crucial development was in the North Pacific and was carried on for the most part from the Japanese islands and the Russian mainland. Eventually, land stations were supplemented by floating factories from these two countries in the late 1950s, and the ability to use their vessels during the "winter" in the Antarctic and during the "summer" off their own coasts, gave the Russians and Japanese a great advantage over their European rivals.

Although there was some slight increase, for a time, in the proportion of whale oil caught outside the Antarctic, the main feature of the revived Pacific fishery was the renewed interest in the sperm whale. Since sperm oil was inedible, and not much use for soap, there had been hardly more effort devoted to it after the war than there had been before it, when it accounted for less than six percent of total oil and Rupert Trouton, for instance, thought it not worth the bother of catching. However, a sudden rise in demand for sperm oil in 1950, which was thought at first to be associated with the Korean war, turned out to be the result of recent discoveries allowing sperm oil to be substituted for certain other oils in soap production, and its future, at least in the market place, was assured. Whereas the catch of whale oil remained fairly stable, because of the quota system, that of sperm oil doubled during the 1950s, with, eventually, less than a third of the total catch coming from areas dominated by European whaling (appendix 20). This failure to secure a reasonable share of the sperm oil trade was especially serious because, in the last few years of British involvement in whaling, sperm oil was rising in price while whale oil was sinking, until in 1961 sperm oil became the more valuable (appendix 21).

Eventually, with the rapid exhaustion of the stocks of baleen whales after 1960, the whaling trade was concentrated once more on the sperm whale, in whose exploitation the British – either in the nineteenth or the twentieth century – had invested relatively little capital or effort, and in whose final extermination they have played no part. In a situation of over-capacity and failing stocks, someone eventually had to stop whaling. The Japanese and the Russians had the better markets to support them to the bitter end, while the British owners realised their assets and turned to more lucrative pursuits.

Conclusion

British involvement in whaling lasted for three and a half centuries. It began with the expansion of Europe, when the whale was located in Arctic waters, and ended only when the virtual extinction of the whale made the trade unprofitable. Those in the last stages of the trade argued, when conscience pricked, that the extermination of the whale was impossible because the cost/yield ratio would prevent the catching of "too many" of the last specimens. It proved, in the event, to be a false argument based, perhaps, on too optimistic a view of human nature, or perhaps on a misunderstanding of the economics of whaling. When Europeans could no longer make whaling pay there were still those – the Russians and Japanese – who worked on different principles, and between them the various whaling nations have brought stocks so low that there are serious doubts if they can ever revive. With such mobile migratory marine animals there has to be a fairly large number before effective breeding can take place and nobody at the moment knows if the surviving specimens can provide for the future. Certainly the Right whale which has been protected throughout the modern phase of whaling has shown no appreciable increase in numbers. The abundance of food may encourage a revival of the blue and fin whales, but it has not yet done so, and scientists are pessimistic. One thing is absolutely clear: whatever happens to the survival of the whales, there can be no whaling in the foreseeable future among the baleen whales. Any attempt to revive the free-for-all slaughter would simply return the species involved to the threshold of extinction.

The problem of over-fishing is in fact a recurring theme of whaling history. Each phase of the trade has undergone the same evolutionary process, the same crisis and the same demise. First came the discovery of the whales and their exploitations in the easiest bay fishery stage. Since, with the ruthless killing of young whales, and of nursing and pregnant females, the breeding bays were easily and rapidly fished out, there followed the seaborne hunting phase when the whales were sought in their feeding grounds or along their migratory routes. This was the more extensive and expensive phase. It was probably also the more arduous phase for those intimately involved in whaling, who now spent months pursing baleen whales along the polar ice sheets, or years searching for sperm whales in the more temperate oceans. But despite the fact that ocean stocks were obviously more plentiful than the numbers to be found in individual bays, they were as likely to be exhausted by constant and heavy fishing. It is a matter of record that every fishery was sooner or later subjected to a rate of catch that exceeded its rate of replacement, so that within a fairly short time whalers were taking a steadily increasing proportion of the whale stock and thus accelerating its decline. At this stage whales became more difficult to find and the trade began to feel the pinch. The weak-hearted – or the wise – withdrew, leaving the remaining owners to squeeze higher profits out of fewer whales, while the more adventurous went off in search of fresh whale stocks. So the cycle began again, many times. There were the broad chronological phases which fell quite happily into geographical divisions: the Arctic – "Northern" – Fishery, the Southern Fishery, the Pacific Fishery, the North Atlantic Fishery, and the Antarctic Fishery. Within the broad phases were the moving centres of activity: Spitsbergen, Greenland and Davis Strait; New England, Brazil, Australia and the Pacific; the Norwegian and Scottish coasts; South Georgia, South Shetlands, Ross Sea, and South Africa; and finally, the Pacific once again. Each of these broad developments depended upon, and encouraged the participation of new people and new influences, new capital and – occasionally – new methods. The trade experienced a Basque, Dutch, British, American, Norwegian and Japanese phase, overlapping to some extent, with experience passed on from one group to the next. Of all the people involved in whaling, the British were the only ones to be extensively involved, admitting brief interludes, throughout the whole period of the trade from the seventeenth to the twentieth centuries.

Thus the whaling trade was not a permanent thing, with a traditional corpus of international merchants enjoying a stable and reasonable prosperity. Even within the longer, seemingly permanent phases of the trade – in the late eighteenth century, for instance – excessive wealth and bankruptcy went hand in hand. In most trades there are "connexions" and agencies which allow experienced merchants to trade with a fair degree of security. In whaling, however, there was nothing to stop the rapid intrusion of rash competition. It is sometimes called a trade and sometimes an industry, but it would be reasonable to treat it as neither. The slightest increase in profits drew ships in from other trades in a way that would have been impossible in a land-based industry with more permanent capital goods. It is, indeed, extremely difficult to identify or quantify capital accumulation in whaling, even in modern times when larger and more expensive ships were involved. Thus rising prices were not enjoyed by the owners of existing capital stock, but had to be shared with newcomers out for a quick kill. Since the produce almost always rose in volume, the price declined again, and the newcomers went out of the trade leaving the established men with their low profits once more. This does not mean that men could not make large sums in the early stages of a rising market, but it does mean that they could not make them for very long. Moreover, whaling shared with agriculture the vagaries of nature. Climate, luck, and things known only to whales, might produce one good season in three before the twentieth century. The men who persevered over good years and bad made a reasonable fortune, but it would be misleading to look only to the good years and describe whaling as a lucrative trade, as writers tended to do in the past. This point is borne out to some extent by the slow growth of whaling in the eighteenth century, and by the failure of even substantial bounties to have much effect on the trade before the price rise associated with the period of industrialisation at the end of the century.

The proceeds derived from whaling were affected by other things than the condition of the fishing grounds and recurring excess capacity. Whale oil for most of its history was valued in terms of vegetable oil, and factors far removed from the Arctic or Antarctic had their influence on whaling: better seed harvests in Europe and Africa, or newer seed-crushing machinery at home. The value of whalebone for corsets was determined by fashion, at least to some extent. Thus in some market conditions a particular geographical fishery might be profitable, and in other circumstances it would not be. Fortunately for those involved in it, demand was seldom so poor that serious gaps developed in the long history of the trade.

The most obvious periods of relative inactivity, so far as Britain was concerned, were in the late seventeenth and early eighteenth centuries, when British whaling owners failed completely to compete with the Dutch, and in the second half of the nineteenth century when they failed to make the technical adjustment that would have allowed them to take part in the early stages of modern whaling. It was in this period, perhaps more than any other, that a sluggish market deterred British shipowners from making the necessary investment in newer types of vessels. In both of these periods there seemed to be no point in going on when adequate oil supplies could be obtained abroad.

If the first theme in whaling history is the rise and fall of particular branches of the fishery; the second is the influence of a changing economy, with changing needs, both at home and abroad. Whaling began for the provision of raw materials for the soapers, and survived in a rather sluggish way as the supplier of lighting oil and stay-bones. Its boom in the late eighteenth century was associated with industrial demand, and growing financial troubles in the nineteenth century owed more to the advances in seed crushing, and competition from American whale oil, than they did to gas lighting. In the twentieth century whaling once more made sense when hydrogenation made it suitable for soap and margarine making. In general it is true to say that the major changes in whaling associated with the growth of the Southern Fishery and the move to the Antarctic were the result of complex changes in the demand for raw materials, and had little to do with the internal affairs of whaling itself. The Northern Fishery owners, fo instance, had little connexion with the Southern Fishery owners in the late eighteenth and early nineteenth centuries, and the last of the "old" British Northern people who hung on in Dundee till the twentieth century had nothing whatever to do with the rise of modern whaling. The Southern

Fishery was learned from the Americans, the Antarctic Fishery from the Norwegians.

Long-term changes in the economy tended, in a growth situation, to work in favour of the whaling industry, though this was not always the case. The rivalry of seed oil has already been noted, but far more important in its consequences was the investment in palm oil and other vegetable oils in the twentieth century. It is doubtful if even a more promising whaling industry could have held back the production of vegetable oil, and in the circumstances it was just as well that the vegetable oil trade was ready to take over as the whaling trade collapsed.

Changes in Europe were as important as changes at home or within the empire. In particular, since whale oil was eminently mobile and could be carried as easily to Hamburg as to Hull, there tended to be an international price which worked for or against Britain in a rather arbitrary fashion which again had little to do with the performance of the British industry itself. The most obvious examples are the rising price following the wars and the general upward trend associated with a growing Continental margarine consumption, and the falling prices associated with the slump.

It would, however, be unfair to blame abstract economic forces for the fluctuations in whaling when much of the blame for its ills lay within the trade itself. The basic problem was the insecure relationship between supply and demand. The demand for whale oil was relatively inelastic, even to the extent that a rise in the consumption of whale oil tended to be determined not by the price of whale oil but by the price of preferred oils such as rape. On the other hand supply was highly elastic by the very nature of whaling. As a result the price of whale oil moved sharply and erratically despite any long-term upward or down-ward trend. Unfortunately, as noted above, this movement of prices tended to attract and repel peripheral, "marginal," owners, and to over-encourage or discourage the committed men, so that a swing in one direction was followed fairly quickly by a swing in the other.

In the very early days of whaling an increase in the number of ships led automatically to an increase in the aggregate catches. However, the number of ships in relation to the available whales soon reached a point where additional ships made no additional catches; in economic terms, marginal efficiency was nil. Since the same amount of whales were now shared between a larger number of ships, individual profits immediately sank, whatever the level of prices. This was as true in the twentieth century as in the eighteenth. Indeed, in the later stages of the various fisheries, the number of ships involved made almost no difference to the aggregate number of whales caught. This was why profits were usually highest during war-time, when the number of ships was artificially kept down to the number it ought to have been all the time if the industry was ever to exist on a sound footing.

There appeared to be no answer to this inability to balance supply and demand, and in this respect whaling differed from most trades and industries. Forward planning was almost impossible because, as with the corn trade, no one knew what next year's harvest would bring. Shipowners therefore equipped their whalers in search of the previous season's prices and hoped for the best. It was, in fact, the same sort of problem that faced shipowning in general, for similar reasons: ships operate in an almost perfect market. By the end of the eighteenth century some at least of the shipowners on regular runs had discovered that the only way to survive was to form shipping "rings," and these have been common in shipping, and in other forms of transport with similar problems, ever since. Whaler owners could not form such rings because, unlike shipowners, they had more to sell than freights. Individual owners could not restrict output because they needed to sell every drop of oil they could lay their hands on, either to make ends meet if the market was poor, or to accumulate funds against a future poor market if conditions were good. Always there was the problem of ignorance: every captain caught as much as he could without knowing how others were faring, and no one knew how much oil would have been the optimum catch until it was too late. The nearest owners came to such a ring was their joint negotiations with the Board of Trade over the bounties in the 1780s. They knew how much profit they needed to break even, but the only way they could conceive of reaching this figure was by government subsidy for any ship that cared to set to sea. Even in the twentieth century owners were generally unable to organize production in their own favour.

There was a tragic consequence of unrestrained competition. For almost the entire history of the trade every captain endeavoured to kill every whale he could, whether or not it was "needed" by the economy as a whole. No thought was given to age or sex until, in the Arctic, there were few whales left, and even then the more ruthless men took small whales which the more sensible men left alone. But who was the sensible man, the one who squandered the future or the one who stood aside and let him? Honourable people may have one answer, but there may be a quite different one from shareholders looking for a maximum return on capital, or for simple economic survival. There was never any chance that the Right whale would survive. So long as there was a demand for oil, so long as whales were to be found in regular locations, and so long as they were caught by a system of free competitive enterprise, there was no hope whatever. There was no restraint except the financial one in traditional whaling, and that was never more than a feeble brake on activity. It is difficult to see how it could have been otherwise. The old whaling captains who devastated the fisheries in various parts of the world had no statistics or scientific knowledge of whales to guide or restrain them; moreover, their fishing was on a pigmy scale taking over two centuries to exterminate the Right whale and over one century to make significant inroads into the sperm whale stocks. It can at least be pleaded for these men that the results of their action were less apparent at the time than they are now.

The modern whaling trade was very different from the old. It was highly mechanised, efficient, and capital intensive to a degree undreamed of in the past. Yet it shared the same intrinsic flaws and pursued the same time-worn path to destruction that seems to day to have been totally suicidal. The exhaustion of Antarctic whaling was forecast before the First World War, but though many people warned of the consequences of overfishing, few people listened; or, rather, few people were able to believe sufficiently in an unwelcome and incredible forecast to give it precedence over traditional market forces. The demand for whale oil after 1906 was apparently insatiable, and so the remaining whales were hunted with the efficiency, speed and precision of modern war.

It was not simply that the hunters were destroying the whale; they were also destroying themselves. The old pattern of rising prices calling forth excessive investment did not stop simply because the pelagic vessels now grossed 15,000 tons and cost £300,000, and the interwar problem was one of excess production and low prices in most years, with many of the leading firms in serious financial trouble. International regulations did nothing to ease the dilemma of Hektor, Christensen, Kerguelan Whaling, Jahre and others who came cap in hand to Unilever offering their fleets or land bases at almost any price because competition was ruining them. The only answer, as the Retionalisers would have argued in the 1930s, was the destruction of capacity; but laid up ships remained for ever ready to put to sea at the least sign of advancing prices.

The Second World War cleared the seas of most of the floating factories, yet the few that remained set about their fishing with as even greater efficiency and ruthlessness, and it took them less than twenty years to complete the destruction of the whale stocks. There was no room for doubt about the outcome of their fishing. The British companies admitted the short-time nature of their investment, and the Japanese companies that bought them out knew that they were attacking the last of the whales. While sentiment or morality has little part to play in economics, this rush to kill the goose that lay the golden eggs would appear to be a rather selfish denial of a great trade to future generations. Once more, however, there is a recurring theme that appears, and which to some extent counters accusations of "greed." As indicated above, whale oil was very nearly "redundant" when the final slaughter began, and its loss is now of little economic consequence because other sources of oil have arisen to take its place. It had happened when the Spitsbergen fishery gave out, when Hobart Bay was deserted, when South Georgia declined. Always there had been another source to take its place. This time the source moved from the roughest oceans to the mildest lands. Some might call it an advance, while others will wonder why, in this case, the last of the whales had to be exterminated. To call it a matter of profit hardly seems enough. The lesson is a hard one: that no amount of good faith and international agreement can prevent the exhaustion of wasting re-sources in international waters so long as they are exploited under a system of free competition and when profit is the sole determinant of the level of activity. But profit is, after all, a reflection of need. In the years following the Second World War people were hungry, and whale oil played a vital part in supporting the fat ration. The whale paid the penalty for being the only easily available source of food, or, rather, the only source which could be expanded rapidly by commercial exploitation, as opposed to the slower process of agricultural development.

The whale may, despite our pessimism, revive. But in the interval a new possibility is arising, and presently receiving the attention of ocean scientists. Just as domestic animals are machines for turning grass into meat and milk, so the whales were krill-converters. The food chains in the Arctic and Antarctic oceans have been altered by the intervention of man. Millions of tons of whales were supported by food that is now, presumably, feeding other forms of life, or multiplying on a large scale. It has been suggested that seals, emperor penguins and certain types of fish are benefiting enormously from the increasing supply of krill, and the last of these may well be brought into use as human food. The krill may also be fished for food, if only after chemical conversion. Unfortunately the whale had a better "nose" for the krill than has man, and it remains true that nothing could so easily have made available the vast potential of the Antarctic food chain as the largest animal of all time. It may yet be a matter of regret that the whale was sold for peanuts.

Appendix 1
Account of Quantity of Train or Animal Oil Imported and Exported, 1701-1785
(tuns)

Year	England Imports Except Greenland*	England Imports From Greenland†	England Exports	Scotland Imports	Scotland Exports
1701	1333	—	84	—	
1702	2645	—	—	—	
1703	630	—	2	—	
1704	566	—	5	—	
1705	1017	—	20	—	
1706	792	—	3	—	
1707	703	11	9	—	
1708	1301	—	—	3	
1709	1181	—	19	2	
1710	1319	—	44	—	
1711	1097	—	10	27	
1712	1375	—	4	10	
1713	1130	—	104	19	
1714	1039	—	75	11	
1715	1539	—	29	3	
1716	1139	—	7	1	
1717	855	—	19	7	
1718	1284	—	3	3	
1719	1100	—	27	1	
1720	1594	—	20	1	
1721	2050	—	9	5	
1722	1819	—	32	4	
1723	2014	—	193	1	
1745	2115	—	31	7	—
1746	2590	60	21	129	1
1747	4274	53	6	20	—
1748	3185	18	682	33	3
1749	3172	59	324	32	—
1750	3173	304	65	73	—
1751	3373	306	334	131	1
1752	3451	513	151	317	2
1753	2519	867	368	461	238
1754	1793	1290	338	353	44
1755	1971	1328	59	447	40
1756	1977	991	215	527	122
1757	1522	866	16	180	27
1758	2114	481	—	140	37
1759	3283	588	1	—	21
1760	2604	738	34	47	58
1761	3259	522	1	193	51
1762	2549	286	—	183	59
1763	5087	265	217	261	76
1764	5294	443	195	219	113
1765	6592	879	213	387	30
1766	6232	620	440	124	142
1767	5726	423	297	125	93

Years 1724–1744

Year	England Imports Except Greenland*	England Imports From Greenland†	England Exports	Scotland Imports	Scotland Exports
1724	2088	—	42	7	
1725	1951	—	92	3	
1726	1791	—	3	4	
1727	3093	—	299	30	
1728	2785	—	202	51	
1729	2473	—	976	14	
1730	2415	—	159	62	
1731	2246	168	37	20	
1732	2711	—	53	8	
1733	2735	—	68	29	
1734	3335	—	72	21	
1735	2717	—	46	28	
1736	2630	132	6	—	
1737	3490	76	206	44	
1738	2534	134	89	—	
1739	2767	123	18	—	
1740	2462	—	8	6	
1741	3104	12	—	27	
1742	2035	6	5	1	
1743	2578	—	7	40	
1744	1811	—	47	41	

Years 1768–1785

Year	England Imports Except Greenland*	England Imports From Greenland†	England Exports	Scotland Imports	Scotland Exports
1768	7077	510	332	143	44
1769	6842	1429	234	474	56
1770	6786	1496	559	393	7
1771	8232	834	671	121	90
1772	7020	1301	508	402	30
1773	7550	1397	54	279	39
1774	6258	3291	92	433	21
1775	7376	1299	37	285	82
1776	3643	2025	157	404	31
1777	3439	2234	28	347	13
1778	3561	1735	105	379	6
1779	2043	1060	345	303	9
1780	2755	2478	116	170	92
1781	1460	1810	397	472	41
1782	1732	2451	4	222	65
1783	3590	1709	207	312	69
1784	3811	3359	67	334	121
1785	5659	4034	380	555	17

Note: *This was initially imported from Holland, but by the 1740s was chiefly colonial-caught oil from America. †This source clearly omits oil imported by the South Sea Company in the 1720s.

Source: Great Britain, Public Record Office (PRO), Board of Trade (BT) 6/93/116-117.

Appendix 2

Number of Greenland Whalers Fitted Out by Major Whaling Ports, and Total English and Scottish Whaling Fleets, All Ports, 1733-1785

	London	Liverpool	Whitby	Hull	English Totals		Scottish Totals	
					No.	Tons	No.	Tons
1733	3	—	—	—	3	920	—	—
1734	3	—	—	—	3	920	—	—
1735	3	—	—	—	3	920	—	—
1736	4	—	—	—	4	1148	—	—
1737	5	—	—	—	5	1431	—	—
1738	6	—	—	—	6	1780	—	—
1739	6	—	—	—	6	1780	—	—
1740	2	—	—	—	2	632	—	—
1741	2	—	—	—	2	632	—	—
1742	3	—	—	—	3	981	—	—
1743	5	—	—	—	5	1329	—	—
1744	5	—	—	—	5	1647	—	—
1745	5	—	—	—	5	1648	—	—
1746	5	—	—	—	5	1648	—	—
1747	2	—	—	—	2	628	—	—
1748	2	—	—	—	2	628	—	—
1749	6	—	—	—	6	2154	—	—
1750	16	1	—	—	19	6264	1	333
1751	22	1	—	—	23	7360	6	1933
1752	26	1	2	—	30	9871	10	3137
1753	27	1	4	4	35	11814	14	4294
1754	36	1	4	7	52	17235	15	4680
1755	41	2	4	7	66	21293	16	4964
1756	42	2	4	7	67	21328	16	4964
1757	34	2	4	4	55	17221	15	4531
1758	32	2	4	4	52	15399	15	4500
1759	23	1	—	3	34	10337	15	4480

	London	Liverpool	Whitby	Hull	English Totals		Scottish Totals	
					No.	Tons	No.	Tons
1760	28	2	1	2	40	12082	14	4239
1761	22	2	—	2	31	9789	14	4239
1762	18	2	—	2	28	8877	14	4239
1763	21	2	—	—	29	9095	10	3110
1764	23	3	—	—	32	10361	10	3141
1765	24	3	—	1	33	10099	8	2560
1766	24	4	—	2	35	10015	9	2798
1767	24	6	2	3	39	12284	9	2798
1768	25	6	2	6	41	12802	9	2798
1769	24	6	4	6	44	13471	9	2798
1770	28	4	4	7	46	14775	9	2798
1771	26	9	4	8	50	14700	9	2798
1772	24	7	5	8	48	15358	9	2798
1773	28	10	5	9	55	16712	10	3017
1774	34	10	8	12	65	19770	9	2774
1775	45	17	14	10	96	29131	9	2774
1776	36	20	15	9	91	27047	7	2252
1777	27	18	14	8	77	21917	7	2252
1778	26	13	14	4	71	20291	5	1588
1779	25	7	14	4	59	16907	3	957
1780	25	5	10	4	52	14900	4	1283
1781	15	2	8	3	34	9859	5	1460
1782	20	3	7	3	38	11122	5	1460
1783	28	3	7	4	47	14268	4	1095
1784	50	7	11	9	89	27224	7	2048
1785	78	10	16	14	140	43565	13	3864

Source: PRO, BT 6/93/98 and 126.

Appendix 3

Number and Tonnage of Greenland Whalers, Quantity of Oil, Bone and Sealskins, and Value of Bounties,
Great Britain, 1733-1800

(Periods Related to the Rate of Bounty; dates inclusive)

	Whalers		Bounty		Oil	Bone	Skins
	No.	Tons	Rate	Total	Tuns	Cwt.	Number
1733-1749	67	20,934	20/-	£19,086	908	765	19
average	*4*	*1231*		*1123*	*54*	*45*	*1*
1750-1776	1534	474,474	40/-	912,956	27,502	19,552	156,498
average	*57*	*17,573*		*33,813*	*1019*	*724*	*5796*
1777-1781	317	91,412	30/-	131,835	6286	2250	139
average	*63*	*18,282*		*26,367*	*1257*	*450*	*28*
1782-1786	534	163,908	40/-	320,438	19,906	11,959	37,824
average	*107*	*32,781*		*64,088*	*3981*	*2392*	*7565*
1787-1792	1028	305,131	30/-	432,813	32,738	38,303	130,355
average	*171*	*50,855*		*72,135*	*5456*	*6384*	*21,272*
1793-1795	203	56,845	25/-	71,761	9871	13,011	14,266
average	*68*	*18,948*		*23,920*	*3290*	*4337*	*4755*
1796-1800	323	89,765	20/-	86,200	26,457	32,951	59,846
average	*65*	*17,953*		*17,240*	*5291*	*6590*	*11,969*
1733-1800	4006	1,202,469		£1,975,089	123,668	118,791	398,927

Source: PRO, BT 6/230, fol 92.

Appendix 4
Number and Tonnage of Ships Clearing for and Entering from Greenland, with Real Value of Imports, 1781-1800, and Great Britain, 1733-1800

| | England (Whalers) | | | | Scotland | | | | Imports | | | | | | | |
| | Clearing | | Entering | | Clearing | | Entering | | Oil | | Bone | | Sealskins | | Total |
	No.	Tons	No.	Tons	No.	Tons	No	Tons	Tuns	£	Cwt.	£	No.	£	£
1781	34	9862	33	9620	5	1460	5	1460	1917	53,674	980	15,168	187	36	68,878
1782	38	11,124	36	10,611	5	1460	4	1095	2367	61,538	1255	16,945	3337	584	79,067
1783	47	14,270	46	13,957	4	1095	4	1095	2028	44,613	880	11,438	3372	422	56,472
1784	89	27,228	88	26,857	7	2047	7	2047	3482	97,495	2053	23,607	4855	931	122,033
1785	140	43,570	137	42,652	13	3865	13	3865	4131	95,036	2293	26,372	8255	1582	122,991
1786	168	52,254	166	51,742	23	6997	23	6997	7898	150,065	5478	62,995	18,005	3151	216,211
1787	217	65,890	216	64,486	31	9057	31	9057	9905	178,298	9115	91,154	30,521	5342	274,794
1788	222	64,987	216	62,960	31	8910	31	8910	7166	121,826	7907	51,398	13,416	2348	175,572
1789	151	46,282	148	45,393	27	7584	27	7584	5518	99,318	9123	59,298	30,432	5706	164,322
1790	103	30,819	99	29,577	23	6297	22	5899	4036	88,799	4063	34,534	49,862	9349	132,683
1791	93	27,546	92	27,324	23	6312	22	6124	3397	78,137	4706	47,063	4285	750	125,949
1792	87	25,956	86	25,393	20	5491	18	4904	2714	66,511	3389	37,276	1819	364	104,151
1793	73	21,286	73	21,287	14	3815	14	3815	3354	77,153	4008	40,084	1126	282	117,519
1794	53	14,772	52	14,493	13	3480	12	3193	3041	79,061	3816	24,801	1453	327	104,189
1795	40	10,877	40	10,877	10	2613	10	2613	3475	109,472	5817	44,089	11,687	2922	156,483
1796	44	12,091	43	11,791	9	2319	9	2319	4468	147,429	5633	33,092	16,731	3764	184,285
1797	57	15,801	55	15,247	10	2614	10	2614	5486	172,795	6923	27,687	17,514	4379	204,861
1798	59	16,597	59	16,597	10	2614	9	2315	5294	153,545	7320	25,620	9379	2345	181,510
1799	60	17,047	60	17,047	10	2629	9	2339	5637	157,832	6910	24,186	6961	2349	184,367
1800	54	15,405	53	15,105	10	2651	10	2651	5572	214,429	6166	20,039	9261	2778	237,247

Source: PRO, BT 6/230/76.

Appendix 5
Vessels Clearing for the Southern Fishery, and Premiums Paid, 1776-1808

	No.	Tons	£
1776	12	1977	n.a.
1777	13	2103	2400
1778	19	3038	1500
1779	4	467	500
1780	7	771	2000
1781	6	757	1400
1782	6	910	1400
1783	9	1040	nil
1784	15	3109	3600
1785	18	4155	1700
1786	34	n.a.	300
1787	44	n.a.	5600
1788	42	8998	n.a.
1789	45	9602	n.a.
1790	46	10,121	n.a.
1791	64	7717	n.a.
1792	42	9544	n.a.
1793	38	8487	5200
1794	37	7948	8100
1795	33	8333	6000
1796	37	9054	13,500
1797	23	6885	4100
1798	34	9143	5100
1799	26	7485	5600
1800	24	6382	7100
1801	34	10,103	5300
1802	54	15,678	6800
1803	39	11,084	6400
1804	49	14,283	7800
1805	25	7642	8500
1806	30	8809	8300
1807	17	5178	8400
1808	30	8050	n.a.

Sources: 1776-1785: PRO, BT 6/93/98 and 135; 1785-1787: PRO, BT 5/5, 7 March 1788; 1789: BT 6/95/197; and 1788 and 1790-1808: PRO, Customs 17, *passim*.

Appendix 6
Regional Sources of Whale Oil, 1772-1805

	Total Europe*	Total America†	Green-land Fishery	Southern Fishery	British North America	New England Colonies
1772	1617	7032	1610	—	3667	2943
1773	1392	7680	1392	—	4051	2925
1774	3300	6874	3296	—	2390	3454
1775	1356	7290	1335	—	2473	4093
1776	2215	3832	2149	—	2895	52
1777	2284	3888	2186	—	2793	2
1778	1797	3740	1746	—	2614	1
1779	1631	2290	1540	—	1826	2
1780	2962	2731	2872	—	2542	2
1781	2383	1621	2351	—	1187	147
1782	2823	1896	2532	—	1415	—
1783	2149	3588	2072	—	2107	669
1784	3843	3881	3843	—	3009	428
1785	4878	5765	4870	—	3500	1084
1786	9053	3639	9011	—	2620	306
1787	12,131	3078	12,096	—	2300	285
1788	7180	8499	7166	3270	3228	327
1789	5519	8608	5517	3415	3486	383
1790	4088	8501	4036	3801	3248	383
1791	3402	7338	3397	3551	2135	64
1792	2715	8024	2715	4321	2632	—
1793	3355	8307	3354	5917	1570	—
1794	3081	7819	3041	4059	2944	—
1795	3573	6452	3475	3102	2739	—
1796	4519	6918	4468	4398	1860	—
1797	5573	7986	5486	5552	1943	—
1798	5347	6716	5295	3679	2369	—
1799	5646	7223	5637	3182	3234	—
1800	5581	7637	5572	3374	3174	—
1801	5320	10,293	5240	5612	3975	—
1802	7479	10,491	7449	6959	2837	—
1803	7080	10,409	7042	7117	2899	—
1804	10,048	11,558	9964	6504	4382	—
1805	12,786	10,840	12,718	5494	5034	—

Note: *Includes Greenland Fishery. †Includes Southern Fishery. Both totals include small parcels of oil from minor sources. The figures are not completely reliable because the Customs officers were rather vague about the classification of oil imports. The Southern Fishery was, for instance, included in America in 1788 and in Europe in 1789 (the table above has been adjusted in this case). The figures are a reasonable reflection of the orders of magnitude, and variations between sources are insignificant.

Source: PRO, Customs 17, *passim*.

Appendix 7
Prices of Oil and Whalebone, 1769-1785

	Sperm	Seal	Whale	Cod	Refined Sperm	Whale-bone
	Tun	Tun	Tun	Tun	Lb.	Ton
1769	£24	£17	£16	£16	14d	n.a.
1770	23	18	17	17	15	£350
1771	27	21	20	19	18	360
1772	34	22	18	20	21	n.a.
1773	37	26	24	23	20	330
1774	38	24	21	21	20	250
1775	40	28	26	27	20	320
1776	43	25	23	23	19	280
1777	54	26	25	24	30	280
1778	70	24	21	23	30	280
1779	85	26	25	24	42	315
1780	70	26	22	22	42	280
1781	67	30	28	30	31	340
1782	65	30	26	32	36	345
1783	46	25	24	23	30	285
1784	46	26	23	26	31	260
1785	40	28	22	24	19	245

Note: Taken during November, "being the time of the most general consume [sic] and the price of each article at that time most settled."

Source: PRO, BT 6/93/137.

Appendix 8
Prices of Oil, Whalebone and Sealskins, 1786-1801

	Green-land Oil	South-ern Oil	Sperm Oil	Green-land Bone	South-ern Bone	Green-land Skins	South-ern Skins
	£	£	£	£	£	*s/d*	*s/d*
1786	19	19	50	230	170	3/6	2/-
1787	18	16	68	200	160	3/6	2/-
1788	17	14	63	130	100	3/6	2/-
1789	18	14	58	130	80	3/9	3/-
1790	22	15	53	170	100	3/9	3/-
1791	23	18	42	200	90	3/6	3/-
1792	24	20	36	220	100	3/9	2/6
1793	23	19	37	200	100	4/3	1/6
1794	26	21	50	130	100	3/9	2/-
1795	31	26	68	170	110	4/-	3/6
1796	33	30	72	118	75	3/9	3/-
1797	32	29	80	80	80	4/3	3/-
1798	29	27	79	70	75	4/3	5/-
1799	29	26	74	70	60	5/6	4/3
1800	39	34	70	65	50	5/-	4/-
1801	40	36	84	65	45	3/9	3/9

Source: PRO, BT 6/230/95.

Appendix 9
The Northern Whale Fishery, 1815-1842

Years	Ships to Greenland and Davis Straits		Total Ships	Total Tons	Ships Lost	Whales Caught	Tuns of Oil	Tons of Bone
	G.	**D.S.**						
1815	98	48	146	47,148	1	733	10,682	528
1816	101	45	146	46,868	1	1330	13,590	632
1817	97	53	150	48,084	5	828	10,871	539
1818	94	63	157	50,362	2	1208	14,482	666
1819	96	63	159	51,082	12	988	11,401	517
1820	102	57	159	50,546	3	1595*	18,745	946
1821	80	79	159	50,709	14	1405	16,853	923
1822	61	60	121	38,144	8	630	8663	422
1823	55	62	117	36,759	3	2018	17,074	921
1824	32	79	111	35,013	1	761	9871	534
1825	21	89	110	34,751	5	500	6370**	350
1826	5	90	95	30,414	5	512	7200	400
1827	16	72	88	28,273	1	1162	13,186	733
1828	14	79	93	28,665	3	1197	13,966	802
1829	1	88	89	28,812	4	871	10,672	608
1830	0	91	91	29,396	19	161	2199	119
1831	8	80	88	28,608	3	451	5104	273
1832	19	62	81	26,393	5	1563	12,610	676
1833	3	74	77	25,294	1	1695	14,508	802
1834	7	69	76	24,955	3	872	8214	442
1835	1	70	71	n.a.	6	167	2632	n.a.
1836	3	58	61	n.a.	2	70	707	n.a.
1837	15	37	52	n.a.	2	122	1356	65
1838	31	8	39	n.a.	1	466	4345	236
1839	29	12	41	n.a.	0	115	1441	79
1840	11	20	31	n.a.	2	22	412	14
1841	11	8	19	n.a.	0	52	647	22
1842	14	4	18	n.a.	0	54	668	n.a

Note: *This figure is from the 1834 edition; the 1155 printed in the 1854 edition is clearly wrong. **This figure from the 1834 edition; there is a blank in the 1854 edition.

Source: J.R. McCulloch, *Descriptive and Statistical Account of the British Empire* (4th ed., 2 vols., London, 1854), I, 642.

Appendix 10
The Price of No. 1 Whale Oil, 1895-1914
(barrels included)

	High		Low			High		Low	
	£	s	£	s		£	s	£	s
1895	16	10	15	0	1905	15	10	13	10
1896	18	0	15	0	1906	23	10	15	10
1897	16	15	15	10	1907	24	0	21	0
1898	16	10	15	5	1908	23	10	17	0
1899	17	0	15	5	1909	20	0	18	0
1900	22	15	21	5	1910	24	0	19	10
1901	21	10	19	0	1911	23	10	18	0
1902	22	0	19	10	1912	23	0	17	0
1903	20	10	17	10	1913	23	5	21	0
1904	16	0	14	0	1914	24	0	19	10

Source: *International Whaling Statistics* (Oslo, 1942), 54.

Appendix 11
Whales Killed off Shetland, Hebrides and Ireland, 1904-1929

	Whales caught	No. of Catchers	Whales per Catcher
1904	327	10	33
1905	533	11	48
1906	710	12	59
1907	600	13	46
1908	727	15	49
1909	830	15	55
1910	734	16	46
1911	634	16	40
1912	498	16	31
1913	549	17	32
1914	685	15	46
1915	—	—	—
1916	—	—	—
1917	—	—	—
1918	—	—	—
1919	—	—	—
1920	749	11	68
1921	—	—	—
1922	358	6	60
1923	347	7	50
1924	632	7	90
1925	379	7	54
1926	461	7	66
1927	312	7	45
1928	186	7	27
1929	85	4	21

Note: No whales were caught before 1904 or after 1929.

Source: *International Whaling Statistics* (Oslo, 1942), 12-13.

Appendix 12
British Whaling: Expeditions and Catches, 1909/1910-1938/1939

Species of Whales Caught

Year	Blue	Fin	Hump-back	Sei	Sperm	Others	Total	Oil (tons)	Shore bases	FFs	Catchers
1909/10	14	43	359	346	2	1140	1904	10,715	13	—	34
1910/11	23	70	1671	195	—	1406	3365	17,016	13	—	36
1911/12	113	334	2130	11	63	1186	3837	20,164	22	2	58
1912/13	304	1273	1142	114	205	398	3436	21,293	19	3	53
1913/14	443	1128	695	245	373	504	3388	22,257	16	3	50
1914/15	1030	951	382	7	505	260	3135	23,508	9	3	40
1915/16	2137	1428	695	49	596	9	4914	33,174	7	1	41
1916/17	1389	929	133	40	118	11	2620	22,088	6	1	29
1917/18	1025	951	67	128	213	123	2507	21,773	6	1	31
1918/19	435	1249	157	193	503	10	2547	17,744	5	1	38
1919/20	792	1460	312	405	401	8	3378	22,908	8	1	46
1920/21	826	1711	315	107	329	12	3300	23,561	5	1	31
1921/22	2219	1215	307	212	148	4	4105	32,681	5	1	34
1922/23	3144	1998	258	154	116	5	5675	47,711	7	3	47
1923/24	1921	2545	324	565	350	54	5759	43,013	9	3	55
1924/25	2913	2759	392	167	604	—	6835	57,923	10	2	56
1925/26	2588	4848	280	387	566	66	8735	63,351	11	3	61
1926/27	3197	2902	201	326	593	29	7248	64,848	11	3	64
1927/28	2930	2498	107	498	996	50	7079	66,694	12	4	69
1928/29	2954	3608	154	387	1098	29	8230	85,435	12	4	65
1929/30	4561	6198	402	307	489	326	12,283	143,138	10	9	102
1930/31	8452	4054	350	117	156	—	13,129	189,066	14	11	78
1931/32	6389	2581	511	34	267	1	9783	134,084	5	5	47
1932/33	8582	3546	307	11	536	2	12,984	196,962	3	8	72
1933/34	8409	4217	1075	30	533	352	14,616	198,746	4	8	79
1934/35	8210	6748	1467	153	953	2	17,533	215,016	6	9	91
1935/36	7798	5243	3130	294	3434	7	19,906	206,727	9	11	131

Species of Whales Caught

	Blue	Fin	Hump-back	Sei	Sperm	Others	Total	Oil (tons)	Shore bases	FFs	Catchers
1936/37	5755	6903	3073	414	5198	44	21,387	214,605	9	15	149
1937/38	4855	10,686	2866	131	1004	—	19,542	218,003	5	11	120
1938/39	4942	6046	4	13	331	—	11,336	149,624	2	9	81

Source: International Whaling Statistics (Oslo, 1942), 126.

Appendix 13

Catches of Major British Antarctic Expeditions, 1922/1923-1940/1941

(whale oil; tons)

	1922/1923	1923/1924	1924/1925	1927/1928	1928/1929	1929/1930	1930/1931	1931/1932	1932/1933
Salvesen									
Leith Harbour	12,000	7167	16,667	10,000	10,833	8926	5550	12,250	–
Neko	2833	1790	–	–	–	–	–	–	–
Sevilla	3792	2800	3383	6383	9033	7018	7833	–	–
Saragossa	–	–	–	6700	8383	9028	10,917	12,933	21,450
Salvesrria	–	–	–	–	–	16,216	18,667	21,967	17,975
Sourabaya	–	–	–	–	–	15,060	15,400	19,500	19,360
New Sevilla	–	–	–	–	–	–	–	–	–
Southern Whaling									
Prince Olaf's Harbour	12,392	8743	12,333	7458	10,467	8842	6667	–	–
Southern Queen	4783	5000	5744	7117	–	–	–	–	–
Southern Empress	–	–	–	–	11,917	11,404	14,450	28,282	28,583
Southern Princess	–	–	–	–	–	10,228	17,597	31,382	31,217
Hector Whaling									
Hektoria	–	–	–	–	–	13,917	20,350	–	19,033
Kerguelan Whaling									
Tafelberg	–	–	–	–	–	–	18,667	–	20,833
Star Whaling									
Svend Foyn	–	–	–	–	–	–	–	–	–
United Whalers									
Terje Viken	–	–	–	–	–	–	–	–	–
Union Whaling									
Uniwaleco	–	–	–	–	–	–	–	–	–

Appendix 13 (cont'd)

	1933/1934	1934/1935	1935/1936	1936/1937	1937/1938	1938/1939	1939/1940	1940/1941
Salvesen								
Leith Harbour	11,035	8583	11,333	5717	6417	7106	4225	–
Neko	–	–	–	–	–	–	–	–
Sevilla	–	–	–	–	–	–	–	–
Saragossa	–	–	–	–	–	–	–	–
Salvesrtria	17,509	19,740	17,920	15,566	21,580	13,727	14,915	–
Sourabaya	14,961	13,674	15,279	14,441	17,982	13,582	14,134	–
New Sevilla	16,740	20,383	16,514	17,916	19,768	14,908	16,839	–
Southern Whaling								
Prince Olaf's Harbour	–	–	–	–	–	–	–	–
Southern Queen	–	–	–	–	–	–	–	–
Southern Empress	37,293	25,778	23,933	20,948	17,547	17,042	14,752	19,307
Southern Princess	10,800*	23,288	19,958	20,919	18,831	14,213	13,100	–
Hector Whaling								
Hektoria	21,683	14,808	17,688	11,767	15,667	13,409	13,533	–
Kerguelan Whaling								
Tafelberg	21,333	21,500	20,833	13,730	19,809	16,533	12,617	–
Star Whaling								
Svend Foyn	–	30,725	21,717	15,783	20,963	16,383	15,933	18,990
United Whalers								
Terje Viken	–	–	–	17,000	18,583	18,164	19,333	–
Union Whaling								
Uniwaleco	–	–	–	12,358	12,833	–	6901	

Note: *Southern Empress* was recalled early in 1933/1934. 1925/1926 and 1926/1927 are missing.

Source: Geddes Statistics.

Appendix 14

Regional Sources of Whales and Oil, 1909/1910-1938-1939* (tons)

	South Georgia		South Shetland		Other Antarctic		Africa		North Atlantic	
	Whales	Oil	Whales	Oil	Whales	Oil	Whales	Oil	Whales	Oil
1909/10	307	3663	–	–			233	1667	901	3923
1910/11	1683	8317	–	–			547	3824	843	3933
1911/12	1764	8647	c.400	c.1833			1006	6452	564	2828
1912/13	1258	8983	511	3217			1039	6191	541	2548
1913/14	1149	9355	585	4348			1061	6186	414	1621
1914/15	1324	13,021	437	3044			980	5709	139	500
1915/16	3064	24,138	435	2658			1415	6918	–	–
1916/17	1698	17,702	–	–			922	4385	–	–
1917/18	1711	16,866	–	–			695	4490	–	–
1918/19	949	7667	316	2083			1282	7750	–	–
1919/20	1224	10,258	414	2394			1310	8654	430	1603
1920/21	1466	12,136	571	3350			1263	8076	–	–
1921/22	1682	18,970	421	3123			1721	9447	281	1142
1922/23	2191	24,535	1248	11,103			1819	10,143	417	1931
1923/24	1401	15,927	963	9594			2583	14,404	812	3089
1924/25	2347	29,176	910	9117			2868	16,564	710	3067
1925/26	3075	26,923	1366	14,349			3473	18,082	821	3997
1926/27	2009	27,359	1434	15,091	–	–	3130	18,525	675	3872
1927/28	1361	17,453	1543	20,084	470	7343	3011	17,571	694	4244
1928/29	2049	21,514	2077	29,317	630	10,950	3007	20,744	467	2911
1929/30	1904	17,750	–	–	7056	102,783	2603	18,027	–	–
1930/31	1143	12,217	–	–	11,053	170,141	823	6181	–	–
1931/32	1355	12,248	–	–	7367	114,393	1043	7352	–	–
1932/33	–	–	–	–	11,563	186,004	1168	8833	–	–
1933/34	1224	11,066	–	–	11,416	174,217	1574	10,154	–	–

	South Georgia		South Shetland		Other Antarctic		Africa		North Atlantic	
	Whales	Oil	Whales	Oil	Whales	Oil	Whales	Oil	Whales	Oil
1934/35	766	9174	–	–	14,557	191,501	1753	11,168	–	–
1935/36	841	11,332	–	–	11,697	154,529	2850	16,062	–	–
1936/37	744	5709	–	–	11,617	157,262	2411	17,082	–	–
1937/38	825	6417	–	–	15,286	185,811	1239	9059	–	–
1938/39	651	7444	–	–	10,541	141,188	n.a.	n.a.	–	–

Note: *In addition there were large catches off Western Australia in 1935/1936, off Peru in 1935-1936, off Peru in 1935-1937, and off Madagascar in 1936-1939. Two shore stations in British Columbia were counted in the British total, bringing in an average of 2361 tons of oil in 1932-1938, and one in New Zealand accounted for 280 tons per annum in the same period.

Source: International Whaling Statistics (Oslo, 1942), 126-131.

Appendix 15
Antarctic Whaling: British, Norwegian and Total Catches of Oil,
1909/1910-1938/1939

	Britain	Norway	Total	
	(tons)	(tons)	(tons)	Catchers
1909/1910	5125	15,730	26,265	37
1910/1911	9258	28,429	48,528	48
1911/1912	10,884	40,915	61,909	58
1912/1913	12,555	52,737	71,429	62
1913/1914	14,451	51,743	72,010	63
1914/1915	17,299	59,130	83,141	61
1915/1916	26,797	58,470	93,134	57
1916/1917	17,702	37,533	60,638	44
1917/1918	16,866	20,731	43,079	48
1918/1919	9750	27,071	40,949	50
1919/1920	12,651	29,433	45,470	44
1920/1921	15,486	44,332	65,105	47
1921/1922	22,092	46,661	75,420	46
1922/1923	35,637	57,789	102,425	60
1923/1924	25,521	46,142	77,446	66
1924/1925	38,292	69,719	116,182	65
1925/1926	41,273	80,208	130,551	70
1926/1927	43,450	92,997	145,394	80
1927/1928	44,879	116,788	172,899	84
1928/1929	61,780	193,999	271,890	111
1929/1930	120,533	288,019	424,460	194
1930/1931	182,358	381,949	601,391	232
1931/1932	126,641	nil	134,760	45
1932/1933	186,004	214,309	409,410	118
1933/1934	185,283	203,009	399,257	126
1934/1935	200,675	197,316	409,000	153
1935/1936	165,861	186,006	406,056	175
1936/1937	162,970	170,744	443,018	196
1937/1938	192,228	162,874	556,722	256
1938/1939	148,632	120,722	470,129	281

Source: *International Whaling Statistics* (Oslo, 1942), 22.

Appendix 16
South African Whaling 1910-1938: Stations, Catchers, and Oil as
a Percentage of Total British Catch

Season	Stations	Catchers	Oil (tons)	%
1909/1910	1	3	1667	15.6
1910/1911	2	6	3824	22.5
1911/1912	5	18	6452	32.0
1912/1913	5	21	6191	29.1
1913/1914	5	22	6186	27.8
1914/1915	4	23	5709	24.3
1915/1916	5	25	6918	20.5
1916/1917	4	16	4385	19.9
1917/1918	3	12	4490	20.6
1918/1919	4	23	7750	43.7
1919/1920	4	25	8654	37.8
1920/1921	3	20	8076	34.3
1921/1922	4	19	9447	28.9
1922/1923	4	21	10,143	21.3
1923/1924	4	29	14,404	33.5
1924/1925	5	30	16,564	28.6
1925/1926	5	34	18,082	28.5
1926/1927	5	35	18,525	28.6
1927/1928	5	35	17,571	26.3
1928/1929	5	37	20,744	24.3
1929/1930	5	43	18,027	12.6
1930/1931	1	10	6191	3.3
1931/1932	1	8	7352	5.5
1932/1933	2	14	8833	4.5
1933/1934	2	17	10,154	5.1
1934/1935	2	17	11,168	5.2
1935/1936	3	32	16,092	7.8
1936/1937	3	29	17,082	8.0
1937/1938	2	16	9059	4.2

Source: *International Whaling Statistics* (Oslo, 1942), 126-131.

Appendix 17
Average Prices of Antarctic Whale Oil, 1920-1939
(Based on available figures, shown as a percentage of total production)

	£	s	%		£	s	%
1919/20	90	8	65	1929/30	25	0	100
1920/21	31	5	67	1930/31	21	19	83
1921/22	32	10	65	1931/32	11	19	100
1922/23	33	0	58	1932/33	13	0	100
1923/24	34	15	59	1933/34	10	8	87
1924/25	35	13	59	1934/35	12	7	91
1925/26	34	0	61	1935/36	17	10	83
1926/27	27	17	64	1936/37	20	7	98
1927/28	28	7	67	1937/38	13	0	100
1928/29	29	17	75	1938/39	14	18	100

Source: *International Whaling Statistics* (Oslo, 1942), 54.

Appendix 18
Antarctic Whale Oil Catches, 1945/1946-1962/1963

						Percentage of Total Whale Oil		
	Total	United Kingdom	South Africa	British Empire	Norway	U.K.	British Empire	Norway
1945/1946	134,151	40,450	--	40,450	86,460	30.2	30.2	64.4
1946/1947	311,284	84,686	30,333	115,019	150,085	27.2	36.9	48.2
1947/1948	328,182	89,777	25,864	115,641	165,713	27.4	35.2	50.5
1948/1949	333,994	91,153	22,242	113,395	155,466	27.3	34.0	46.5
1949/1950	338,033	78,887	22,537	101,424	173,915	23.3	30.0	51.4
1950/1951	342,089	68,318	23,000	91,318	162,367	20.0	26.7	47.5
1951/1952	365,218	72,157	27,737	99,894	169,460	19.8	27.4	46.4
1952/1953	332,974	72,323	23,700	96,023	130,742	21.7	28.8	39.3
1953/1954	356,705	80,786	23,150	103,936	164,696	22.6	29.1	46.2
1954/1955	325,899	69,052	13,692	83,014	121,501	21.2	25.5	37.3
1955/1956	327,359	68,148	13,431	81,579	119,481	20.8	24.9	36.5
1956/1957	337,941	58,764	13,761	72,525	150,674	17.4	21.5	44.6
1957/1958	334,280	59,650	--	59,650	121,500	17.8	17.8	36.3
1958/1959	314,855	42,430	--	42,430	122,467	13.5	13.5	38.9
1959/1960	325,098	44,478	--	44,478	102,295	13.7	13.7	31.5
1960/1961	336,362	39,765	--	39,765	111,265	11.8	11.8	33.1
1961/1962	307,300	24,648	--	24,648	83,120	8.0	8.0	26.2
1962/1963	215,597	11,210	--	11,210	30,634	5.2	5.2	14.2

Source: Geddes Statistics.

Appendix 19
The Performance of British Whaling Expeditions in the Antarctic,
1945/1946-1962/1963
(Whale Oil; tons)

Season	Salvesen				United Whalers	Union Whaling
	Leith Harbour	*Southern Venturer*	*Southern Harvester*	Total	*Balaena*	*Empire Victory*
1945/1946	2335	14,293	—	16,628	23,822*	—
1946/1947	8672	26,109	19,071	53,853	30,833	30,333
1947/1948	10,210	33,866	20,486	64,554	25,223	25,864
1948/1949	9969	28,135	24,484	62,686	28,467	22,242
1949/1950	7793	23,065	17,111	47,970	30,917	22,537
1950/1951	9096	20,926	18,510	46,551	21,767	23,000
1951/1952	8715	19,834	19,659	48,207	23,950	27,537
1952/1953	6723	16,249	23,801	46,773	25,550	23,700
1953/1954	10,578	25,985	19,373	55,536	25,250	23,150
1954/1955	11,561	14,790	17,881	44,252	24,800	13,692
1955/1956	10,684	20,061	25,750	56,548	11,600	13,431
1956/1957	7808	16,772	17,242	41,822	16,942	13,761
1957/1958	11,559	9679	16,320	37,558	22,092	—
1958/1959	5224	11,878	10,785	27,888	14,542	—
1959/1960	4908	10,515	15,722	31,145	13,333	—
1960/1961	8297	18,008	13,460	39,765	—	—
1961/1962	—	11,415	13,233	24,648	—	—
1962/1963	—	—	11,210	11,210	—	—

Note: *Using *Empire Victory*, hired from the government. *Balaena* was the first used in 1946/1947. There is a slight discrepancy in the figures for 1952/1953 in two tables, possibly because one has the estimated and the other the final total. The alternative figures are 47,016 tons for Salvesen, 25,459 for United Whalers and 23,482 for Union Whaling.

Source: Geddes Statistics.

Appendix 20
Antarctic Share of World Production of Whale and Sperm Oil, 1945/1946-1961/1962
(tons)

	Whale Oil				Sperm Oil			
	Antarctic	Other	World	Antarctic share of world %	Antarctic	Other	World	Antarctic share of world %
1945/46	134,151	12,875	147,026	91.2	n.a.	n.a.	n.a.	n.a.
1946/47	311,284	13,003	324,287	96.0	12,007	27,659	39,666	30.3
1947/48	328,182	20,110	348,292	94.2	22,796	28,108	50,904	44.8
1948/49	333,994	39,358	373,352	89.5	33,772	12,502	46,274	73.0
1949/50	338,033	39,467	377,500	89.5	23,051	24,533	47,584	48.4
1950/51	342,089	45,607	387,696	88.2	42,140	63,339	105,479	40.0
1951/52	365,218	44,590	409,808	89.1	47,737	26,735	74,472	64.1
1952/53	332,974	40,452	373,426	89.2	20,132	30,343	50,475	39.9
1953/54	356,705	48,317	405,022	88.1	24,225	45,994	70,219	34.5
1954/55	325,899	44,762	370,661	87.9	47,842	42,135	89,977	53.2
1955/56	327,359	50,194	377,553	86.7	57,046	51,552	108,598	52.5
1956/57	337,941	51,615	389,556	86.8	36,993	60,701	97,694	37.9
1957/58	334,280	53,224	387,504	86.3	52,527	68,875	121,402	43.3
1958/59	314,855	55,211	370,066	85.1	43,770	69,894	113,664	38.5
1959/60	325,098	47,109	372,207	87.3	32,391	74,057	106,448	30.4
1960/61	336,362	44,103	380,465	88.4	35,868	71,623	107,491	33.4
1961/62	307,300	39,689	346,989	88.6	35,878	78,871	114,747	31.3

Source: Geddes Statistics.

Appendix 21
Whale Oil and Sperm Oil Prices, 1945-1962
(per ton)

	Whale Oil				Sperm Oil			
	Highest		Lowest		Highest		Lowest	
Year	£	s	£	s	£	s	£	s
1945	44	15	44	0	44	15	44	15
1946	67	10	44	15	99	0*	67	10
1947	101	10	67	10	146	0*	80	0
1948	110	0	90	0	130	0*	72	10
1949	100	0	80	0	68	0	50	0
1950	127	10	80	0	80	0	48	0
1951	172	10	110	0	120	0	85	0*
1952	120	0	67	10	54	0*	42	0
1953	80	0	67	10	61	0	47	10
1954	86	0	73	10	73	10*	62	10
1955	90	0	76	4	74	0	66	0
1956	93	0	84	0	83	10	69	0
1957	94	0	75	0	88	0	79	0
1958	79	0	67	10	73	10	55	0
1959	79	0	72	10	55	0	50	0
1960	77	15	69	10	76	0	65	0
1961	74	10	60	0	82	0	75	0
1962	56	0	36	10	92	0	85	0

Note: *Drums included.

Source: Geddes Statistics.

Select Bibliography

Anonymous. *Monthly Supplement of the Penny Magazine of the Society for the Diffusion of Useful Knowledge,* No. 74 (1833).

Anonymous. *Sufferings of the Ice-Bound Whalers.* 2nd ed., Hull, 1836.

Anderson, A.J.C. and Williams, P.N. *Margarine.* 2nd ed., Oxford, 1965.

Barron, W. *An Apprentice's Reminiscences of Whaling in Davis's Straits. Narrative of the Voyages of the Hull Barque Truelove, from 1848 to 1854.* Hull, 1890.

Barron, W. *Old Whaling Days.* Hull, 1895.

Beale, T. *A Few Observations on the Natural History of the Sperm Whale.* London, 1835.

Bennett, A.G. *Whaling in the Antarctic.* Edinburgh, 1931. (A graphic account of life and labour on the first generation of modern floating factories).

Blainey, G. *The Tyranny of Distance: How Distance Shaped Australia's History.* Melbourne, 1966. (Refers to Australian whaling).

Browne, J. Ross. *Etchings of a Whaling Cruise, with Notes of a Sojourn on the Island of Zanzibar, and a Brief History of the Whale Fishery, in Its Past and Present Condition.* London, 1846.

Budker, P. *Whales and Whaling.* London, 1958. (A modern survey).

Conway, W.M. *Early Dutch and English Voyages to Spitsbergen in the Seventeenth Century.* London, 1904.

Conway, W.M., *No Man's Land: A History of Spitsbergen.* Cambridge, 1906. (An excellent survey of early whaling in Spitsbergen).

Dakin, W.J. *Whalemen Adventurers.* Sydney, 1934; rev. ed., Sydney, 1963. (An old-fashioned but useful account of whaling in Australasian waters, containing many extracts from Enderby letters preserved in the Mitchell Library, Sydney).

de Crèvecœur, J.H. St. J. *Letters from an American Farmer*. Philadelphia, 1782; reprint, London, 1962. (A valuable account of New England whaling towns.

Dundee Year Books. Dundee, 1881-.

Elking, H. *A View of the Greenland Trade and Whale Fishery, with the National and Private Advantages Thereof*. London, 1722. Reprinted in J.R. McCulloch (ed.). *A Select Collection of Scarce and Valuable Economical Tracts*. London, 1859, pp. 61-103. (The earliest English survey of whaling, by the director of the South Sea Company's operations).

Ellis, C. *The Hydrogenation of Oils*. London, 1914.

Ferguson, H. *Harpoon*. London, 1932. (A lively account of life on a modern floating factory, written from the point of view of the workmen).

Hadley, G. *A New and Complete History of the Town and County...of Kingston-upon-Hull*. Hull, 1788. (Contains an interesting account of the whaling trade from Hull).

Hansard. *The Parliamentary History of England*. London, 1816. (Debates on whaling in vols. XXV and XXVIII).

Harlow, V.T. *The Founding of the Second British Empire*. 2 vols., London, 1952-1964. (Vol. II, chapter 5, section 3 is an account of the "search for oil" in the late eighteenth century).

Harmer, S.F. "History of Whaling" and "Southern Whaling," *Proceedings of the Linnaean Society of London*, CXL (1928), pp. 51-95 and CXLII (1931), pp. 85-163.

Hawes, C.B. *Whaling*. London, 1924.

Hilditch, T.P. *The Industrial Chemistry of the Fats and Waxes*. London, 1927; 2nd ed., London, 1941.

Hohman, E.P. *The American Whaleman: A Study of Life and Labor in the Whaling Industry*. New York, 1928. (One of the better surveys of American whaling).

Jackson, G. "Government Bounties and the Establishment of the Scottish Whaling Trade, 1750-1800." In Butt, J. and Ward, J.T. (eds.). *Scottish Themes: Essays in Honour of Professor S.G.E. Lythe*. Edinburgh, 1976, pp. 46-66.

Jackson, G. *Hull in the Eighteenth Century. A Study in Economic and Social History*. London, 1972. (Chapter VII deals with whaling).

Jenkins, J.T. "Bibliography of Whaling." *Journal of the Society for the Bibliography of Natural History*, II, part 4 (1948), pp. 71-166.

Jenkins, J.T. *A History of the Whale Fisheries*. London, 1921.

Jenkins, J.T. *Whales and Modern Whaling*. London, 1932. (As a well-written appeal for a deceleration in whaling this is far more valuable than his attempt to write history).

Lawrie, R.A. *Meat Science*. 2nd ed., Oxford, 1974.

Lubbock, B. *The Arctic Whalers*. Glasgow, 1936. (A chronological survey concerned more with the ships than with the trade).

Lythe, S.G.E. "The Dundee Whale Fishery," *Scottish Journal of Political Economy*, XI (1964), pp. 158-169.

Mackintosh, N.A. *The Stocks of Whales*. London, 1965. (A major analysis of the zoological background to the decline of modern whaling).

Mackintosh, N.A. and Wheeler, J.F.G. *Southern Blue and Fin Whales*. Cambridge, 1929. (Very useful).

Macpherson, D. *Annals of Commerce, Manufacturers, Fisheries and Navigation*. 4 vols., London, 1805.

Martin, G. *Animal and Vegetable Oils, Fats and Waxes*. London, 1920.

Matthews, L.H., *et al. The Whale*. London, 1968.

Maynard, F. and Dumas, A. *The Whalers*. London, 1937. (An interesting account of French involvement in Southern Whaling).

Moorehead, A. *The Fatal Impact. An Account of the Invasion of the South Pacific, 1767-1840*. London, 1966. (European entry into the Pacific including a section on whaling).

Morely, F.V. and Hodgson, J.S. *Whaling North and South*. London, 1927.

Ommanney, F.D. *Lost Leviathan*. London, 1971. (A lively modern account of whaling).

Purchas, S. *Hakluytus Posthumus, or Purchas His Pilgrimes*. 20 vols., Glasgow, 1905-1907. (Volumes XIII and XIV contain eyewitness accounts of the opening of the Spitsbergen fishery).

Robertson, R.B. *Of Whales and Men*. New York, 1956. (A semi-fictional account of a modern whaling voyage with Salvesen. Good descriptive material).

Ruud, J.T. "International Regulations of Whaling." *Norsk Hvalfangsttid*, XLV, No. 7 (1956), pp. 374-387.

Salvesen, H.K. "Modern Whaling in the Antarctic." *Journal of the Royal Society of Arts*, LXXXII (1933), pp. 408-429.

Salvesen, T.E. "The Whaling Industry of Today." *Journal of the Royal Society of Arts*, LX (1912), pp. 515-523.

Sanderson, J. *Voyage from Hull to Greenland in the Year 1789*. Hull, 1789.

Scoresby, W. *An Account of the Arctic Regions, with a History and Description of the Northern Whale Fishery*. 2 vols., Edinburgh, 1820. (Volume 2 is the standard work on the Greenland fishery).

Scoresby, W. *Memorials of the Sea*. London, 1835.

Scott, W.R. *The Constitution and Finance of English, Scottish and Irish Joint-Stock Companies to 1720*. 3 vols., Cambridge, 1910-1912.

Sheahan, J.J. *General and Concise History and Description of the Town and Port of Kingston-upon-Hull*. London, 1864.

Sheppard, T. and Suddaby, J. "Hull Whaling History and Miscellaneous Material." *Hull Museums Publications*, Nos. 30-31 (1906).

Sibree, J. *Fifty Years Recollections of Hull*. Hull, 1884. (Chapter VII dwells on the disaster of 1835).

Slipjer, E.J. *Whales*. London, 1962. (A good general survey).

Smith, C.E. *From the Deep of the Sea*. London, 1922. (The edited diary of the surgeon of the *Diana* during her enforced wintering in Davis Strait in 1866-1867. Undoubtedly the best account of the sufferings involved in whaling).

Spencer, J. *The Messmate. A Companion for Sailors*. Hull, 1836. (Account of life on the *Jane*, caught in the ice in 1835).

Stackpole, E.A. *The Sea-Hunters: The New England Whalemen during Two Centuries, 1635-1835*. Philadelphia, 1943. (One of the best accounts of American whaling).

Starbuck, A. *History of the American Whale Fishery*. Waltham, MA, 1878. (A standard work still of great value).

Tawney, R.H. and Power, E. (eds.). *Tudor Economic Documents*. 3 vols, London, 1924-1951.

Thompson, D'A.W. *On Whales Landed at the Scottish Whaling Stations During the Years 1908-14 and 1920-27*. Glasgow, 1928. (Essential for the revival of whaling in British waters).

Tressler, D.K. and Lemon J. McW. *Marine Products of Commerce*. New York, 1951. (Chapter 33 is a useful survey of whaling products).

Vamplew, Wray. "The Evolution of International Whaling Controls," *Maritime History*, II (1973), pp. 123-139.

Vamplew, Wray. *Salvesen of Leith*. Edinburgh, 1975.

Van Stuyvenberg, J.H. *Margarine: An Economic, Social and Scientific History, 1869-1969*. Liverpool, 1969.

Villiers, A.J. *Whaling in the Frozen South. Being the Story of the 1923-24 Norwegian Whaling Expedition to the Antarctic*. London, 1925. (An account of the first Antarctic pelagic expedition in the *Sir James Clark Ross*).

Waugh, N. *Corsets and Crinolines*. London, 1954. (One of the best surveys of the unseen use of whalebone).

White, A. *A Collection of Documents on Spitsbergen and Greenland*. London, 1855.

Willan, T.S. *The Early History of the Russia Company, 1553-1603*. Manchester, 1956.

Williams, K.A. *Oils, Fats and Fatty Foods*. 3rd ed., London, 1950.

Wilson, C. *The History of Unilever. A Study in Economic Growth and Social Change*. 2 vols., London, 1954.

Wilson, C. *Profit and Power: A Study of England and the Dutch Wars*. London, 1957.

Young, G. *A History of Whitby*. 2 vols., Whitby, 1817.

Additional Bibliography

Note: The following important articles on British and other whaling/sealing activity are contained in the *International Journal of Maritime History*.

Basberg, B.L. "A Ship Ashore? Organiation and Living Conditions at South Georgia Whaling Stations, 1904-1960." XIV, No. 1 (2002), 93-113.

Dickinson, A.B. "Some Interrelationships between Twentieth Century Sealing and Whaling at South Georgia." V, No. 2 (1993), 175-188.

_____ and Sanger, C.W. "Modern Shore-Station Whaling in Newfoundland and Labrador: Expansion and Consolidation, 1898-1902." II, No. 1 (1990), 83-116.

_____ and _____. "Modern Shore-Station Whaling in Newfoundland and Labrador: The Peak Season, 1904." V, No. 1 (1993), 127-154.

Goddard, J.M. "The Rissmuller Factor in North American Shore Whaling, 1900-1912: The Atlantic Years." V, No. 2 (1993), 135-155.

Hacquebord, L., Steenhuisen, F.; and Waterbolk, H. "English and Dutch Whaling Trade and Whaling Stations in Spitsbergen (Svalbard) before 1600." XV, No. 2 (2003), 117-134.

Sanger, C.W. "'Oil is an Indispensable Necessity of Life:' The Impact of Oscillating Oil and Baleen Prices on Cyclical Variations in the Scale and Scope of Northern Commercial Whaling, 1600-1900." XV, No. 2 (2003), 147-157.

_____ and Dickinson, A.B. "The Origins of Modern Shore-Based Whaling in Newfoundland and Labrador: The Cabot Steam Whaling Co. Ltd., 1896-98." I, No. 1 (1989), 129-157.

_____ and _____. "Renewal of Newfoundland and Labrador Shore-Based Whaling, 1918-1936." VII, No. 1 (1996), 83-103.

Steele, M.W. and Caiger, J.G. "On Ignorant Whalers and Japan's 'Shell and Repel' Edict of 1825." V, No. 2 (1993), 31-56.

See also these other contributions that were either omitted in the original volume or have appeared since its publication:

Anonymous. *Monthly Supplement of the Penny Magazine of the Society for the Diffusion of Useful Knowledge,* No. 74 (1833).

Barrow, Tony. *The Whaling Trade of North-East England, 1750-1850.* Sunderland, 2001. (An excellent regional survey)

Basberg, B.L.; Ringstad, J.E.; and Wexelsen, E. (eds.). *Whaling and History: Perspectives on the Evolution of the Industry.* Sandefjord. 1993. (Contains a varied collection of important articles throwing light on the British experience)

Busch, B.C. *Whaling will Never Do for Me: The American Whaleman in the Nineteenth Century.* Lexington, 1994. (One of the best, erudite, discussions of the social history of whaling from the American perspective)

Credland, A.G. (ed.). *The Journal of Surgeon Cass aboard the Whaler Brunswick of Hull, 1824.* Hull, 1988.

Davis, L.E.; Gallman, R.E.; and Gleiter, K. *The Pursuit of Leviathan: Technology, Institutions, Productivity and Profits in American Whaling, 1816-1906.* Chicago, 1997. (A valuable study of the technology and economics of US whaling which illuminates our understanding of fluctuations in British whaling in that period)

Does, W. van der. *Storms, Ice and Whales: The Antarctic Adventures of a Dutch Artist on a Norwegian Whaler.* 1934; English translation, Cambridge, 2003. (A very instructive account of every aspect of whales, catching techniques, vessels and social life in the Antarctic fishery on board Larsen's Factory ship *Sir James Clark Ross*)

Fairley, J. *Irish Whales and Whaling.* Belfast, 1981. (A zoologist's survey of whales, and accounts of beachings, whaling in the eighteenth century and two little-known "modern" whaling stations, Arranmore and Blacksod)

Francis, D. *Arctic Chase: A History of Whaling in Canada's North.* St John's, 1984. (Local detail about British whaling in Canadian waters, chiefly in the nineteenth century)

Francis, D. *A History of World Whaling.* London, 1990. (A useful guide to international whaling, though chiefly of European and American efforts)

Hart, Ian B. *Pesca: A History of the Pioneer Modern Whaling Company in the Antarctic.* Salcombe, Devon, 2001. (The most important company study in recent times which illuminates many aspects of twentieth century whaling and its ultimate decline)

Jackson, G. "State Concern for the Fisheries, 1485-1815." In D.J. Starkey, C. Reid and N. Ashworth (eds.). *England's Sea Fisheries: The Commercial Sea Fisheries of England and Whales since 1300.* London, 2000. (Considers, briefly, support for whaling as part of general fishing)

_____. "The Rise and Fall of English Whaling in the Seventeenth Century." In A.G.F. van Holk (ed.). *Early European Exploitations of the Northern Atlantic, 800-1700.* Groningen, 1981. (This published "Proceedings of the International Symposium" contains many important articles by leading scholars on various aspects of Arctic whaling)

_____. "The Battle with the Arctic: 1785-1839." in G. Jackson and S.G.E. Lythe (eds.). *The Port of Montrose: A History of its Harbour, Trade and Shipping.* Tayport, 1993. (A detailed account of whaling from Montrose)

_____. "Whaling," "Whaling Vessels" and "International Whaling Commission." In *Encyclopaedia Britannic,* recent editions.

_____. "Why did the British not Catch Rorquals in the Nineteenth Century?" In Basberg, Ringstad and Wexelsen (eds.), *Whaling and History.*

_____. "The Whaling Trade," "Sail Whalers," "Steam Whalers" and "Catchers." In *Oxford Encyclopaedia of Maritime History* (forthcoming).

_____. "The Whaling Trade." In *Encyclopaedia of World Trade* forthcoming.

Jones, A.G.E. *The Greenland and Davis Strait Trade 1740-1865.* NP, 1996. (A transcription of Lloyd's Register and the Register of the Society of Merchants, Ship-owners and Underwriters, this reveals the ships, owners, masters, and activity in every whaling port, Unfortunately this source is not easily available: only 100 copies were made. [see G. Jackson, review in *Mariners Mirror*, 1997])

Leinenga, Jürgen R. *Arctische walvisvangst in de achttiende eeuw.* Amsterdam, 1995. (A very useful wide ranging comparative study of the chief European participants in Greenland and Davie Straight whaling in the eighteenth century, with important graphs and tables showing compartative activity. Useful details of whaling from Anstruther, Newcastle, Whitby and Exeter. In Dutch, with English summary, but graphs and tables are easily understood.)

Morton, H. *The Whale's Wake.* Honolulu, 1982. (An important discussion of British and American whaling in terms of imperial annexations in the Pacific, especially around Australasia)

Sanger, C.W. "The Nineteenth Century Newfoundland Seal Fishery and the Influence of Scottish Whalemen." *Polar Record*, XX (1980), 232-252.

Schmitt, F.P.; De Jong, C.; and Winter, F.H. *Thomas Welcome Roys: America's Pioneer of Modern Whaling.* Charlottesville, 1980. (A valuable account of a pioneer of explosive and rocket propelled harpoons, and of power-driven winches for recovering whales. He established whaling in the seas north of Scotland but was ultimately a failure)

Stoett, P.J. *The International Politics of Whaling.* Vancouver, 1997. (An impartial examination of attempts to control whaling by the International Whaling Convention written against the background of whaling history.)

Watson, L. *Whales of the World.* London, 1981. (A "Complete Guide" to the numerous species of whales, their habits, migrations and distribution)

INDEX

Printed and bound by CPI Group (UK) Ltd, Croydon, CR0 4YY

16/04/2025

14658576-0004